Liberty, Rationality, and Agency
in Hobbes's *Leviathan*

Liberty, Rationality, and Agency in Hobbes's *Leviathan*

David van Mill

STATE UNIVERSITY OF NEW YORK PRESS

Published by
State University of New York Press, Albany

For information, address State University of New York Press,
90 State Street, Suite 700, Albany, NY 12207

Production by Diane Ganeles
Marketing by Michael Campochiaro

Library of Congress Cataloging-in-Publication Data

van Mill, David.
  Liberty, rationality, and agency in Hobbes's Leviathan / David van Mill.
    p. cm
  Includes bibliographical references and index.
  ISBN 0-7914-5035-X (alk. paper)—ISBN 0-7914-5036-8 (pbk. : alk.
  paper)
  1. Hobbes, Thomas, 1588–1679. Leviathan. 2. Liberty. I. Title.

JC153.H659 V35 2001
320.1—dc21   00-045053

10 9 8 7 6 5 4 3 2 1

To my parents

Contents

Part III: External Freedom

Part IV: Conclusion

Acknowledgments

I would like to thank *Polity* for allowing me to reprint the article "Rationality, Action and Autonomy in Hobbes's *Leviathan*" that originally appeared in *Polity* 10, no. 2 (winter 1994) and *Journal of Politics* for permission to publish "Hobbes's Theories of Freedom" in *Journal of Politics* 57, no. 2 (May 1995).

I begin my list of people to thank with Preston King, a Hobbes scholar himself, who started me on the path of political philosophy while I was an undergraduate at Lancaster University. I have profited from the friendship and academic assistance of a number of people over the period of time it took to produce this work: Adam, Shelley, Sarah, Rich, Vince, Roger, Matt, Laura, Caroline, Frank, Chris, Alicia, Mary, Stef, and Kathy were all great friends to me throughout the process and I thank you all. I would like to express my appreciation to Brent Pickett for being a friend, but also for reading most of the chapters at one stage or another. Horst Mewes and Tim Fuller also provided many useful comments that helped me refine my arguments. Simone Chambers has been a great source of support over the last ten years and went beyond the call of duty in her assistance with the manuscript. I can do nothing but commend her tenacity in maintaining her interpretation of Hobbes (despite my best efforts to persuade her otherwise;) one day, perhaps, I will be able to convince her to change her mind. My biggest debt is to David Mapel. It is a debt so large that I am well aware it can never be fully repaid. As an advisor, and now as a friend he has worked tirelessly for me over many years and I could not have asked for better guidance. He read every chapter several times, and whatever coherence there is to the book is largely due to him. (It goes without saying, of course, that the flaws that remain are Mapel's alone.)

Part I

Introduction and Theoretical Framework

1

❧

Introduction

Thomas Hobbes, at first glance, provides a coherent and easily identifiable concept of liberty. He seems to argue that agents are free to the extent that they are unimpeded in their actions by external obstacles. In fact, Hobbes's theory of liberty tends to be more complicated, vague, and is at times, contradictory. Studies by J. R. Pennock, A. Wernham, Ralph Ross, Brian Barry, J. W. N. Watkins, and a variety of others lead one to conclude that there is no single, easily identifiable "Hobbesian" theory of liberty.[1] My aim in this book is to reformulate Hobbes's ideas on liberty in terms of his wider discussion concerning the requirements for rational agency. I hope to demonstrate that Hobbes's theory of agency is just as concerned with "internal" as with "external" conditions of action, although he was not inclined to discuss the former in terms of liberty. Instead, one has to examine his more general discussions of reason and rationality, power and felicity, endeavor, worthiness, and personality to piece together a coherent argument concerning the internal requirements for action. Without ever explicitly saying so, Hobbes takes us beyond his limited definition of "negative" liberty to discuss a kind of conduct similar to notions of *autonomous rational action*.

In the terminology of Richard Flathman,[2] Hobbesian liberty does not extend much beyond the idea of basic movement. Flathman characterizes this kind of liberty as

3

freedom$_1$ by which he means: "Self-activated movement plus the possibility of impediments to the movement in question."[3] On Flathman's scale of types of freedom this category fails to incorporate the major requirements of agency. I argue that Hobbes's discussion goes considerably beyond this minimal view of liberty and is actually closer to Flathman's notion of freedom$_5$, in which action is "attempted by an agent in the pursuit of a plan or project self—critically chosen to satisfy, and in fact satisfying, certifiably worthy norms or principles."[4]

In other words, Hobbes extends the discussion from the question of external impediments on movement to an examination of the requirements for coherent and long-term rational action. My discussion examines Hobbes's arguments concerning many different aspects of civil society and human psychology, which when pieced together provide a fairly comprehensive theory of agency. Much of the confusion in the scholarly literature over Hobbes's ideas on action can be clarified by finding a distinction in *Leviathan* between movement, which is more concerned with "external" circumstances, and agency, which concerns "internal" conditions. I suggest that although Hobbes does use the terms *liberty* and *freedom* to refer to the lack of physical impediments to motion, he also has a broader discussion of action, agency, and autonomy and the requirements for rational conduct. The distinction between internal and external conditions of freedom draws on the work of Joel Feinberg[5] and I will use it to replace the more usual categories of "positive" and "negative" liberty.

Summary of the Chapters

Chapter Two: The Scope of Freedom

The aim of this chapter is to lay out the analytical framework I use to examine Hobbes's major ideas on liberty and action. Feinberg has made an interesting argument concerning the nature of freedom. Rather than drawing upon the usual division between negative and positive concepts of freedom, he distinguishes instead between the categories of internal and external requirements for freedom. Freedom, for Feinberg, is largely about the exercise of control: constraints that limit internal and external control over actions also limit our freedom. A constraint is anything that prevents one from doing something and can be an internal condition such as psychosis or fear, or an external constraint such as a locked door. This approach allows me to draw out the intricacies of Hobbes's argument concerning the requirements for full agency in a manner that the positive/negative categories do not allow.

I wish to extend Feinberg's argument by placing constraints and conditions for action along a continuum; this will allow us to consider actions in terms of how much liberty they exhibit internally and externally. For example, when examining internal requirements for liberty and action we can evaluate Hobbes's discussion in relation to passions, habits, fear, and rationality. I will argue that Hobbes thought that the more an action exhibits rationality, then the more the agent demonstrates control over internal conditions and hence the more capable she become of living an autonomous life. I will also discuss some aspects of contemporary notions of liberty and autonomy. I will focus in particular on recent arguments by Flathman and Charles Taylor in order to clarify my subsequent discussion of Hobbes.[6]

Chapter Three: Hobbes and Negative Freedom

Chapter 3 is an analysis of what Hobbes has to say in *Leviathan* concerning liberty. The current scholarly consensus interprets Hobbes purely as a theorist of negative liberty. According to this view, Hobbes argues that liberty exists where external impediments do not restrict movement. It is understood that Hobbes does not make a link between rationality and freedom; one can be insane and free because the internal conditions of the agent are of no consequence to the question of whether the agent is free. This also allows Hobbes to argue that fear and liberty are compatible with one another.

The interpretation of Hobbes as a theorist of what I call "pure" negative liberty is supported by Hobbes's claim that when an impediment to motion is internal to a thing itself, it is not "a want of liberty but of the power to move."[7] Liberty is defined in terms of physical impediments to motion and we are free to the extent that we can move our limbs unimpeded by external barriers. We are unfree only to the extent that we are prevented by barred windows, locked doors, and so forth, from pursuing our passions and desires. Flathman characterizes this kind of liberty as freedom$_1$ by which he means "Self-activated movement plus the possibility of impediments to the movement in question."[8] This is not quite correct, because Hobbes does not even make the minimal demand that free movement has to be self-activated. A rock that has been pushed down a hill is free according to Hobbes's most basic definition of liberty even though the motion comes from an external source. On Flathman's scale of types of freedom this category fails to incorporate the major requirements of agency.

My discussion of Hobbes as a theorist of negative liberty will challenge the main body of literature on the topic. I argue that Hobbes's discussion goes considerably beyond this minimal view of liberty and that he in fact discusses freedom in a much richer way than has previously been identified. In opposition to the standard view of Hobbes as a theorist of "pure" negative freedom, I argue instead for what I term a more *extended* theory of freedom.

Chapter Four: The Internal Conditions of Freedom:
Complex Instrumental Rationality and Autonomy

This chapter presents the first stage of the key theoretical argument in the book. The major aim is to show that Hobbes's argument advances beyond external requirements for liberty to a discussion of the necessary conditions for rational agency. I argue that Hobbes was interested primarily in promoting the development of rational individuals as a necessary condition for a peaceful society. Only with such rational persons as subjects can we live collectively and at the same time pursue our individual conceptions of the good life. Extended rationality is crucial in this interpretation of Hobbes's political theory because without persons capable of rationally ordering their preferences, the chances of political stability and the maintenance of a commonwealth over time are radically reduced.

I will present a theory of rationality that goes beyond the game-theoretical interpretations of Hobbes currently in vogue. This latter view presents Hobbesian rationality in terms of calculations that individuals would make in situations such as the "prisoner's dilemma." Under such conditions, the individual supposedly makes judgments based on maximizing short-term utility. I will demonstrate that Hobbes's view of rational calculation goes considerably beyond the maximization of immediate preferences.

I show that the sum total of Hobbes's ideas concerning reason, intellectual virtue, wit, dexterity of the mind, discretion, prudential design, the need to balance and guide desires and passions, wisdom, experience, the desire for power, deliberation, felicity, authorization, and worthiness, add up to a sophisticated concept of the self. The rational person Hobbes describes, who lives in a well-ordered society, bears little resemblance to the self-interested maximizer that most commentators find in the pages of *Leviathan*. I demonstrate in this chapter that Hobbes's theory of extended rationality, when pieced together, is very similar to modern theories of agency.

I will demonstrate that those who live by the dictates of the laws of nature do not fit the usual interpretation of Hobbesian individuals who are presented as being constantly swayed by a random procession of passions. As a supporting argument for the claims presented in this book, I will relate this discussion back to the general schema of the modern liberal understanding of autonomy discussed in chapter 2.

Chapter Five: The Internal Conditions of Freedom: Substantive Rationality and Autonomy

In this chapter, I develop the theory of volition discussed in chapter 4 and suggest that Hobbes has a substantive theory of rationality. By substantive rationality I mean that a person ultimately has to be able to formulate and act upon a life-plan in relation to the laws of nature that apply to civil society. The laws of nature are a crucial aspect of my interpretation of Hobbes. Hobbes's idea of agency mandates that we live by norms or "laws" of conduct that we impose upon ourselves. The interpretation offered in this chapter and in chapter 4 suggests that Hobbes utilized the laws of nature to fulfill this requirement. I argue that these laws provide a universal code in the sense that everyone can agree that the laws of nature are good; they alone promote peace and well-being. The goal of peace (the reasonable) sets limits on the goods pursued (the rational). I argue that his theory of agency suggests that a person becomes fully free only when he or she lives by self-imposed rules. Reason allows us to discover certain universal principles that help us structure a civil society and our individual life-plans within that society. Once peace has been secured we are able to live felicitous lives, pursuing long-term goals in a manner that augments our lives as a whole.

Chapter Six: Voluntarism and Morality

It is usually argued that Hobbes only gives prudential, as opposed to moral reasons, for why people should keep promises, obey the sovereign, and cooperate with others. In this chapter I will suggest that a robust moral theory can be found in the pages of *Leviathan*. To make such an argument I begin by addressing the old question of whether Hobbes presents a theory of psychological egoism. This question is of some importance because it bears directly on the issue of whether Hobbes presents a theory of morality or one of prudential self-interest. I argue that Hobbes's theory of volition, presented in chapters 4 and 5, precludes him from supporting psychological egoism and also allows him to present a coherent moral theory that sits well with the theory of the self discussed throughout this book. This means that Hobbes was not a moral relativist; good and bad may often appear to mean different things to different people, but there is still a basic moral code that dictates how we pursue the good. This chapter concludes the attempt to establish that Hobbes was concerned with something comparable to a modern ideal of agency. The next task is to consider how Hobbes thought society should be arranged in order to promote rational, autonomous beings. I turn, therefore, in chapter 7, to the external conditions of liberty and agency.

Chapter Seven: Freedom, Equality, and the Laws of Nature

Here I examine Hobbes's understanding of the external conditions necessary for liberty and action. I will discuss not only physical barriers as impediments to liberty, but will also consider Hobbes's views on the state of nature, economic conditions, property relationships, the power of the church, the power of the sovereign, civic education, free speech, and freedom of association.

It has usually been argued that Hobbes favored a form of government more conducive to tyranny than liberty. I argue instead that we can find a theory of liberal constraints embedded in Hobbes's discussion of the laws of nature. These constraints, which I argue are an embryonic form of a "harm principle," protect citizens from abuses by the sovereign and from fellow subjects of the commonwealth. In particular, natural law, when made into positive law by the sovereign, creates a prior condition of equality that is essential for each individual to act freely. In this chapter, I extend the analysis of the laws of nature and claim that natural law, because it is the guiding force of reason, also establishes the conditions most advantageous for freedom within a commonwealth. My intention is to demonstrate that Hobbes was concerned mainly with creating a society characterized by civil freedom.

Hobbes leaves us in no doubt as to the requirement for an absolute sovereign and many commentators have argued that because of this there is precious little freedom available for the members of the commonwealth that Hobbes prescribes. I will examine this requirement in terms of the need for peace and order and suggest that Hobbes was concerned with absolutism, not because of any authoritarian leanings on his part, but because he saw no other means of securing a safe environment for agency. In other words, civility and agency depend upon absolutism. Hobbes's discussion of the state of nature is meant to support the need for an authoritative sovereign and describes the very opposite of what a civil society should look like. In place of arts, science, peace, prosperity, and civility we get instead, insecurity, fear, invasion, and death. It is necessary, therefore, that we rationally place limits on ourselves and live under a self-imposed authority that can curtail natural liberty through civil law; only then is agency available to all.

It is the capacity for rational agency that makes us capable of acting in accordance with the laws of nature; this is why education becomes such a vital concern in Hobbes's work. Parts 3 and 4 of *Leviathan* are devoted to promoting religious reeducation, without which we are likely to continue to fight and to place the commonwealth in danger. We have to be schooled in order to overcome such passions as partiality, pride, revenge, and vainglory. We also have to be capable of making contracts with each other, and Hobbes tells us repeatedly that without reason we cannot be the authors of our deeds and hence cannot be held responsible for our actions and promises. In sum, we have to acquire opinions that do not threaten the very existence of the commonwealth. We must be taught that the laws of nature that relate specifically to civil society dictate that we do unto others as we would have them do unto us. Hobbes was convinced that a commonwealth would fail without some form of tutelary sovereign, and so once again I argue that the aim of involving the sovereign in education and religion is not to tyrannize the subjects but to foster peace as a prior necessity of agency. I claim that the task of the sovereign is to be tolerant toward religious beliefs, the expression of ideas, and to groups and assemblies that do not threaten the survival of the state or the lives and interests of the subjects.

Chapter Eight: Hobbes's Dualism

In the conclusion I claim that the theory of rational action developed throughout the book does not sit well with other concepts in Hobbes's overall system of thought. In particular, it causes problems for his theories of determinism and consent. There are, in fact, many discrepancies in Hobbes's descriptions of such topics as freedom, equality, and power. One could explain this away by suggesting that Hobbes is simply careless and inconsistent in his work. I suggest that there is another and better answer to the puzzle, namely that Hobbes deliberately presents his readers with two different descriptions of each of these issues. One description relates to life lived according to the right of nature in the state of nature, and the other relates to life lived by the laws of nature within a well-ordered commonwealth.

2

~

The Scope of Freedom

Introduction

The basic starting point for writing a book on Hobbes and liberty is that the concept of freedom and the related issues of liberalism, rationality, and agency, hold such great import within our Western political tradition. The word *freedom* is today universally accepted as a good to be promoted and pursued. Supporters of every political persuasion embrace and support the idea. And yet it is a rare occasion when we are provided with a clear definition of what the term means by those who so wholeheartedly champion its cause. The Gulf War, for example, was fought under the banner and rhetoric of freedom; and communism, we are told, has fallen in surrender at the feet of the Western ideals of liberty and "free" trade. Yet throughout these conflicts, economic and military, the meaning of the terms *liberty* and *freedom* has been left largely unexplained. It seems that in contemporary political debate, it is enough to embrace (without having to explain or defend) freedom as a good.

This chapter is an attempt to define what is at stake when we enter the discourse on the psychology and politics of freedom. It is fitting that the discussion hinges on the work of Thomas Hobbes because we discover in his works a great understanding of the rhetorical power of the word *freedom*, and we find also, what is often missing in contemporary discussions of the concept, an analysis of the dangers as well as the benefits of liberty. I hope that it will become apparent that Hobbes's discussion also demonstrates the difficulty of presenting a coherent concept of freedom; a mind as keen as Hobbes's was still apt to wander in some confusion over this difficult topic.

I will engage what Hobbes has to say in more detail later in the book. The aim of this chapter is to lay out what I hope will be a useful analytical framework to examine his ideas on liberty and action. I focus on the work of three prominent contemporary theorists: Charles Taylor because he is perhaps the primary modern defender of the theory of positive freedom; Richard Flathman, who presents the best recent defense of negative freedom; and Joel Feinberg, because, I will argue, he offers a more persuasive terminology of freedom than the usual positive/negative dichotomy (even though I claim that his theory can still be placed within the negative theory camp).

I first outline Taylor's theory of freedom. Then I examine Flathman's response to Taylor and focus in particular on his distinction between freedom and autonomy. I argue that this distinction is inadequate for understanding the complex nature of freedom and in its place I offer a competing set of distinctions based on the arguments of Feinberg. I then argue for a theory of freedom that blends some of the arguments of Feinberg and Flathman into a liberal theory of freedom. Much of the disagreement between Feinberg, Flathman, and Taylor is at the semantic rather than at the substantive level, or so I will argue. In particular, Flathman distinguishes between freedom and autonomy; Feinberg divides liberty into the categories of partial and full, and internal and external freedom; and Taylor distinguishes between partial and full freedom. Very often the three authors mean much the same thing when they use these different terminologies. In place of Flathman's distinction between freedom and autonomy I will argue for a theory of "freedom on a continuum," although I will also utilize Flathman's categories when they prove to be helpful. The goal of the discussion of these three authors is to formulate a more defensible theory of freedom than either negative or positive theorists have managed to date, and to utilize a vocabulary that is more helpful for understanding the theory of freedom presented by Hobbes.

Charles Taylor and Positive Freedom

In "What's Wrong with Negative Liberty,"[1] Taylor has presented a complex, although not always clear, defense of what Isaiah Berlin has termed *positive freedom*.[2] Freedom for Taylor is essentially about "the exercising of control over one's life,"[3] both internally and externally. Hence he presents "An exercise concept of freedom [that] requires that we discriminate among motivations. . . . If we are free in the exercise of certain capacities, then we are not free, or less free, when these capacities are in some way unfulfilled or blocked."[4] It is part of our nature, he argues, that we make strong evaluations about things that mean more to us in relation to our normative frameworks.[5] We distinguish between our desires and impulses according to the worth they hold for us and if we are prevented from pursuing what we see as the good because of external forces or because of certain false desires, we are made unfree. When we act upon a desire we do not identify with, we are controlled by, rather than having control over, our passions: "Freedom is important to us because we are purposive beings. But then there must be distinctions in the significance of different kinds of freedom based on the distinction in the significance of different purposes."[6]

Taylor seems to identify different types of desires, and he distinguishes between "brute" and "import-attributing" desires, and "lower" and "higher" (first-and second-order) desires. We can examine each of these categories of desires according to how they enhance the self. Brute desires are often little more than sensations. Some of these can make us unfree if they rob us of control of the self, but we can also be free when acting upon such desires. I may, for example, have a strong desire for wine that would classify as a brute desire, but as long as I identify with this desire and exercise control over it then I am acting in a free manner. In this sense, brute desires can also be import-attributing, representing something I strongly identify with, providing authenticity to my identity, and fitting well with my fundamental purposes: "being brute is not what makes desires repudiable . . . we could not say in general that we are ready to envisage losing our brute desires without a sense of diminution. On the contrary, to lose my desire for, and hence delectation in, oysters, mushroom pizza, or Peking duck would be a terrible deprivation. I should fight against such a change with all the strength at my disposal."[7] These are rather strong statements to make concerning the loss of a desire for certain foodstuffs, but we get the general idea that brute desires can be valuable.

Desires and their relationship to freedom are, however, mostly about weightier things than our basic appetites: "we have to see our emotional life as made up largely of import-attributing desires."[8] These are a more sophisticated form of desire than the base variety because they are not simply the result of "the throbs, elans, or tremors I feel"[9] but are desires that to a greater or lesser extent define who I am as a person. They "are of great significance for me, meet important, long lasting needs, and represent a fulfillment of something central to me."[10] Despite import-attributing desires being so central to identity, Taylor argues that we can be made unfree by them (this is a crucial point that will be taken up in the section on Flathman). According to Taylor, an import-attributing desire can make us unfree when the good that is aimed at is not really a good for the person: "Now how can we feel that an import-attributing desire is not truly ours? We can do this only if we see it as mistaken, that is, the import or the good it supposedly gives us a sense of is not a genuine import or good."[11]

Hence, whether we are mistaken seems to depend on whether we identify with the import-attributing desire. If we do, and if we see it as truly promoting what is important to us, especially in relation to our framework, then we can be free when we act upon it. If we do not identify with the desire and feel restricted by it, then we can at best be described as exercising an impoverished form of freedom: "what is it to feel that a desire is not truly mine? Presumably, I feel that I should be better off without it, that I do not lose anything in getting rid of it, I remain quite complete without it."[12] "Losing these desires we lose nothing, because their loss deprives us of no genuine good."[13] We recognize that the good we get from the desire is not a genuine good: "Thus we can experience some desires as fetters, because we can experience them as not ours."[14] The examples Taylor provides here are of the woman whose fear prevents her from fulfilling a real desire to engage in public debate, and of the man whose feelings of spite are ruining a relationship he holds dear. Such people can be very aware of their second-order desires (desires that are hierarchically superior in relation to our most fundamental purposes), and yet are still unfree because they are moved to certain behavior that prevents realization of these desires. We can, therefore, divide these import-attributing desires into "first-order" (lower), and "second-order" (higher), desires.

A further complication arises; Taylor suggests that we can also be unfree if we follow desires that we identify with and that we promote to the rank of higher, second-order desires: "We can quite easily be doing what we want in the sense of what we can identify as our wants, without being free; indeed, we can be further entrenching our unfreedom."[15] We make a fundamental mistake in how we discriminate between our desires. Here we may fully identify with the desire, it may well be our strongest desire, and yet we are still mistaken about what is good for us: "Freedom now involves my being able to recognize adequately my most important purposes, and my being able to overcome or at least neutralize my motivational fetters . . . I must be actually exercising self-understanding in order to be truly or fully free."[16]

This is where Taylor introduces the notion of second-guessing into his discussion. An external agent may be able to recognize that what we see as promoting self-realization may actually be preventing it; being free is not just about doing what we most want to do, it is about doing what is actually good for us and we are only fully free when our actions promote our most valuable goals. The mistake here is "public" because the decision of whether or not I am free is an external one: "the subject himself cannot be the final authority on the question whether he is free; for he cannot be the final authority on the question whether his desires are authentic, whether they do or do not frustrate his purposes."[17]

When we examine freedom in light of this understanding of desires, it seems that we can be unfree in several distinct ways. We can be unfree, as the theorist of negative freedom would also agree, when we are prevented from acting on certain goals by external impediments. We can also be unfree if we spend all of our energy and resources on pursuing only the brute desires. This is not because brute desires necessarily make us unfree, but because we also need to develop our import-attributing desires in order to be fully free. Making things more complicated, we can be unfree if we are prevented from pursuing a correct second-order desire by a more powerful first-order desire. Here we recognize that we are "acting" according to the less important desire that we do not necessarily identify with. We would be happy to be rid of this desire because we fully realize that it adds nothing of meaning to our life, and in fact prevents self-fulfillment. And, finally, we can be unfree when we are mistaken about a desire we promote to the rank of second-order.

It is clear from these arguments that Taylor thinks there is a close relationship between freedom and rationality. Rational action, in relation to freedom, is judged according to how well a person fits his or her behavior to a "framework" within a coherently organized life-plan (as opposed to, e.g., akratic behavior). In this respect, to be fully rational and fully free are much the same thing, or at least one cannot be fully free if not also fully rational. Always acting according to "first-order" desires prevents one from organizing one's desires in the most rational manner; the result is that one's actions are not in line with one's contrastive evaluations, and consequently are not free, or at the most, are only minimally free. To be free for Taylor requires a considerable degree of reason and rationality.

Taylor makes the point that part of our understanding of ourselves as human beings is that we are rational choosers and suggests that anything that limits our ability to choose also limits our freedom, whether this happens to be fear, mental illness, narrow horizons, external impediments, or mistaken import-attributing desires. The talk here is not of trivial choices of whether to wear blue or red shoes, but of crucial choices that help to define who we are in relation to our authentic self. The rationality of an action, is, therefore, tied up in the worth of the act. When we are in a certain relationship to the things that are important to us and that allow us to arrive at contrastive evaluations, then we can be described as rational actors.

It is not entirely clear from Taylor's writings when he thinks agents can be classed as fully free. Sometimes he describes people who do not live in the rational harmony as just described as unfree; other times he says they are less free, and it would seem the more a human life is rationally organized the more free it becomes. The latter seems to be much more sensible and, as will be argued later, is along the same lines as the theory of freedom on a continuum. But the bulk of his writing suggests that the former is a more accurate representation of Taylor's position. On the occasions when he suggests that we are less free when we are not in rational harmony, he is only willing to admit to a "very impoverished" form of freedom.

Exactly how closely our behavior has to coincide with *moral* criteria in order to be classed as free action is also unclear and it is to this question that I turn. As already noted, Taylor suggests that we may be acting in full accord with our second-order desires, which actually promote our most valuable purposes, and yet still be mistaken. One can make this claim and suggest that the fault lies in the agent making an incorrect assessment of what is most valuable to her. But Taylor also seems to make the stronger claim that certain goals make us unfree because they are not morally justifiable. He tells us that our "fundamental purpose . . . (can be) shot through with confusion and error"[18] and provides Charles Manson as an example.

Even a strong identification with our fundamental purposes, arrived at through contrastive evaluations, is not always enough for us to be free. Sometimes, for second-order desires to be free, they also have to be desires that promote morally praiseworthy actions. Our lack of freedom in this sense stems from the fact that we have a severely flawed sense of what *should* be important to us: "the capacities relevant to freedom must involve some self-awareness, self-understanding, *moral* discrimination and self-control, otherwise their exercise could not amount to freedom in the sense of self-direction."[19] Although Taylor does not signal the fact, his argument concerning freedom has taken a fundamental shift and we now find that liberty is judged according to the *moral* content of fundamental purposes. The discussion has moved from an assessment of the rationality of ends, to a judgment of the moral worth of the ends. The mistake made by the agent in this sense is fully public because it is judged according to generally understood communal norms of morality.

At the highest level, freedom and the morally good life seem to become inseparable. Taylor's discussion of Manson makes it clear that we can identify with, rationally pursue, hierarchically organize, and fully attain fundamental purposes and still be unfree if all of these things do not fit with a framework that also sits well with the moral norms of one's community. Such freedom requires a considerable level of self-awareness and probably a fair amount of social engineering. We must be able to recognize that what we most want is not what is always best for us, and we must be able to choose the most worthy of our desires. We must also be willing to accept that others know better than we do about the best path to our own self-fulfillment, and accept that on occasions desires we strongly identify with are limiting our freedom. And we have to be able to piece together all of the disparate elements of our lives and prioritize them into a consistent whole that fully manifests what it is to live the good life, as an individual and as a member of a moral community.

The manner in which Taylor links freedom and virtue suggests that we need more than a life-plan that we more or less rationally follow; we need a life-plan that is aimed at the "incomparably higher," and that blends the aspects of my life (beginning, middle, and end) as though I was a character in a novel with a continuous moral unity to my existence. It is unlikely that one organizing framework for life will suffice to provide all of the answers to the questions we ask, especially given the plurality of moral and instrumental goods in the contemporary world, and hence to be fully free we will need to balance a variety of frameworks to create a coherent whole. Freedom is a tricky thing that is not easily realized!

To summarize briefly, I have suggested that Taylor proposes five ways in which we can be unfree. The first is if we are blocked by external forces from pursuing what we deem to be the good. The second is if we pursue brute desires at the cost of all other higher desires. The third is that we can be made unfree if we pursue an import-attributing desire so fanatically that we do not pursue at least some of our other import-attributing desires. The fourth is that we can be unfree if we pursue an import-attributing desire about which we are rationally mistaken (we think the thing is good for us but really it is not). And finally, we can pursue an import-attributing desire that is morally mistaken (the thing we pursue is bad for other people). How compelling is this argument? In the next section I will focus on three aspects of Taylor's argument that seem to be particularly troublesome.

a. First it is worth noting that Taylor himself seems to stray from his own categories of agency. He tells us that it is important to recognize that much of what he says about the relationship between freedom and desires does not hold in the case where a person has an internal conflict between two desires, with both of which the person identifies; here the person retains freedom of choice. He gives as an example the tension in a man's life between, on the one hand, going to a bar with his friends, and on the other hand, maintaining a happy marriage by staying at home. In this case the individual recognizes each choice as crucial to his identity, as giving meaning to his life, as an expression of his self, and hence as being valuable. As a consequence there is tension in his life that is not easy to resolve, but because both desires give his life meaning his choice is difficult but free: "If the conflict is between two desires with which I have no trouble identifying, there can be no talk of lesser freedom, no matter how painful or fateful."[20]

He is quite clear about this person exercising freedom because he identifies with both desires: "my marriage may be breaking up . . . I may feel unequivocally that my marriage is much more important . . . but nevertheless I would not want to talk of my being freer if I could slough off this desire."[21] Such a person is free even if he feels "unequivocally that my marriage is much more important than the release and comradeship of the Saturday night bash . . . [t]he difference seems to be that in this case, I still identify with the less important desire."[22] This is a very strange example for Taylor to use because it seems to contradict the claim that we are only really free when we pursue the "higher" desires, arrived at through a contrastive evaluation of our import-attributing desires. Such evaluations seem to be the real barometer of freedom for Taylor, but if this is the case both of these choices cannot be free, because the person accepts that the marriage is the much higher good. At most the husband seems to demonstrate a very impoverished freedom when he chooses a night out with his friends over his spousal obligations.

Taylor suggests that this person could still be free because he identifies "with the less important desire."[23] I do not really know what to make of this. It seems to be inconsistent to claim that we are only fully free if we prioritize "higher" desires, and then argue that we are equally free when following the "lower" desire if we identify with it. If this is the case then he will have to agree that the smoker who identifies with her smoking, the bully who identifies with his bullying, and the racist who identifies with his racism is as free as the person who pursues the "higher" desires. Certainly Manson identified with his desires! In order for Taylor's overall position to be consistent he has to retain the "higher/lower" distinction, and yet once he introduces the notion of identifying with a desire as a major criteria for freedom this distinction begins to crumble. We can, of course follow a higher desire that we also identify with, but Taylor's position seems to be inconsistent when he argues that we can also be free if we act on a "lower" desire with which we identify. The whole point of introducing the higher/lower distinction is to suggest that we are somehow very limited in our freedom and that we do not identify with the desire that leads us down the more base path, even if we really do think we prefer this option. If Taylor wishes to argue that identification with a desire is the key to freedom, he will have to abandon the dichotomy between higher and lower, but he cannot really do this because so much of his argument is based upon this very tension.

This highlights a further problem with identifying freedom with higher and lower desires; one would suspect that the wife would not be very sympathetic to the argument that her husband was not fully to blame for his actions (and hence not fully free) because he was in the grip of a demon lower desire. To put the argument in such a way sounds like a distortion of Taylor's argument, but it is the example he chooses to best represent his own theory, and it does highlight the problem of robbing people of responsibility once we say they are unfree if they are following "base" or "lower" desires.

b. To talk of our ability to make strong moral evaluations as a defining part of what makes us human, and then to suggest that we can be very mistaken about what we really want, and hence are *unfree* also seems to border on inconsistency. My fundamental desires, Taylor says: "are of great significance to me, meet important long lasting needs [and] will bring me closer to what I really am."[24] This suggests that we will only be driven from their path by other desires we identify with even more strongly and which, therefore, do not rob us of freedom. We can certainly be mistaken in some sense about what we want. But if we go through the reasoning process necessary to recognize our fundamental desires, it seems to be very dubious to then say the end result is not a free choice. As Flathman argues, a person cannot at one and the same time make a mistake and be unfree. The very idea of something being a mistaken decision suggests that there were alternative choices available.

The examples provided by Taylor of "import-attributing desires" that make us unfree, such as an irrational fear that prevents us speaking in public, or spiteful behavior that ruins a relationship, are not very convincing. In these examples Taylor does suggest that we are unfree and not less free; in such cases we can "talk of the absence of freedom without strain."[25] I would suggest that his argument is under considerable strain at precisely this point. One problem is that these examples used by Taylor are not desires at all, but emotional states of mind. Of course, we may not identify with a particular fear, such as public speaking, but this is different from not identifying with a desire, the definition of which according to the OED is something "directed to the attainment of some object." I do not think we try to attain "fear" or "spite"; rather, they are things that prevent us from pursuing our desires. Taylor says that some import-attributing desires give us a good that is not a genuine good, and yet in the examples he provides the individuals do not seem to experience a good of any sort.

The idea Taylor posits of a contrastive evaluation is that we calmly evaluate all the options open to us, weigh the likely consequences of our actions, and make the best judgment according to the available evidence. Now we can of course make the wrong decision because we do not possess full knowledge, and we cannot predict the future, but can we possibly say that a choice made through such a well-ordered thought process is not a free one? If such a person is not responsible for her actions it is hard to imagine anybody who possibly could be.

When we move beyond brute desires and onto desires of some import to us, I do not see how Taylor can maintain the argument that we can have a desire and not also identify with it. I will grant that we can be mistaken in this identification, and that we are less free than we could otherwise be, but I cannot accept that such desires make us unfree. Taylor's argument depends upon promoting emotions to the level of desires and he never presents us with a genuine desire as an example of something that a person would not also identify with. I would suggest that almost all of the things that we act upon we do to a greater or lesser extent identify with. It is only when we get to the level of severe mental illness and very strong emotions that we can say people do not, at least to some extent, identify with their behavior.

    c. My interpretation of Taylor's argument suggests that there is a clear link in his thought between freedom, rational action, and moral virtue. This link is a *necessary* one for Taylor because of the intricate manner in which freedom, morality, and epistemology are intertwined. The question we must pose to Taylor is whether he thinks those who do not engage in morally praiseworthy actions are free or unfree. Are we to criticize the racist, the sexist, the mugger, and the murderer? If so, then we must also hold them accountable for their actions and hence as having acted freely. Taylor argues that those who do not live up to moral ideals should be "open to censure"[26] and worthy of our contempt. But one may ask why this is so if to act immorally is, if not to behave unfreely, at least to wallow in an impoverished form of freedom? If such people are not free they cannot also be held responsible for their words and actions.

    Flathman contends that Taylor (along with most theorists of positive freedom) links together the concepts of liberty and virtue in a manner that ultimately provides an incoherent theory of freedom. As a result of the broadening of the moral (how we treat others) to incorporate the wider category of the ethical (how we ought to live), the concepts of agency and freedom become inescapably and unjustifiably tangled up with issues of virtuous behavior. By mixing these concepts together, Taylor obscures the crucial distinction between questions concerning the worth of an action and questions concerning the freedom of an action. Criticism of Taylor is not meant to suggest that the higher/lower distinction is not valuable in relation to the morality of an action, only that we cannot at the same time link it to the freedom of an act. The two have to be kept distinct. Nor am I trying to suggest that identification with a desire is not useful for understanding the freedom of an act, but it helps us judge the amount of control over the action, not the moral value of the act. I am quite willing to accept that we should evaluate preferences in terms of the importance they hold for agents, and if we cannot pursue these things we are less free. The idea of freedom on a continuum that I will develop later is based on this being the case in many instances. But we can identify with desires that most would see as unworthy of moral praise and, consequently, freedom should not be based upon some notion of the "incomparably higher" in relation to communal moral norms.

Flathman and Negative Freedom

Flathman argues for what he calls a "modified Hobbesian version of freedom:" we are free as agents to the extent that we are unimpeded in the pursuit of our desires by external forces. Action involves deliberation concerning objects pursued, and hence demands a more extended concept of rationality than the one found in Hobbes's discussion of freedom. Flathman claims that we can judge if a person is pursuing a given end in the most rational manner, and we can examine the logical and practical consistency of a set of ends, but we are on shaky ground if we try to assess one end as rationally better than another. Rationality is more an aid for attaining our ends than for ranking them, although this is not to suggest that we cannot provide cogent reasons for pursuing our objectives. Flathman is willing to say that we can make judgments about ends in regard to claims for autonomy but not in regard to freedom. He agrees with positive theorists that people may well be under the influence of habits and brute desires, but he argues that actions driven by such forces are usually the result of a free choice originally and continue to be in large measure free. We may realize we are in the grip of a habit or brute desire, recognize it as mistaken behavior, and still not be able to rid ourselves of it, suffering from a "weakness of the will."[27] But this does not mean we are unfree; we "cannot at once be unfree and make a mistake."[28] "I contend that such actions are the agent's own" based upon evaluative choices "authentic to the actor."[29]

It is only in the case of severe mental illness that we can say a person does not identify with given behavior. Aside from this extreme type of example, Flathman claims that we can identify to a greater or lesser extent with our actions, that we can exercise different levels of control over our behavior, and thus that we are free. He argues that we must, to some extent, identify with our desires that are always pursued through a process of reasoning. They are acted upon as the result of a rational understanding of alternatives, and must, therefore, be something with which the actor identifies. In the act of pursuing one desire rather than another we have demonstrated our capacity to place our desires on a scale of worth; once we can do this we have developed "a self that exercises control over itself."[30] Provided there are no external barriers preventing us from acting in the manner we wish, we have achieved genuine freedom in relation to our desires simply by choosing among, and acting upon them.

Hence freedom, as opposed to autonomy, is a pretty simple thing to gauge; as long as we are not impeded by external objects and we are capable of a minimum level of rationality we are free. Along with many other theorists of negative freedom, Flathman does allow that there are levels of agency that express more control of the self than so far acknowledged. He readily admits that the autonomous agent may demonstrate greater self-control than the person who is only marginally rational. Whether Flathman will also agree that the autonomous individual is more free is the question to which I now turn.

Flathman on Autonomy

Autonomy and freedom have different meanings according to Flathman, and they are not necessarily compatible with one another. The major difference between the two is that the requirements for a person to be described as free are less stringent than those required to describe a person as autonomous. In particular, a free action only has to be minimally rational to be counted as fully free, whereas defensible reasons have to motivate an agent before her action can be classed as autonomous. According to Flathman, autonomy requires more than acting in pursuit of ends and desires. We must also act in a manner that fits with the norms, rules, conventions, and traditions "that provide the setting in which day to day activities occur."[31]

It is not enough to be a "chooser" to be autonomous because we may choose according to standards that are held uncritically. We need to have arrived at our beliefs through a process of rational critical reflection. Beyond this, an autonomous agent needs to act according to a rationally conceived life-plan in which actions are integrated in such a manner that they correspond to long-term goals. Flathman argues that such a person does not have to be concerned with "good" or "higher" ends and principles to be classed as autonomous; a person can be both autonomous and immoral. Autonomy is about greater control of the self, but the self can be controlled in pursuit of both moral and immoral ends.

Given Flathman's analysis, we cannot differentiate between degrees of freedom because either we are not freedom evaluable, or we are exercising *full* freedom. Freedom for Flathman boils down to being able to pursue minimally rational desires unmolested by others. There are no intermediate possibilities because rationality is removed as a bench mark for freedom and becomes only a measure of autonomy. He argues that persons unencumbered by obsession, compulsion, psychosis, and so forth, are free; the issue then becomes one of how people use their freedom, not of whether they are free. Some choices will be harder than others, as with the smoker who recognizes that the habit is unhealthy but who is addicted to nicotine. Other choices can lead to a sad use of our liberty, as when a person slowly descends from one drink a day into alcoholism. But these are choices all the same, and if they are choices then the chooser must be a free person.

Having presented a clear demarcation line for freedom, Flathman suddenly introduces a different and apparently conflicting argument. On the one hand, he goes to great lengths to maintain a very definite distinction between freedom and autonomy. On the other hand, he now introduces a new claim and states that it is important to recognize that we are not all *equally* free. This is why at certain points in his book he posits the notion of freedom on a continuum: "it makes good sense to talk of *more or less* freedom."[32] When Flathman talks of freedom in terms of a continuum, he starts with psychosis; a condition that is not even "freedom evaluable." From this point, he considers habits which, to a greater or lesser extent, influence our lives and our degrees of freedom.

Flathman suggests that the continuum could progress from psychosis and neurosis, to habits we would rather abandon. From here the progression moves to akratic behavior, then onto habits of a benign kind. The plus side of the continuum goes from rational, instrumentally calculated actions, and then onto ever more positive character traits until we reach the status of Plato's philosopher-king. This continuum "is calibrated . . . from little or seriously inadequate control over inner forces to entire control over them."[33] Flathman suggests that the further along this continuum we can place a person, the more free we can say that person becomes.

How can we judge such freedom of action? The best demonstration according to liberal theories of freedom seems to be how well the agent rationally pursues goals. It seems logical, therefore, to argue that the more rational a person is the more free she is. This seems to be the conclusion we should arrive at if we think of freedom as a continuum. However, when Flathman distinguishes between freedom and autonomy, he argues that only a minimal form of rationality is required for *full* freedom. One can agree with Flathman that only a small amount of rationality is required for a person to be classed as minimally free (and, as a consequence, responsible for her actions), but it is unclear why Flathman will not agree that being more rational makes a person more free. Rationality is an aid to the pursuit and achievement of ends and must, therefore, be important in increasing the range of alternative choices available to the actor. The more rational we become, the more free also; freedom is again being measured on a continuum on which freedom and autonomy eventually blend into the same thing. This seems to be a sensible way to evaluate how free a person is and seems more precise than describing people as "unfree," as Taylor sometimes does, if they do not exercise full control over themselves. But it also seems to oppose the point of Flathman's distinction between freedom and autonomy.

When Flathman distinguishes between freedom and autonomy he argues that we should only differentiate between the psychotic and the more mentally stable in terms of the presence or absence of freedom. By positing a minimal rationality as a necessary and often as a sufficient condition of freedom, Flathman does make it easier to distinguish between freedom and autonomy. However, if an integral part of freedom is *choice* it becomes difficult to make subtle but important distinctions. In particular, we cannot say that persons are more free if they are more rational. Flathman does not deny that autonomy is in most cases an important good to be pursued, but he worries that it can potentially encroach upon freedom. It is important to remember that to be autonomous is not to be more free as far as Flathman is concerned. Autonomy "makes us better able to protect and profit from . . . (our) individual freedom,"[34] but it does not increase it. He sees the possibility of a slippery slope where the end result is an unjustified sacrifice of freedom for the sake of autonomy; freedom and autonomy can and do come into conflict. This is the main reason why he draws a clear distinction between the two concepts, and why he promotes a narrow definition of freedom. Without such clear boundaries, Flathman thinks the potential exists for interfering with a person's present exercise of freedom of choice for the sake of promoting more or "better" freedom in the future. It seems that Flathman does recognize that freedom is more complicated than his definition allows for (hence his discussion of freedom on a continuum) but he is unwilling to admit this because he fears opening the floodgates for coercion in the name of autonomy. This is what Taylor calls the "Maginot Line" defense of negative freedom that is based on the fear of the "totalitarian menace" of more expansive concepts of liberty.[35]

Is Flathman correct in arguing that his terminology provides better protection from unwarranted interference? Perhaps it does make us think more carefully before we decide to limit a person's freedom. I will argue, however, that the slippery slope cannot be escaped simply by separating freedom from autonomy. Once this has been demonstrated, the reasons for differentiating between freedom and autonomy become less pressing and we can use a more precise terminology that better addresses the complexities of the concept of freedom.

Consider the following example. A person may perform an action that was fully intended, an action that was identified with at the time of the act, and one for which full responsibility is accepted. Despite these factors the action may undermine certain long-term goals of the agent, and render impossible, future choices that are very important to self-realization. A concrete example of this may be an intravenous drug user. In this case, we may wish to say the action was free but that the person was not fully free or autonomous. We may conclude that freedom does clash with autonomy in this sense. But could we legitimately argue that an external agent would have been justified in intervening in a coercive manner to prevent the action? Maybe so, maybe not. The point is that we are faced with the same difficult choice whether we say it is a choice between freedom and autonomy or whether we say it is a choice between partial freedom and full freedom.

In the same manner that we need to debate whether we should interfere to make the partially free person fully free, Flathman has to face the choice of whether to make the free person autonomous. The problem is more of a semantic than a substantive kind. Flathman cannot avoid difficult choices and the threat of the slippery slope simply because he distinguishes freedom from autonomy; we are stuck on the slope whichever terminology we use. Given this dilemma, it is better to couch the discussion in terms of partial and full freedom because the alternative is to lose a lot of the ordinary meaning of the word *freedom*.

Flathman also makes too much of the danger of the slippery slope. If we examine the definition of autonomy we find that it rules out intrusive intervention in all but the most extreme cases. Autonomy requires a large degree of rationality, integrated behavior, and *self*-control, not control of the self by others. Flathman seems to recognize this and hence that autonomy cannot often be imposed at the expense of freedom. He states that "autonomy is self-rule . . . it is rule of one's own thought and action by oneself" and "it seems to follow that the absence of autonomy is its opposite, namely the rule of the self by someone or something apart from or other than the self."[36] One can be free and not autonomous as when one acts with limited rationality, but one cannot be autonomous and unfree because being autonomous means acting according to *one's own rationally chosen* ends. I do not see how we can claim that autonomy and fully rational freedom can be in conflict given a definition of autonomy that seems to rule out interference by others unless a person is going to cause herself serious harm. Joseph Raz defines autonomy in a similar manner: "The ruling idea behind the ideal of personal autonomy is that people should make their own lives"[37] and "his choice must be free from coercion and manipulation by others."[38] Once the problem is so defined, it seems better to talk of being more or less free in which "higher" levels of freedom blend into autonomous behavior. Autonomy becomes something that is not distinct from freedom but is instead a fuller or higher form of freedom.

It is clear that Flathman's sympathies lie with making a clear distinction between freedom and autonomy. My analysis suggests that the discussion of freedom measured along a continuum is the stronger argument, not because it represents a large substantive difference from the distinction between freedom and autonomy but because it allows for a more detailed description of free action.

Internal and External Freedom

If discussing freedom as a continuum provides a better terminology than Flathman's distinction between freedom and autonomy, how can we develop this view? Following Feinberg, we can differentiate between the categories of positive and negative, and internal and external constraints and opportunities, where negative and positive relates to the absence or presence of things affecting action. Freedom, for Feinberg, is largely about the exercise of control; constraints that hinder internal and external control over actions limit freedom, whereas opportunities, especially external ones, tend to promote freedom. A constraint is anything that prevents one from doing something and can be an internal condition such as psychosis or fear, or an external condition such as a locked door.

Although Feinberg does not spell it out in detail, his typology provides us with four categories: "internal positive," "internal negative," "external positive," and "external negative." He does not use the terms *positive* and *negative* in the traditional sense but instead uses them to refer to the presence or lack of something that may prevent a person from performing a desired action. Internally this could be a lack of knowledge, mental skills, or physical strength (negative constraints), or the presence of severe headaches, mental illnesses, or obsessive desires (positive constraints). Externally it may be the lack of money or basic material goods necessary to achieve one's goals (external negatives) or the presence of physical barriers such as barred doors, handcuffs, or prison cells (external positives) that limit our freedom. Freedom boils down to the presence of certain internal abilities and external opportunities and the absence of obstacles that prevent one from acting upon these abilities and opportunities: "Freedom from a negative constraint is the absence of an absence, and therefore the presence of some condition that permits a given kind of doing. The presence of such a condition when external to a person is usually called an opportunity, and when internal, an ability."[39]

To summarize, a negative constraint is the absence of something, the very absence of which prevents or limits freedom, and a positive constraint is the presence of something which, because of its presence, limits or prevents action. Following Gerald C. MacCallum Jr.'s well-known argument,[40] Feinberg argues that we should abandon the usual negative/positive freedom distinction; such a dichotomy does not exist because "freedom from," the heart of negative freedom also gives us "freedom to" things: "'Freedom from' and 'freedom to' are two sides of the same coin, each involved with the other, and not two radically distinct kinds of freedom, as some writers have suggested. Indeed it is difficult fully to characterize a given constraint without mentioning the desires it does or can constrain."[41]

MacCallum claims that all intelligible statements about freedom can be truncated into one concept of freedom expressed by the following triadic relationship: "X is (is not) free from Y to do (not do, become, not become) Z,"[42] where X is an agent, Y is an impediment of some kind, and Z is the goal/objective. If one of these three elements is missing then we are not really talking of freedom. The key, therefore, to understanding what different authors mean by freedom is not to separate them into positive and negative camps, but to delve more closely into what they specify as the criteria for conditions X, Y, and Z.

I do not think that MacCallum and Feinberg do justice to the differences between the two traditional concepts of freedom. The key to the success of their argument rest on the Y component: "[w]henever the freedom of some agent or agents is in question, it is *always* freedom from some constraint or restriction on, interference with, or barrier to doing, not doing, becoming, or not becoming something."[43] Do all theorists, negative and positive, say that freedom is about the lack of restraint on action? I do not think so. Is a dog as free as Einstein? We tend to think that it is not because it lacks the intellectual and rational capacities of the famous scientist. Hence it does not have the same knowledge, interests, and choices as Einstein. The only way round this problem for MacCallum is to claim that the absence of certain physical or mental faculties counts as a constraint, or as an interference. But note that the terms *restraint, interference, restriction,* and *barrier* (the terms MacCallum uses) suggest that something is getting in the way of agency, that is, that something is present, not that something is lacking, or absent. Only if we become extremely loose with our use of the word "constraint" can we cram all arguments about freedom into one neat package. The term constraint now becomes so elastic that it no longer acts as a useful conceptual tool.

Some theorists of positive freedom (as we noted with Taylor) go even further and suggest very clearly that even when there are no restraints on my actions I can still be unfree because my actions are morally unworthy. Freedom in this sense demands that we do certain things and refrain from doing other things. At its extreme, the argument suggests that we are unfree because we are pursuing ends that do not fit with our telos as human beings. This argument has nothing to do with barriers or constraints; it has everything to do with an evaluation of the right and wrong goals that should be pursued.

It is also worth noting that Hobbes's statements on liberty do not always fit into the triadic construction because his more extreme formulations of freedom do not specify a requirement for either agency (category X), or objectives (category Z), in his definition of freedom: "LIBERTY, or FREEDOM, signifieth, properly, the absence of opposition . . . and may be applied no less to irrational, and inanimate creatures than to rational."[44] A rock rolling down a hill and a river flowing between its banks is fully free according to Hobbes. Unless we are willing to say that one of the most famous expositions of all time on freedom is actually not about freedom, we will have to abandon the idea that the triadic formulation encompasses all that there is to say about liberty.

MacCallum and Feinberg are not blending positive and negative freedom into a "single concept analysis"[45] as they suggest because they do not address many of the other traditional concerns of theorists of positive freedom. For example, Feinberg's four categories cannot help us get to the heart of whether certain desires make us unfree (unless he wants to make the dubious assertion that desires are also constraints); neither author concerns himself sufficiently with the question of whether we can split the self into higher or lower faculties; nor do they fully examine the question of whether it is necessary to participate politically in order to be free. Hobbes himself ridiculed the idea of democratic freedom for precisely the reason that such statements did not relate freedom to the absence of impediments. The idea that I am only free when I live according to laws that I have imposed upon myself may not be terribly persuasive, but it is certainly an idea that is distinct from the one linking all notions of freedom to the issue of constraints.

Feinberg's method of analysis remains useful, however, because it allows me to demonstrate that Hobbes's theory of freedom is much richer than has previously been noted and I will extend his analysis to include some of the traditional concerns of theorists of positive freedom. Rather than providing a theory that does away with the differences between positive and negative theories of freedom, I think it is fair to say that MacCallum and Feinberg, by limiting themselves to the triadic formulation are really presenting an expansive, complex and, I think, more defensible reinterpretation of negative freedom. In particular, Feinberg allows for external hindrances to freedom that go beyond actual physical barriers. Although a lack of material goods is not a physical obstacle to freedom in the same way as a brick wall, it nevertheless makes sense to argue, as Feinberg does, that a pauper is not free to buy an expensive car even if nothing is physically stopping him from doing so: "If only positive factors are counted as constraints, then a pauper might be free of constraints to his (actual or possible) desire to buy a Cadillac, and yet, of course, he is not free *to* buy a Cadillac."[46]

Feinberg also allows us to delve more deeply into the internal limitations on freedom. He is willing to recognize that habits, desires, and passions can sometimes grip us (and make us do something rather than constrain us from doing something) in such a way as to limit our freedom:

> A person who had no hierarchical structure of wants, and aims, and ideals, and no clear conception of where it is within him that he really resides, would be a battlefield for all of his constituent elements, tugged this way and that, and fragmented hopelessly . . . [o]ur picture of the undisciplined or anomic man is not that of a well-defined self with a literal or figurative bayonet at his back, or barriers, locked doors, and barred windows on all sides. Rather it employs the image of roads crowded with vehicles in the absence of traffic cops or traffic signals to keep order: desires, impulses, and purposes come and go at all speeds and in all directions, and get nowhere . . . he is a man free from external shackles, but tied in knots by the strands of his own wants.[47]

This is a perfectly legitimate way to talk of freedom as long as we recognize that all of the internal limitations on freedom cannot be bulldozed into the single category of constraint.

I think a more coherent theory of freedom can be developed by taking Flathman's discarded concept of a continuum and adding it to Feinberg's distinction between internal and external conditions of freedom. For example, when examining Hobbes's discussion of internal conditions of liberty and action, we can evaluate it in relation to his views of passions, habits, fear, and rationality. In chapters 4 and 5, I will argue that Hobbes thought that the more an action exhibits rationality, the more the agent demonstrates control over internal conditions of freedom. The internal/external categories allow me to draw out the intricacies of Hobbes's argument concerning the requirements for full agency in a manner that the positive/negative categories do not allow.

A continuum for internal conditions for freedom could start with the completely catatonic person who is not really capable of agency and hence freedom at all. We can move from here to the schizophrenic and onto the obsessive, both of whom may be free in certain aspects of their lives but gripped by mental illness in other aspects. We can perhaps continue on to lesser habits and desires, such as smoking or kleptomania and from here to people who cannot distinguish well between long-and short-term goals. At the upper end of the continuum are those who can organize desires and goals into a coherent life-plan. Finally, one who is fully free resembles the Kantian ideal of an autonomous individual. Such a person is able to organize a life around norms and principles that go beyond personal preferences. It is no longer enough to pursue goals in a rational manner—such goals have to be measured in terms of reasonableness. The further along this continuum we can place a person the more free we can say that person becomes.

On a continuum illustrating external conditions of freedom, we can begin with a person in a straitjacket deprived of all physical movement. Handcuffs and prison cells allow for slightly more external freedom and their absence allow a person free unimpeded movement. We can then consider the material conditions affecting physical movement; money, tools, equipment, transportation, and so forth, as well as barriers that are imposed from outside the person but that are not physical, such as legal systems and coercive threats. The defining feature of internal and external freedom is not necessarily the existence of a lot of choices because one may have many choices and yet still lack the capacity for action, or have only a few desires that one wishes to act upon. The key is how much control we can exercise over the choices we wish to make. When we recognize that freedom has such a complex character, we can say that we are free in some areas of our lives, less free in others, and that perhaps in a few areas we have no freedom at all. This is because in some areas we may exercise full control, in other areas only partial control, and in still others, none at all.

This view of freedom helps us in some hard cases. Take, on the one hand, Hobbes's claim that a person held hostage by a highwayman to give up either his money or his life, is completely free to choose either option. On the other hand, many have objected that this is not a situation where freedom exists at all, because the person has no real freedom to choose between the two options. Neither of these answers seems to be satisfying. As G. A. Cohen notes, the latter argument fails because it entails making the claim that someone was unfree in performing an action, when in fact, the person would not have been able to perform the action if he was unfree.[48] If one was not free to do what one was coerced to do (give up the money) there would be no point in the coercing agent exerting his power; it is the very fact that the person is free in some sense to give up the money that motivates the highwayman to hold him up in the first place.

But Hobbes's claim also fails because freedom judged solely in terms of the lack of external impediments cannot capture the rich variety of ways in which we can be free. What we should say about the unfortunate victim of the crime is that he is partially free; he could choose to give up his life; he could choose to fight back; he could choose to give up the money. Certainly we can say that the latter choice is the easier of the three. It is perhaps better to suggest that he is free to give up the money but that he is not doing so fully freely. One could perhaps reply that he is still fully free; he is acting upon his considered desires, it is just that his preferences have taken a sudden change. Before the intervention of the highwayman, his preference was to keep his money; after the intervention his preference changed to protecting his life. This, however, simply confuses the issue. The man's preferences have in fact not changed; he would still like to keep his money, it is just that it has become significantly more difficult for him to act on this preference. This is why he is only partially free; he is forced to *act* (and hence in some sense he is free) but his action is not in line with his rational preference (and hence he is not fully free).

Let us look at another example which, although supplied by Flathman, demonstrates why his sharp distinction between freedom and autonomy is inadequate. Flathman argues that Sakharov, in his prison cell, is unfree but autonomous. I argue that this is not the best way of describing Sakharov's condition. Instead, we should use the vocabulary of internal and external conditions of freedom. Let us begin with external conditions; here we can conclude that Sakharov is largely unfree, trapped within his prison walls. He is better off than if he was in chains, but this freedom is still very limited. What about internal conditions of agency? He appears to be very rational and capable of considerable self-control, enough for Flathman to class him as autonomous. But this also is not the case. Firstly, Sakharov's circumstances severely limit any chance of an extensive life-plan. Secondly, he will still have a variety of desires, ends, and purposes necessary to his self-realization that he is unable to pursue because of his prison walls. His external conditions necessarily preclude autonomy or full freedom because they limit both his external and internal freedom. We must conclude that he is hardly free at all externally, and only partially free internally; Sakharov, or anyone else, cannot be fully autonomous if denied external freedom.

This is not to deny that internally, Sakharov may be able to attain a significant degree of self-realization that is unattainable for most people who are not coerced and imprisoned. But surely we can argue that Sakharov would be more self-actualizing and free if he were not coerced. It is hard to imagine that a person can be as self-fulfilled when coerced as when not coerced; this is what coercion is—a limitation (but, as just noted, not a complete denial) of one's freedom. Once we conceptualize freedom as divided into internal and external categories, it becomes much more difficult to justify coercing people (imposing external limits) for the sake of autonomy (enhanced internal control). Freedom as a continuum allows us to make such fine gradations regarding the liberty available to individuals; Flathman's distinction between freedom and autonomy, and the general distinction between positive and negative liberty does not.

The distinction between freedom and autonomy creates difficulties for any meaningful discussion of coercion. Despite Flathman's concern that without clear demarcations people may be coerced into autonomy, the logic of his distinctions actually suggests the counterintuitive position that the coerced person, while lacking autonomy, is still free. I can be coerced and yet still maintain minimal rationality and remain physically unmolested (the two requirements for freedom according to Flathman). Only if Flathman extends the discussion of freedom beyond these minimal criteria can he say that coercion limits freedom. Hence, Flathman distorts much of what we mean by the term *freedom* and robs it of much of its value. He ends up on the same side of the fence as Hobbes who claims that the person with a gun to his head is still free to give up his money or his life. Such claims lead us to ask: "if freedom is so compatible with coercion, why do we value it so highly?"

Conclusion

I do not deny that there may very infrequently be a clash between full and partial freedom as just discussed. But it is better to think of it as such, rather than as a clash between freedom and autonomy. We can be much more precise about the limitations and improvements in conditions of freedom if we use the internal and external terminology. And I think this is a vocabulary that allows us to see clearly that at the "top" end of the continuum freedom and autonomy blend into the same thing. We are able to discuss a lot of behavior we normally want to talk of in terms of freedom and unfreedom by expanding the concept of freedom beyond Flathman's narrow definition while avoiding Taylor's complicated categories of desires. For example, Flathman argues that smokers are free because they have chosen to smoke, and because they have chosen to smoke they must be *fully* free. Taylor, however, suggests that smokers are unfree if they do not identify with their habit. Surely the all-or-nothing approach by both authors to this question is unhelpful and it is better to say that the smoker who wants to give up the habit but has great difficulty doing so is less free in this regard than the person who does not smoke. It does not get to the heart of the matter, however, to say that the person who does not smoke is autonomous whereas the smoker is free because the nonsmoker may also be in the grip of some other habit or compulsion, or may display irrational behavior in many other aspects of her life.

Is somebody with a physical handicap less free than a person without such a disability? Berlin's distinction makes it difficult to answer such a question; the person may be free from external impediments, and hence fully free from the point of view of negative freedom. My argument suggests that in terms of external freedom the handicapped person is not as free as the able-bodied because she does not have the same capacity to act in the physical world; but it may also be the case that having to overcome such a disability fosters all sorts of internal capacities that make the person freer in other ways. It is not to be denied that discussing liberty in these terms often makes judging the freedom of actions very difficult—so be it. It is better to have realistic complexity than unhelpful and misleading parsimony. Thinking about freedom as a continuum also deflects one of the major criticisms of negative theories of liberty, namely that such theories cannot fully embrace the notion of self-realization. The theory of freedom on a continuum suggests that we become more free the more we are rationally able to realize our desires, purposes, and ends. The person who attains full self-realization (if such a thing is possible) would also be fully free.

I have argued that the vocabulary of internal and external, and partial and full freedom, is more useful than the more popular vocabulary that distinguishes between negative and positive freedom. It addresses the complex nature of freedom in a way that the traditional distinction cannot. I conclude that, despite appearances to the contrary, Flathman and Taylor agree on many of the requirements for free agency. In his more persuasive moments, Flathman is willing to accept that freedom demands more than the absence of external obstacles to minimally rational behavior. And Taylor, I think, would agree that there are many aspects of his formulation of positive freedom that fit well with the idea of freedom on a continuum. We can also throw Raz into the pot to strengthen the consensus: "Autonomy in both its primary and secondary senses is a matter of degree. One's life may be more or less autonomous."[49] Discussing freedom in terms of the internal and external boundaries of agency, rather than in terms of a dichotomy between philosophical traditions of positive and negative liberty highlights the wide-ranging terrain of agreement. Even Hobbes could not hold to drawing the boundary of freedom at physical impediments to motion. Although he suggested that "Liberty, or Freedom, signifieth, properly, the absence of opposition"[50] we will see that in his more reflective moods he admitted that internal conditions of the agent also limit freedom. Where the consensus between Taylor and Flathman breaks down is when Taylor shifts the debate from the realm of freedom to the realm of virtue. I agree with Flathman that this is an illegitimate move; it perverts our understanding of liberty and moves the boundaries of the discussion of freedom from the *rationally* defensible to the *morally* permissible.

Part II

Freedom, Autonomy, Rationality, and Morality

3

⁓

Hobbes and Negative Freedom

Introduction

On first reading, Hobbes seems to provide a simple and logically consistent concept of freedom. Agents are at liberty to the extent that their actions remain unimpeded by external obstacles. A majority of commentators have interpreted Hobbes as a theorist of pure "negative" freedom who discusses freedom solely in terms of external impediments to motion, although J. R. Pennock and Brian Barry note that Hobbes sometimes seems to link together freedom and obligation.[1] But even these commentators do not argue that Hobbes's theory extends much beyond discussing freedom as the lack of external impediments. While there is some diversity among Hobbes scholars, nonetheless, differences in interpretation are limited.

I argue, however, that his theory of freedom tends to be considerably more complicated than previously thought. Hobbes actually uses the term *liberty* in several ways, which sometimes complement one another and that at other times lead him to contradictory positions. Indeed, once we examine his argument carefully, we find a rich, although occasionally contradictory, view of freedom. In this chapter, I explain the extent to which Hobbes is consistent in his different usages of the terms *liberty* and *freedom*, words he uses synonymously. As just noted, the consensus among scholars rests in favor of interpreting Hobbes as a theorist of pure negative freedom. J. W. N. Watkins, for example, sums up Hobbes's theory by saying that "a man is free if he can do what he has the will to do,"[2] and Alan Ryan argues that for Hobbes: "Liberty as unimpededness is the only sort of liberty there is."[3] Quentin Skinner also suggests that "Hobbes bequeathed a classic statement of this point of view [negative freedom], one that is still repeatedly invoked."[4]

I will demonstrate that Hobbes also discusses a great many other conditions of freedom besides the absence of external impediments. Throughout the chapter, I call the predominant view of Hobbes's theory "pure" negative freedom and the view expounded here as Hobbes's "extended" theory of freedom. I will proceed, therefore, to examine the relationship between Hobbes's version of external freedom and such concepts as causality, fear, obligation, endeavor, punishment, and the laws and right of nature.

External Freedom and Causality

In chapter 6 of *Leviathan,* Hobbes argues for what seems like a very mechanistic theory of movement. All actions are caused by something and in this sense everything is determined. As he says in *Liberty and Necessity:*

> For he is free to do a thing, that may do it if he have the will to do it, and may forbear if he have the will to forbear. And yet if there be a necessity that he shall have the will to do it, the action is necessarily to follow; and if there be a necessity that he shall have the will to forbear, the forbearing also will be necessary. The question therefore is not whether a man be a free agent, that is to say, whether he can write or forbear, speak or be silent, according to his will; but whether the will to write and the will to forbear come upon him according to his will, or according to anything else in his power. I acknowledge this liberty, that I can do if I will; but to say that I can will if I will, I take to be an absurd speech . . . liberty from necessitation, yet I understand not how such a liberty can be.[5]

As Ralph Ross, Richard S. Peters, and others note,[6] this immediately introduces a potential problem for Hobbes, who wants to argue that the universe is causally determined, and yet who also wishes to discuss freedom of action in a meaningful way. Somehow, Hobbes must make freedom and determinism compatible.

Hobbes distinguishes between two kinds of negative freedom. The first is simply the unhindered movement of any material body. Here there is no distinction between inanimate, animate but irrational, and animate and rational bodies. For example, Hobbes does not distinguish between water running downhill, the physical movements of irrational animals, and the movements of human beings. As long as they are all unimpeded in their movement they are described as free: "LIBERTY, or FREEDOM, signifieth, properly, the absence of opposition . . . and may be applied no less to irrational, and inanimate creatures, than to rational."[7] Included in this category, which he calls "involuntary movement," are such things as coursing of the blood, blinking of the eyes, and breathing. Freedom does not require rationality, and fear and freedom are compatible with one another, which suggests that Hobbes was unconcerned with conditions that are "internal" to the actor: "I conceive of liberty to be rightly defined in this manner: Liberty is the absence of all the impediments to action that are not contained in the nature and intrinsical quality of the agent."[8]

Hobbes also distinguishes a realm of freedom based on volition and this is where the potential tension between freedom and determinism appears. In the case of voluntary acts, our thought processes are still determined by previous events and hence we have no free will in the sense of uncaused thoughts. An act of the will, for Hobbes, simply demonstrates that we have stopped the causal chain of thoughts that move us to a particular action. We do have the choice of acting in certain ways in response to external stimuli, however and this is the realm of voluntary freedom. Hobbes now says that man is free when he "is not hindered to do what he has the WILL to do."[9] "Voluntary presupposes some precedent deliberation, that is to say, some consideration and meditation of what is likely to follow, both upon the doing and abstaining from the action deliberated of."[10]

The difference between the two types of negative freedom is that in the case of voluntary motions the line of causality runs through the human thought process, whereas with involuntary motion it does not. Involuntary refers "to which Motions there needs no help of Imagination," whereas voluntary motion can involve considerable calculation: "And though a man have in every long deliberation a great many wills and nills, they use to be called inclinations, and the last only will, which is immediately followed by the voluntary action"[11] that consists in moving "any of our limbs, in such a manner as is first fancied in our minds."[12] Spontaneous actions are still caused by a previous thought; it is just that there is not as much deliberation involved: "I call them voluntary because those actions that follow immediately the last appetite are voluntary, and here where there is one only appetite that one is the last . . . for no action of a man can be said to be without deliberation, though never so sudden."[13] Such causal links can be very complicated, but Hobbes drives home the fact that, no matter how complicated the process, nothing moves without being caused by a prior phenomenon:

> Nor does the concourse of all causes make one simple chain or concatenation but an innumerable number of chains joined together, not in all parts, but in the first link God Almighty; and consequently the whole cause of an event does not always depend on one single chain, but on many together . . . the last dictate of the judgement, concerning the good or bad that may follow on any action, is not properly the whole cause, but the last part of it; and yet may be said to produce the effect necessarily, in such manner as the last feather may be said to break a horse's back, when there were so many laid on before as there wanted by that to do it.[14]

This form of voluntarism is still a theory of pure negative freedom. Hobbes, at this juncture, does not wish to make any judgment concerning the rationality of the choices a person wills. Although Hobbes distinguishes between voluntary and involuntary movement, it does not affect his theory of freedom because freedom only begins when will and deliberation end. Freedom is still defined by whether there is anything outside of the agent impeding the pursuit of what is willed: "the liberty of the man . . . consisteth in this, that he finds no stop, in doing what he has the will, or desire, or inclination to doe."[15]

At this point, Hobbes is saying that there is nothing to be achieved by drawing the line between freedom and unfreedom according to different states of mind. Instead, he defines the limits of liberty in terms of things external to our consciousness. Any movement, therefore, whether the line of causality runs through the mind or from an external force, is a free movement if it is unimpeded. It is important to note that when Hobbes talks of external impediments he means some *material body* that *physically* impedes motion, such as a wall, a door, chains, or the banks of a river:

> For whatsoever is so tyed, or environed, as it cannot move, but within a certain space, which space is determined by the opposition of some externall body, we say it hath not Liberty to go further. And so of all living creatures, whilest they are imprisoned, or restrained, with walls, or chayns; and of the water whilest it is kept in by banks, or vessels, that otherwise would spread it selfe into a larger space, we use to say they are not at Liberty, to move in such a manner, as without those externall impediments they would."[16]

According to this definition of freedom, very few things curtail our liberty completely. If I am locked in a room I am still free to decide whether to sit or stand, or walk or lie down. And if these things are the only things that I will, then the prison walls are not impinging upon my freedom at all; it is only to the extent that the walls prevent what I will that I am unfree.

According to Hobbes, I would have to be chained and incapable of physical movement to be totally unfree: "If a man should talk to me of. . . . A free subject; A free-will; or any free, but free from being hindered by opposition, I should not say he were in an Errour; but that his words were without meaning, that is to say, Absurd."[17] This is a very strong claim by Hobbes because he is saying that to talk of freedom in *any* way other than the lack of external impediments is nonsense. If Hobbes is correct in this statement it seems that there can never be any such thing as absolute freedom because there would be no movement at all without external objects. In the case of human beings who move according to responses to sensory experience and imagination, there would be no movement if there were no objects or actions stimulating movement. And in the case of movement itself, whether of an animate or inanimate object, it could not take place at all without external friction that can only occur with physical contact.

Hobbes continues by stating that when the impediment to motion is internal to the thing itself, this is not a want of liberty but of the power to move. Hobbes does not say that a person who is inhibited by internal factors is lacking in freedom; rather the person is lacking in the power necessary for free movement: "when the impediment of motion is in the constitution of the thing itself . . . not to say, it wants the liberty, but the power to move."[18] In this context, Hobbes is using the term *power* somewhat differently than when he talks of power in general terms as the "present means, to obtain some future apparent good."[19] Here, power also relates to internal limits to motion. Hence, anything internal to agents, whether it be a lack of willpower, irrationality, physical sickness, fear, or obligation, does not limit freedom; such agents are powerless but not libertyless. Although power and liberty are different, we need the former to perform voluntary actions. We need the will to act (power) and a lack of external obstacles that prevent us acting upon our will (freedom). It is not surprising, therefore, that most students of Hobbes present him as one of the foremost proponents of the purest form of negative freedom. Despite what some commentators have thought, the distinction between involuntary and voluntary movement and the discussion of the will being the last act of deliberation makes no difference to Hobbes's theory of pure negative freedom. Freedom of movement in both cases has nothing to do with the thing moving but only with whether it is impeded in its movement.

It follows that a theory of pure negative freedom does not contradict a deterministic view of the world because the theory is only concerned with what stops motion, not with what causes it. Hence, Hobbes can say without contradiction: "that to him that could see the connection of those causes, the *necessity* of all mens voluntary actions would appear manifest."[20] This is not to say that there is no difference between the effects of impediments to voluntary as opposed to involuntary movement; there are many more avenues of movement for a person than for an inanimate object because humans can will to perform actions. But, because Hobbes's theory of external freedom only looks at impediments and not at the genesis of movement, it applies equally to all movement whether willed or unwilled. Hence, there is no real reason for Hobbes to distinguish between the two.

Hobbes can argue in this way because he defines liberty in a very narrow sense that does not include thought processes; instead, all things internal to the actor come under the heading of power. Because his theory severely limits what is to be counted as impinging upon freedom, it is quite compatible with determinism. One may respond, correctly I think, that Hobbes's theory of freedom, as discussed so far, is inadequate because one cannot get rid of internal obstacles to freedom simply by redefining them in terms of power. But however inadequate, to this point Hobbes is at least consistent. This consistency begins to crumble, however, when we examine some of the other ways in which Hobbes utilizes the term *liberty*.

Freedom and Will

The first internal beginnings of motion, springing from imagination, Hobbes calls "Endeavor." Endeavor directs us toward some object of desire or appetite, or away from something we dislike. Motion, therefore, is caused by things we perceive as good or bad. Hobbes does not want to say that these internal passions can count as restrictions on freedom; actions "that have their beginning from Aversion, or Feare of those consequences that follow the omission, are voluntary actions."[21] To make this argument he must continue to maintain the distinction between power and liberty. Hobbes argues, therefore, that we only enter the realm of freedom once we have finished deliberating. Liberty only relates to impediments to motions that occur after one has deliberated. The will is what puts an end to deliberation and we express our freedom once we put our will into motion.

And yet at other times it seems it is the act of deliberation itself that puts an end to liberty: "And it is called deliberation; because it is a putting an end to the liberty we had of doing . . . because till then we retain the liberty of doing or of omitting, according to our appetite or aversion."[22] Hence, it seems that Hobbes argues that deliberation is not freedom evaluable because it is internal to the actor, but also that it is the putting to an end of the liberty of making a choice, that is, that once we act and express our will we are no longer free. Hobbes seems to be arguing that we are free and unfree at the same time, and yet we cannot be both. He at times also suggests that freedom is about choice itself and not whether one can act upon one's choices: "When a man is hungry, it is in his choice to eat or not eat; this is the liberty of the man."[23]

The claim that deliberation is connected with freedom is inconsistent with his notion of pure negative freedom; if deliberation is linked to freedom then so too must things internal to the actor. The problem is that in his discussion of deliberation and endeavor, Hobbes sometimes links movement (and hence freedom) to aversions that are internal to the actor. As we have seen, endeavor either moves us toward or away from external objects (or, if we are indifferent to the thing, there is no motion at all). In the case of something we desire, there does not seem to be a problem in Hobbes's formulation; we desire something, we move toward it, and we are either successful or not in attaining the desire depending upon whether something external to us gets in our way.

But what of things we are averse to? In this case, what prevents motion is not an external obstacle, but our own passions. It is true that what sparks the passion is external to us, but it does not prevent motion in the same way as a straightjacket or a brick wall. What prevents motion is deliberation on the passions; this in turn results in an aversion that limits motion because of a fear of the likely consequences of the action. Hence, the external object cannot itself be the thing that stops motion because the motion itself never takes place. He goes as far as to say that things we find *offensive* result in "hindering, and troubling the motions vitall." The inconsistency is explained by the fact that Hobbes no longer refers to internal features of action only in terms of power. He begins to talk of them, instead, as a "putting an end to liberty," which implicitly assumes that internal conditions of the agent affect and, more particularly, limit freedom. In Hobbes's discussion of will and deliberation, therefore, we see the first signs that he was not always comfortable with maintaining the power-liberty distinction.

Fear and Freedom

Hobbes wishes to argue that fear and freedom are compatible; to forego an action because of fear is not a lack of liberty, but once again a lack of power: "Feare and Liberty are consistent; as when a man throweth his goods into the sea for *feare* the ship should sink, he doth it very willingly, and may refuse to doe it if he hath the will: It is therefore the action, of one that was free."[24] He continues by claiming that "generally all actions which men doe in Commonwealths, for *feare* of the law . . . had *liberty* to omit."[25] Hobbes tells us that we are bound even to pay the highwayman if we promise to do so: "where no other law (as in the condition of meer nature) forbiddeth the performance, the covenant is valid," for "covenants entered into by fear . . . are obligatory,"[26] because they are done voluntarily. We are free to give up our lives or our wallets to the highwayman because we are acting voluntarily in each case.

Hobbes's arguments concerning obligation must dictate that contracts entered into in the state of nature through fear of death are voluntary and hence valid, binding, and free. Otherwise, the covenant we make to give up our right of nature would not be binding, and there would be no foundation for our obligations to the sovereign:

> And this kind of Dominion or Soveraignty [by acquisition] differeth from Soveraignty by Institution, onely in this, that men who choose their Soveraign, do it for fear of one another, and not of him whom they Institute: But in this case, they subject themselves, to him they are afraid of. In both cases they do it for fear: which is to be noted by them, that hold all such Covenants, as proceed from fear of death, or violence, voyd: which if it were true, no man, in any kind of Common-wealth, could be obliged to Obedience.[27]

Hence, whether a commonwealth is instituted by contract or conquest makes no difference to its validity because in both cases the subjects are free to agree to obey even though they do so from fear (I will suggest later in the book that the distinction between contract and conquest does in fact make a difference to Hobbes's theory of freedom).

Hobbes tells us that laws gain their force not from the difficulty of breaking them, but from the danger of so doing. The laws are "artificiall chains"[28] that place limits upon our actions. In *De Cive*, Hobbes says that in civil society laws do not hinder liberty because "no man . . . is so hindered by the punishments appointed by the city . . . how cruel soever, that he may do all things . . . necessary to the preservation of his life and health."[29] A person who refrains from action because of fear of punishment "is not oppressed by servitude, but is governed and sustained."[30] By stating that liberty stands in opposition to servitude, Hobbes is making the claim that we are still free in relation to law, although law does tend to temper our actions. Laws give us cause for thought but they do not imprison us. To maintain consistency he must mean that laws put limits upon our power, but not upon our liberty.

Up to this point, therefore, there is no contradiction because Hobbes is still maintaining the distinction that fear and liberty are compatible, even though fear and power are not. What stops us from disobeying the law is not an external obstacle but fear of the consequences, which limits our *power* but not our freedom. In *De Cive*, he says that to do things "according to our desires without impediment and WITHOUT PUNISHMENT is liberty."[31] There can be no city without some limitation on freedom because all cities have laws, the breaking of which bring punishment. According to this argument, the fewer punishments there are the more freedom there is, as long as Hobbes means by punishment the imposition of external barriers to our movements, such as prison walls and chains, and not psychological punishments, which would have to involve internal considerations.

As an aside, Hobbes argues that the person who contemplates the consequences of his or her actions when committing a crime is more blameworthy than the one who acts from sudden passion: "A crime arising from a sudden Passion, is not so great, as when the same ariseth from long meditation . . . he that doth it with praemeditation, has used circumspection, and cast his eye, on the Law, on the punishment, and on the consequence thereof to humane society."[32] This suggests that there are different levels of freedom depending upon how premeditated the action is. The contemplative action is deemed more an expression of the person's will than the act of immediate passion. The implication is that Hobbes is aware of the fact that internal rationality has a strong impact upon the freedom of an action. My argument is supported by Hobbes's claim that only those who are capable of rationally making promises to the sovereign are obliged by the law: "Over naturall fooles, children, or mad-men there is no Law, no more than over brute beasts; nor are they capable of the title of just or unjust; because they had never power to make any covenant, or to understand the consequences thereof."[33] Hence, for Hobbes, freedom is linked to responsibility and rationality that again introduces internal considerations into the question of liberty.

To return to the question of fear and freedom, in *Leviathan* Hobbes changes his position from *De Cive*. As a consequence, he runs into severe inconsistencies when he expands his discussion from the example of the fear of the highwayman to fear of the law. In *Leviathan*, Hobbes refers to people who are under the dominion of laws as having the *liberty* of *subjects*. For such individuals, liberty is *only* found in those areas of action that "the Sovereign hath praeter-mitted."[34] The end of civil laws, Hobbes tells us, "is no other . . . but to *limit* the naturall *liberty* of particular men, in such a manner, as they might not hurt, but assist one an-other."[35] And this limit to liberty comes "from *Feare* of some evill consequence"[36] of breaking contracts and promises. Hobbes states as much in the introduction to *Leviathan* where he says that his task is to find the correct balance be-tween authority and freedom. The suggestion here is that authority is a necessary limitation upon freedom. He makes this clear when he states that the sovereign is "a Power set up to constrain those that would otherwise vio-late their faith."[37]

Hobbes has suddenly changed his argument; rather than laws limiting only an individual's power, they now limit her liberty. And, crucially, they limit her liberty not because they are physical externalities (as he says, they are only "artificial chains") but because of the *fear* of punish-ment. Even in his works devoted solely to demonstrating his theory of freedom he falls into the same mistake. In *Liberty and Necessity* he states: "[b]ut the distinction of free into free from compulsion and free from necessitation I ac-knowledge. For to be free from compulsion is to do a thing so as terror be not the cause of his will to do it. For a man is then only said to be compelled when fear makes him willing to it, as when a man willingly throws his goods into the sea to save himself. . . . But free from necessitation, I say, no man can be."[38] Now Hobbes seems to be using the example of the person on the ship to distinguish between acts that are compelled by fear and those that are not in terms of freedom. It makes no sense to talk of being free from compulsion given his strict definition of freedom because compulsion is not an external object. But to show his confusion on this matter, on the very next page he says "it cannot be conceived that there is any liberty greater than for a man to do what he will. One heat may be more intensive than another but not one liberty than another. He that can do what he will has all liberty possible, and he that cannot has none at all."[39]

The potency of the law to limit liberty is also found in Hobbes's claim that "when we speak freely, it is not the liberty of voice, or pronunciation, but of the man, *whom no law hath obliged to speak otherwise*."[40] It is clear from this statement that Hobbes thought fear of the law was enough to limit our freedom of speech. Freedom now exists where the sovereign allows it: "such as in the Liberty to buy, and sell, and otherwise contract with one another; to choose their own aboad, their own diet, their own trade . . . and the like."[41] This statement means that liberty exists where the law is silent and that within this realm, freedom includes the liberty to *choose*.

This is not to suggest that laws are not in some sense external to the agent, but Hobbes does not count them as external impediments in the same sense as, for example, handcuffs. They are different because they cannot stop motion in any way other than by affecting the psychological nature of the individual. For example, a law or an obligation cannot stop the motion of an animal or a falling rock. The only way that they stop a human from acting, therefore, is psychologically, either through a sense of obligation or through the fear of consequences. Hobbes makes the same argument in relation to God. He tells us that for the religiously inclined, the obligation to God limits what we can and cannot do. The fear of God, albeit a lesser fear for most people than the fear of civil punishment, also checks us from breaking our promises.

These considerations necessarily introduce internal properties of the agent into the question of freedom. In

Hobbes's pure theory of negative freedom he cannot claim that such things limit freedom and this is why he argues that checks on movement that are internal to the thing moving, limit its power and not its freedom. Laws and obligations cannot, by definition, be *external impediments* in the sense Hobbes originally uses the term because they cannot limit freedom in the same way that being chained to a brick wall limits freedom.

Hobbes is compelled to make these arguments because he does not wish to argue that we are in the same condition of freedom living under laws as we are in the state of nature. This comes through particularly clearly in the following exchange from *Behemoth or the Long Parliament* when he specifically notes, during a discussion of the Rump Parliament, that his raw definition of liberty is inadequate:

> A. They took also afterwards another name, which was *Custodes Libertatis Angliae* which title they used only in their writs issuing out of the courts of justice
>
> B. I do not see how a subject that is tied to the laws, can have more liberty in one form of government than in another
>
> A. Howsoever, to the people that understand by liberty nothing but leave to do what they list, it was not a title not ingrateful.[42]

If liberty is only to be understood as the absence of external impediments, however, there is no difference in liberty in the state of nature or in society. Civil society does not put more *physical* impediments in our path. In fact, the tone of Hobbes's arguments suggests the opposite, that is that in civil society we will be less impeded in our movements. Natural liberty (negative freedom) is the only kind of liberty that coincides with the lack of external impediments and this has to be abandoned when Hobbes argues in favor of civil society.

Hobbes is really presenting not just two similar *kinds* of liberty, natural and civil, in which one is a little more expansive than the other, but two *concepts* of liberty, external and internal. His definition of natural liberty is as much a literary device as a philosophical argument. What he wants to show is how deplorable the state of nature is when we each have the external liberty to do as we please. Once we enter society we give up this liberty; we are less free in an absolute and abstract sense, but better for it. But to maintain this distinction, Hobbes now has to argue that things other than external obstacles limit liberty as well as power, because laws are not physical impediments.

Hence, his discussion of the liberty of subjects is a significant move from his discussion of natural liberty. There is no difference in principle between the sovereign's sword and the highwayman's gun, yet Hobbes wishes to say that the fear of one leaves us free and the other does not. It is now states of mind (internal properties of the agent) that affect liberty as well as external obstacles, and consequently fear is no longer compatible with freedom. Hobbes must try to conceal this change of position otherwise the whole idea of contract through fear loses its legitimacy; as he says repeatedly, an involuntary contract is not valid.

When he talks of the liberty of the subject in civil society, Hobbes now seems to be linking freedom with justice. Liberty is related to what we can do in relation to the laws of the sovereign, and hence it is dictated by what is just or unjust in civil society. This is why we are still at liberty to do those things that we never contracted away, such as defending ourselves against force. Even people who commit capital crimes can defend themselves: "have they not the Liberty then to joyn together, and assist, and defend one another? Certainly they have."[43] It would seem, therefore, that Hobbes also uses the term *liberty*, when it suits his purposes, to mean freedom of association.

Limits on liberty are identified not only with external obstacles but also with those things of which one is the author. Hence, under this new definition, liberty is found in "the silence of the Law."[44] We do, therefore, have liberty to disobey in certain circumstances. Only when "our refusall to obey, frustrates the End for which the Sovereignty was ordained; then there is no Liberty to refuse: otherwise there is."[45] Here again Hobbes uses the term liberty as an internal concept; "liberty to refuse" can only be a liberty of the mind and not a liberty from external impediments. If, as this suggests, liberty is closely related to justice, understood as voluntary commitment, it is necessary to examine what Hobbes has to say concerning freedom and obligation and it is to this topic I turn next.

Obligation and Freedom

The State of Nature

Hobbes's discussion of freedom and obligation is perhaps the most confusing area of his argument regarding moral association among people. Are we free to treat others in any way we see fit to promote our own interests? Or do we have certain obligations to one another in the state of nature that limit our freedom because we have made promises that in turn create obligations? It seems clear that we can have obligations created through promises in the state of nature; if I promise to give the highwayman my wallet, then I am obliged to do so (if no further cause for suspicion arises). Importantly for this discussion, Hobbes says that such an obligation is an infringement upon my liberty. He tells us that we can be freed from our obligations only by performing or being forgiven, forgiveness being the "restitution of *liberty*."[46]

There are two important points to note here. The first is that if the restitution of liberty comes with the end of an obligation, that obligation itself must limit our freedom. The second is that if forgiveness restores liberty, Hobbes is telling us that internal conditions of *other* actors affect our liberty. This is not to say that forgiveness is not a speech act, and therefore an action of another. But it is not an action that removes a physical impediment; what it does is to remove an obligation, and hence restores liberty. To remove an obligation, however, is much different than, for example, removing chains or other things that physically impede motion. Neither of the two points in this paragraph can be properly identified as external barriers to movement, which means that once again, Hobbes is extending his theory of freedom.

Hobbes is quite insistent that obligation stands opposed to liberty. He says that "obligation is thraldome; and unrequitable obligation, perpetuall thraldome."[47] In a similar vein, he says that "Law and Right, differ as much as Obligation and Liberty: which in one and the same manner are inconsistent."[48] Obligations actually limit freedom for two reasons; they limit what we can do because they create a moral requirement and because they have sanctions attached to them that create fear in the agent. Words are "bonds that have their strength, not from their own nature . . . but from the fear of some evill consequence upon the rupture."[49]

Another example where obligation limits freedom can be found in the passage concerning gift giving: "And when we say a guift is free, there is not meant any liberty of the guift but of the giver, that was not *bound* by any law or contract."[50] This suggests that such bonds would limit freedom. If we make such a promise, therefore, we are obliged and this in turn limits our freedom: "I am bound by it. For it is a Contract."[51] It is also clear that such obligation exists in the state of nature: "Covenants entered into . . . in the condition of meer nature, are obligatory."[52] Such covenants may be more difficult to enforce without the rule of law, but this does not invalidate the moral claims of the promisee.

The Laws of Nature and the Right of Nature

A question immediately arises; is what has been said concerning obligation in the state of nature compatible with what Hobbes has to say about the right of nature? In places, he describes such a right as the "right to everything: even to one another's body."[53] This suggests that in the state of nature freedom is unlimited because nothing prevents persons from acting in any way they please. This freedom may of course be illusory in that "free" agents will tend to collide with one another frequently and in this sense freedom entire will tend to destroy freedom in practice.

In the state of nature, the exercise of the right of nature can actually place external impediments upon action because everyone tends to hinder everyone else. The result is that the more freedom is unlimited, the more we are hindered in our pursuit of power, that is, in our ability to attain future goods. In the state of nature, therefore, the right limits both our liberty and our power. But from the standpoint of moral obligations, the argument that we have the right to anything seems to suggest that there is nothing that morally limits action, as long as we carefully distinguish the absence of normative obstacles from an absence of external obstacles. It is, after all, a "liberty-right."

It is important to recognize, however, that Hobbes argues that there is a difference between the right and the laws of nature and they differ in the same way as do liberty and obligation. Right and law "ought to be distinguished; because Right consisteth in liberty to do, or forbeare: whereas Law, determineth, and bindeth to one of them: so that Law, and Right, differ as much as Obligation, and Liberty: which in one and the same manner are inconsistent."[54] In other words, the right seems to allow us to do anything, whereas the laws place limitations upon us.

When we look at this argument in detail, however, the difference between right and law is not as distinct as this suggests. Hobbes actually argues that in nature man must act to preserve himself according to "his own best judgement and *reason* . . . as conceived to be the aptest means thereunto."[55] A. G. Wernham interprets this to mean that under the right of nature we can do anything we *reasonably think* necessary to preserve life, while under the laws of nature our actions are only legitimate if they actually are aimed at preservation.[56] *Sincerity* is the means of judging actions according to right, while *correctness* becomes the measure according to the laws of nature. As J. R. Pennock argues, Hobbes does not equate the right with unlimited liberty but with *blameless* liberty.[57] As Pennock also notes, this means that Hobbes sees the need for people to justify their use of liberty. The right of nature, therefore, is really nothing more than the freedom from obligations to others.

In the state of nature we are governed by reason to preserve ourselves and as we are extremely vulnerable in this condition, we can do anything we reasonably think will preserve ourselves, which means that liberty is extensive. In the state of nature, the limits imposed by what counts as reasonable will be few because we never know the power of our potential enemies. Hobbes's first law of nature, therefore, is *"That every man, ought to endeavour Peace, as farre as he hope of obtaining it; and when he cannot obtain it, that he may seek, and use, all helps, and advantages of Warre."*[58] The fundamental law of nature actually includes a duty, which helps us to seek peace, *and* the right of nature, which dictates that we are free to defend ourselves according to reason. If reason dictates that we have to kill or use another's body to preserve ourselves then we are entitled to do so. But if reason and judgment dictate that we do not have to act in this manner then we are obligated (by the first part of the first law of nature) and hence are not free to do so. Rather than the laws and the right of nature being incompatible, as Hobbes sometimes says, the right is actually subsumed within the laws and if we do not have a sovereign to protect us then the law of nature dictates that we act according to the right.

Hobbes's argument boils down to saying that we should always act according to the laws of nature, which include the right of nature as a crucial clause of the first law. In civil society, this clause will not often be engaged; in the state of nature it will. Hobbes is correct in saying that the right and the laws are not identical, but it is important to remember that there is no necessary contradiction between the two; it is simply that one or the other takes precedence depending upon the circumstances. Hence, it is obviously better as far as Hobbes is concerned to live in civil society where the laws dominate and where we can basically disregard the second clause of the first law. It is only when the sovereign or other citizens are threatening our lives that we will have to seek recourse in the right of nature.

If this interpretation is correct, it must mean that Hobbes thinks that the morality of an action is to be judged according to the circumstances in which the actor finds herself. In the state of nature, we are more justified in exercising the right of nature and performing actions normally thought to be objectionable in civil society. But in society, where the laws of nature are transformed into positive law, it is much more difficult to justify self-interested actions in terms of self-preservation. This means two things; first, because Hobbes is willing to blame people for breaking their contracts, even under severe conditions, he cannot simply be arguing that we should be solely concerned with maximizing our interests. Secondly, such maximizing behavior in society is seen by Hobbes as an evil, and not as somehow natural, as many commentators have suggested. In both cases, Hobbes argues for limits on freedom based on *reason*, which once more introduces internal considerations into his discussion of liberty. The whole point of Hobbes's discussion of the right of nature is to tell us that we are free to do anything we deem necessary for our preservation, but this can only mean that he is discussing freedom in terms of the lack of moral rather than physical constraints. Hence the second law of nature refers to the necessary limits to the freedom offered by the right of nature in moral, not materialist, terms: "From this fundamental law of nature, by which men are commanded to endeavor peace, is derived this second law: *that a man be willing, when others are so too, as far-forth as for peace and defence of himself he shall think it necessary, to lay down this right to all things, and be contented with so much liberty against other men, as he would allow other men against himself.*"[59]

In the state of nature, there is no impartial judge to rule on the reasonableness of actions and so the right of nature will always tend to "trump" the laws; in civil society this relationship is reversed. For Hobbes, the right of self-preservation is only meant to be exercised when faced by a very real threat, whether in the state of nature or in civil society. It is not something to be abused when we can live in a reasonable manner according to the laws of nature.

It seems, therefore, that liberty is almost complete in the state of nature. But we are obliged in certain instances, and because Hobbes sees obligations creating limits upon liberty, we are not always free to act in any way we wish. In particular, we are not *normatively* free to act against the laws of nature if reason dictates that it is safe to follow them. This is, therefore, a further limit on liberty that is internal to the agent. As Brian Barry has argued, Hobbes did not think we are free to break an obligation if the other party has already complied, because the worry of noncompliance, which can sometimes justify breaking a promise, is no longer a reasonable fear.[60] Only if we equate freedom solely with the right to use unlimited force will we conclude that freedom in nature is complete. Hobbes will not go this far and we find in his discussion of obligation a theory of freedom that has considerably more content than the one he first presents to us. Even within his argument concerning natural liberty, Hobbes is forced by his own reasoning to move beyond a simple mechanistic understanding of freedom. And once the right of nature has been renounced then liberty is restrained in significant ways by the demands of morality.

Civil Society

The problem for Hobbes is that even given certain natural duties, as long as we reasonably believe our actions are justified for our preservation, then they are indeed justified. What is right, and consequently the extent of our liberty, depends upon our personal opinion. Without a common judge there is no one to decide who is, and who is not, acting in a reasonable fashion, hence the need to exchange natural liberty for the liberty of subjects. With this exchange, our liberty becomes limited and exists only where the law is silent. It also exists within those rights that cannot be handed over to the sovereign, which means that "Natural liberty, which is unhindered by law is retained in part even in civil society."[61]

The difference between civil law and civil right is that the latter is the liberty left to us by the law, but civil law is what obliges us, and hence in those areas where the law speaks, it removes liberty from us. "Civil right" is really the same as the right we have in the state of nature; we are still free to do as we wish because there is no law limiting action. Because injury and injustice are defined in terms of promises to the sovereign, they do not exist in those areas not defined by the law.

However, Hobbes does sometimes discuss right in a different sense than in the state of nature. In the state of nature, Hobbes talks of the right of nature as the liberty to perform actions; in civil society he talks of *rights* one has not given up to the sovereign, such as the right to life. As he says himself: "There be some rights, which no man can be understood . . . to have abandoned or transferred."[62] The liberty of the subject lies not only in the silence of the law, but also in those areas where the sovereign has commanded, yet where the subject "may nevertheless, without injustice, refuse to do" because "every subject has liberty in all those things, the right whereof cannot by Covenant be transferred."[63]

What Hobbes means is that we are free in those areas where the sovereign interferes, but where we have not made a promise and hence where we are not obliged. This in turn means that our liberty is affected by what we *do* and *do not* say. This may be why Hobbes says that speech is a voluntary motion. Civil freedom is affected much more by speech acts than by external obstacles and where we have not made a promise we retain "the liberty to disobey."[64] We also have the freedom to petition the sovereign: "if a subject have a controversie with his sovereign. . . . He hath the same liberty to sue for his right . . . and consequently . . . the liberty to demand the hearing of his cause."[65] Hobbes's theory of freedom is enlarged once more and now incorporates speech acts, a justification for disobedience, and the right of appeal.

Hobbes's discussion of freedom and right leads to considerable confusion in *Leviathan*. On the one hand, right refers to unimpeded acts; on the other it takes on a more modern sense of the word *rights*, which suggests that freedom resides in capacities we hold simply by being persons. This in turn suggests that rights rest upon a positive claim we can make against others. The use of the term *right of nature* is confusing because the point Hobbes is trying to make in *Leviathan* is that we lay down the right, that is, the freedom to all things. But if freedom only relates to things external to the agent, then it is difficult to see what exactly is being laid down, unless it is something that is linked to the agent. Simply saying that we *give up* freedom must contradict Hobbes's original definition of freedom by stretching the term to include more than the absence of external obstacles. One cannot simply give up obstacles to action.

This confusion can be seen most clearly when Hobbes argues that for a man to lay down the right, "is to devest himselfe of the liberty of hindering another of the benefit of his own right to the same thing."[66] Here liberty must mean something more than external impediments because we lay down a liberty in the sense of surrendering a right to act. In this description, to have liberty is to be morally prohibited from acting in a way that may hinder *others*. This may seem to be a trivial distinction, but it is important to keep in mind that Hobbes's original definition of external liberty refuses to allow for such ephemeral differences, and is concerned only with concrete physical obstacles that prevent motion. Yet the distinction Hobbes makes between being hindered and giving up the right to hinder clearly goes far beyond his original starting point.

In civil society we are again expected to live according to the laws of nature, but now the expectation is more binding because the laws have the added status of bearing a relationship to the civil law. This relationship gives us an added incentive to live by the dictates of reason. Because we have contracted to obey the sovereign's laws through our own will, we are also the authors of the laws, which provides an additional reason to obey. Only when a person has given up the right is she obliged or bound not to hinder others. By giving up the right, each has taken on a moral duty, "not to make void that voluntary act of his own."[67]

Conclusion

Hobbes tells us that to talk of freedom in any other way than freedom from being hindered by opposition is as absurd as to talk of "a *round Quadrangle;* or *accidents of*

Bread in Cheese; or *Immateriall Substances.*"[68] We have to conclude that he does not follow his own advice and often uses language in an absurd manner. In addition to what has been discussed so far, he also talks of the "liberty of the church"[69] which is absurd because a church is not capable of motion and hence of being impeded by an external object. Such absurdity continues when he also claims that people have the "liberty to vote,"[70] the liberty to dissent, the "liberty of private revenges,"[71] and that they can act as the *"Custodes libertatis"* (guardians of liberty).[72] In all of these cases Hobbes is using the term *liberty* in a more conventional sense than his strict definition allows for because he is talking about civil liberties rather than whether one is being impeded or not by physical external barriers. Such confusion can be found at the very heart of his definition of freedom, which properly understood signifies *"motion*, as to *go*, to *speak*, to *move* any of our limbs."[73] Note that these are not the same because to speak is not the same as moving one's limbs, precisely because it does not require motion, unless Hobbes here is suggesting that free speech refers not to a particular right but to the actual movement of the lips, which seems to be highly doubtful.

The liberty of the subject actually has very little to do with the absence of external obstacles. What Hobbes is really concerned with is not unimpeded movement, but "a right or liberty of *action.*"[74] Clearly Hobbes thinks that civil society limits absolute freedom, but that this is necessary for a more worthwhile bounded liberty: "Fear of oppression, disposeth a man to anticipate, or to seek ayd by society: for there is *no other way* by which a man can secure his life and liberty."[75] As Hobbes says himself when discussing freedom in civil society, "such Liberty is in some places more, and in some lesse; and in some times more, in other times lesse."[76] He says this not because there are sometimes more and sometimes less external impediments, but because freedom expands and retracts depending upon our own speech acts, and upon the legislative activity of the sovereign.

Hence, we are bound to obey, and our promise adds weight to the force of the law that already limits our liberty through fear of punishment. Hobbes realized that we cannot rely solely upon the goodwill of men, and so the power of the sword is required to reinforce covenants. In civil society, therefore, we obey from a mixture of fear and duty, both of which are now described as internal constraints on liberty. In fact, because we can also take on obligations in the state of nature, the only real difference in civil society is that now our obligations are enforced by a body external to ourselves. In nature we can break a contract "upon any reasonable suspicion,"[77] but not so in society where both obligation *and* force provide protection.

In this chapter I have laid out some of the inconsistencies in Hobbes's use of the terms *freedom* and *liberty* and have hinted that Hobbes draws away from his theory of pure negative freedom. In the next 3 chapters the argument concerning the internal conditions for freedom will be fleshed out in much greater detail to demonstrate why his more bold statements concerning pure negative freedom are not adequate.

4

~

The Internal Conditions of Freedom: *Complex Instrumental Rationality and Autonomy*

Introduction

As we have seen in chapter 3, there is no single, easily identifiable "Hobbesian" theory of *liberty*; he uses the term in a variety of ways and ultimately moves a substantial distance from his most forceful definition of freedom as the absence of external physical obstacles. The intention of this chapter is to build on these insights and show that Hobbes had something more important in mind for the state to protect than unencumbered movement. By focusing on liberty rather than on his wider understanding of *action*, the literature on Hobbes has missed his concern with autonomy, or what I call, "full freedom."

I will demonstrate that Hobbes's theory of rational action is concerned as much, if not more, with *internal* conditions for agency, even though he was not inclined to discuss these as liberty. In terms of freedom being measured along a continuum, my analysis shows that Hobbes is not describing people who are incapable of self-government because they are ruled by passion. Hobbes extends his discussion to include an analysis of the necessary internal conditions for coherent and long-term rational action. Richard Flathman only discusses Hobbesian liberty in terms of basic movement; he describes this as freedom$_1$, by which he means: "Self-activated movement plus the possibility of impediments to the movement in question."[1] On the typology of freedom developed by Flathman this category fails to incorporate the major requirements of agency. In this chapter I claim that Hobbes's extended theory of freedom moves into the realm of what Flathman calls Freedom$_3$ (autonomy) in which "action is attempted by an agent in the pursuit of a self-critically chosen plan or project that the agent has reason to believe is consonant with defensible norms or principles."[2]

Much of the confusion over Hobbes's ideas on liberty can be cleared up by drawing a sharp distinction between internal and external conditions for freedom. To make such an argument one has to examine his more general discussions of reason and rationality, power and felicity, endeavor, and worthiness and personality to piece together a coherent argument concerning the internal requirements for action. I contend that Hobbes held up an ideal of autonomy which, although perhaps out of reach for some people, is nevertheless a goal he thought worthy of our efforts. Further, I argue that the usual interpretations of Hobbes's political writings, which state that his overwhelming concern was order, actually miss what he regards as the fundamental purpose of political community. This purpose is the creation of peace through order so that we may live autonomous lives. The creation of order, usually seen as the primary end for Hobbes, is in fact an a priori requirement for his "deeper" concern with autonomous living.

In the following 3 chapters, Hobbes's theory of action is presented as a two-tiered model in which there is a division between "thin" and "thick" properties of rationality. In the "thin" version, rationality is defined in a neutral manner relating to ends. In the "thick" version, rational action extends to a consideration of ends. To be fully autonomous, individuals have to formulate a rational life-plan in terms of finding the best means to ends, and choosing the best ends dictated to us by reason. Or as Hobbes might have said, the latter is really a requirement that reason dominate the passions in order that we may live by the dictates of the laws of nature. This chapter focuses on some of the major requirements of a liberal conception of autonomy with each section taking us further along the internal continuum of freedom discussed in chapter 2. The first of these is the general requirement of rational thought; the second proceeds to the more specific demand that such thoughts need to relate to one another in a coherent manner in the pursuit of ends.

Instrumental Rationality

It is usually asserted that Hobbes is the founding figure of the concept of instrumental rationality that is today called "rational choice theory." Contemporary theorists of rationality suggest that Hobbes provides the first systematic account of the "economically rational man" who has become such a pervasive presence in contemporary philosophy and social science. Those who support a more substantive concept of rationality, such as Jurgen Habermas, look back through history to Immanuel Kant in order to find a more compelling concept of human agency. What I will attempt to demonstrate in this chapter is that Hobbes is not an ally of contemporary rational-choice theory and that Habermas and his supporters should reexamine Hobbes's masterpiece, *Leviathan*; here they will find a concept of rational agency that they will find much to agree with. In chapter 5 I will claim that Hobbes's view of rational agency is not identical to that of Habermas because it does not stretch to an idea of consensus formation through dialogue; Hobbes requires a theory of rationality that is intersubjective but not in a deliberatively democratic manner.

I will be somewhat brisk in my description of the main characteristics of rational choice theory because the main tenets are by now well-known and much discussed. As Donald P. Green and Ian Shapiro note,[4] there is debate among rational choice scholars about the precise features of rational choice theory and Morris P. Fiorina states that "RC today is not a monolithic movement—if it ever was. I suspect the only thing that all RC people would agree upon is that their explanations presume that individuals behave purposively."[5] There is perhaps more agreement than this comment suggests and Green and Shapiro seem closer to the mark when they suggest that most RC theorists do agree about certain assumptions concerning "utility maximization, the structure of preferences, decision making under conditions of uncertainty, and, more broadly, the centrality of individuals in the explanation of collective outcomes."[6] For example, Kenneth J. Arrow, Mancur Olson Jr., David Gauthier, and William Riker may disagree about what exactly is being maximized, or how agents go about the task of maximizing, or how strongly preferences may be held, but all agree that rational individuals have some preference ordering that they try to maximize.[7]

For the purposes of this chapter I am going to sketch out a "thick" version of rational choice because it is still probably the dominant and most parsimonious version today, and because it is the one that is most associated with Hobbes. Very briefly, and somewhat broadly, this particular view of instrumental rational agency suggests that actions are judged rational or not depending on how well they help an individual to attain his or her goals given different conditions of uncertainty. This is a means/ends form of calculation and is hence instrumental, which is to say that an act is judged rational if it is instrumentally successful in bringing about the desired goal. One measure of rationality, therefore, is the successful attainment of ends; if agents A and B both try to attain goal C, *all things being equal* (e.g., information, and correct calculation) the most successful in attaining goal C is also the most rational. Goal C itself is not open to rational evaluation, and certainly not to an evaluation of a moral kind. Following Hume (and most would also say Hobbes), rational choice theory suggests that reason itself is not motivational nor can it tell us which end is more rational than another; it performs to the directives of the passions, but cannot choose among them. As Gauthier notes: "On the economist's view preference is revealed in choice and has no independent operational significance."[8] Hence, most rational choice scholars would agree with Jeffrey Friedman when he says that "I mean by 'rational choice theory' the claim that, regardless of what sort of ends people pursue, they do so through strategic, instrumentally rational behavior"[9] and with Dennis Chong who claims that "Rational choice theory builds on the assumption that people choose, within the limits of their knowledge, the best available means to achieve their goals. They are presumed to be instrumentally rational, meaning that they take actions not for their own sake, but only insofar as they secure desired, typically private ends."[10] Collective action is also explained in the same manner, and any form of "cooperation must be explained in terms of the individual's cost-benefit calculus."[11]

Pursuing a goal can in fact be described as irrational, but only if by pursuing it one is prevented from attaining other more valuable goals in one's preference orderings. The domain of the rational is limited to examining how preferences are held and how they relate to one another. Hence the rational agent has a preference structure that is rank-ordered and transitive. As stated by Green and Shapiro: "Rational choice theorists agree that certain *consistency* requirements must be part of the definition of rationality [and] assume the possibility of rank-ordered preferences over all available outcomes for every individual. Rational choice theorists also assume that preference orderings are transitive. If A is preferred to B, and B is preferred to C, then this consistency rule requires that A is preferred to C."[12] As just noted, rational agents are also supposed to be primarily interested in maximizing their own interests (whatever these may be). Gauthier makes the following claims:

> Practical rationality in the most general sense is identified with maximization. Problems of rational choice are thus of a well-known mathematical type; one seeks to maximize some quantity subject to some constraint. The quantity to be maximized must be associated with preference [and] the theory of rational choice defines a precise measure of preference, *utility*, [of the agent] and identifies rationality with the maximization of utility. [U]tility is to

be assigned to each possible outcome in such a way that
one may infer the person's preference between any two
outcomes from the utilities. For any two possible outcomes
the one with the greater utilities must be preferred.[13]

Jon Elster summarizes all of this in the following
manner:

Ideally, then, a rational-choice explanation of an action
would satisfy three sets of requirements. First, there are
three optimality conditions. The action is the best way for
the agent to satisfy his desire, given his belief; the belief is
the best he could form, given the evidence; the amount of
evidence collected is itself optimal, given his desire. Next
there is a set of consistency conditions. Both the belief and
the desire must be free of internal contradictions. The
agent must not act on a desire that, in his own opinion, is
less weighty than other desires which are reasons for not
performing the action. Finally, there are a set of causal
conditions. The action must not only be rationalized by the
desire and the belief; it must also be caused by them.[14]

The unit of analysis in rational choice theory, as should
be clear by now, is the individual: "By tracing social institutions, collective action, and social change to the actions of
individuals, the theory follows the principle known as
methodological individualism."[15] An agent ideally has the
same value scale for decision making that is transferable
over the different spheres of human life. Hence the rational
individual will decide using the same systematic criteria
for action whether he or she is buying a can of beans, voting
for a political candidate, or deciding to engage in revolu-
tionary activity. As James Buchanan and Gordon Tullock
put it: "the representative or the average individual acts on
the basis of the same over-all value scale when he partici-
pates in market activity and in political activity."[16] Ultimately, the hope is that the deductive methodology of
rational choice will be able to provide a blanket understanding of human behavior and explain individual and collective action through reference to strategic rational choice:

"What sets contemporary rational choice scholarship apart is the systematic manner in which propositions about the micro foundations of political behavior are derived. In their efforts to explain political outcomes, rational choice theorists appeal to deductive accounts of incentives, constraints, and calculations that confront individuals."[17] Rational choice theory, therefore, is a bold theory indeed that starts from simple and parsimonious assumptions and tries to build from these an explanation of human behavior that stretches from the most insignificant to the most earth-shattering.

Hobbesian Rationality: Good as the Promise of Things to Come

Attempting to demonstrate a concern for autonomy in Hobbes's writings may seem to be an unfruitful task given the usual view that Hobbes saw humans as narrowly self-interested pursuers of immediate gratification, who are ruled by passion rather than by reason. There seems little room at all to place individuals on the internal continuum of freedom if Hobbes really does describe them as most commentators suggest. Gauthier, for example, interprets Hobbes as presenting "a straightforwardly maximizing view of rational action."[18] Stanley I. Benn states quite explicitly that human beings as found in Hobbes's writings cannot be described as autonomous: "So long as we act only for the sake of our desires, we are not self-governing; as in Hobbes's mechanistic theory of man, we are merely attracted and repelled by things external to us, determined to action, not freely determining."[19] Other commentators who agree with this line of thought include Leo Strauss, Michael Oakeshott, and A. P. Martinich.[20] It is, in fact, almost universally accepted that Hobbes argued that reason is a slave of the passions.

Richard Flathman is one recent Hobbes scholar who still maintains that the passions dominate reason in Hobbes's work and argues in a similar manner to Benn that, for purposes of conceptualizing liberty, Hobbes "refuses to differentiate between the freedom of action and the freedom of movement."[21] Gregory S. Kavka states that Hobbes's theory of action is inadequate because it is aimed only at physical objects rather than at "states of affairs."[22] In other words, it does not account for "cumulative considerations of reasons for or against performing an act."[23] Hence Kavka takes more or less the traditional view that Hobbes sees action only in terms of immediate short-term preference. Even the most favorable interpretation of Hobbes's theory of action is unsatisfactory, Kavka claims, because he "ignores . . . the fact that deliberation involves weighing the merits of alternative courses of action and taking account of different sets of possible consequences of each one."[24] I will show that Hobbes's theory is immune to such criticism precisely because the theory does involve considerations of rational deliberation.

Nevertheless it would be idle to deny that this description of people can be found in Hobbes's work. But if this is his position, then, as Gary Herbert observes, Hobbes's theory of movement stands in stark contract to his theory of psychology. It is hard to imagine human "machines" having passions and desires: "the word 'endeavour' . . . would be inconsistent with his main mechanistic line of thought."[25] However, even some of the more straightforward comments about motivation do not fit the strict mechanistic view, as, for example, when Hobbes says that "the Thoughts, are to the Desires, as Scouts, and Spies, to range abroad, and find the way to things desired."[26] Whether the traditional views of Hobbes's psychology and mechanistic determinism are conjoined or held separately is not important, however, because I will demonstrate that both are false representations of Hobbes's understanding of people in civil society. Like Herbert, I contend that "Hobbes does not ground his mature theory of human nature on a crude mechanics . . . even though . . . [t]he belief that he does is admittedly almost universal."[27]

Hobbes's claim, discussed in chapter 3, that we do not have a free will does not mean that he believes we are incapable of making choices. The will is unfree only in the strict sense that every thought is causally related to a previous one. His intent is to show that thoughts do not simply spring from nowhere, or from nothing, but have a causal link to previous deliberations. But in terms of decision making the will represents the last act of deliberation. It is the point at which we decide to act, or refrain from acting, according to something we desire and is, therefore, the final expression of choice. Thus, the lack of *free will* in Hobbes's narrow use of the term does not preclude the possibility of rational calculation.

It is apparent on first reading that Hobbes was not presenting the most naive form of mechanistic theory because he does not link motion simply to the movement of the limbs but also to desires and thoughts. The whole point of part 1 of *Leviathan* is not to show how we *react* but to show how we *think*. Indeed, Hobbes goes further, stating that we are creatures capable of rational behavior and that reason can and will direct the passions given the appropriate circumstances. Hobbes states in the introduction to *Leviathan* that the commonwealth imitates "that *Rationall* and most excellent worke of Nature, Man."[28] The point Hobbes is making here is not that a select few are capable of rationality but that humans as a species are rational. One of the problems for maintaining peace is precisely the fact that men are so equal: "Nature has made men so equall, in the faculties of body, and mind . . . that . . . when all is reckoned together, the difference between man, and man, is not so considerable, as that one man can thereupon claim to himselfe any benefit, to which another may not pretend. . . . And as to the faculties of the mind . . . I find yet a greater equality among men than that of strength."[29] Hobbes's whole enterprise fails if humans are irrational because, as he also says in the introduction, the only way we can understand humans is through rational introspection. Hobbes would not have written the book if he thought humans could not reason.

Hobbes locates his actors in a complicated decision-making situation, and as Benn notes: "A necessary constituent of the model decision situation is, accordingly, a decision-making subject satisfying certain minimal conditions of both cognitive and practical rationality."[30] It is clear, therefore, that Hobbes does take an interest in the internal condition of the agent and introduces the question of *why* an action is performed when we evaluate the freedom of the agent. We can place the Hobbesian individual on the internal continuum of freedom; how far along is yet to be determined.

The title of chapter 8 of *Leviathan* should give us a clue that Hobbes is concerned with the thoughtful pursuit of ends; it is titled "Of the Vertues commonly called Intellectual; and their contrary Defects." Intellectual capacities are called "virtues" because they are "valued for eminence and . . . are always understood [that] such abilities of the mind, as men praise, value, and desire should be in themselves."[31] Those who lack these virtues are called by "names that signifie *slownesse of motion*, or difficulty to be moved."[32] Chapter 8 of *Leviathan* is basically a discussion of what makes us either rational and reasonable, or "mad" and "giddy." Vainglory, pride, self-deception, self-conceit, envy, and rage, are damaging. All of these lead to "dejection" because to live in such a manner is to be prone to "causeless fears"[33] that are a form of madness Hobbes calls "melancholy." Such irrationality is dangerous because these afflictions result in social unrest when they become widespread.[34]

Intellectual virtue is, therefore, clearly valued by Hobbes, who identifies it as "good witte," or as dexterity of mind. This in turn divides into two categories; "natural" and "acquired witte." The former is explained as the sort of wit that is gained through experience and consists of quickness of thought, and more importantly through the "*steddy direction* [of thinking] to some approved end."[35] The celerity and structure of these thoughts is governed by the strength of our commitment to our ends; without the guidance of desired ends "men's thoughts run one way, some another."[36]

Those who display "good witte" are capable of "*Discerning*, and *Judging* between thing and thing . . . this virtue is called Discretion" and a "Fancy, without the help of Judgement, is not commended as a vertue."[37] Hobbes's discussion of discretion continues when he says: "if the defect of discretion be apparent, how extravagant soever the fancy may be, the whole . . . will be taken for a signe of want of wit. . . . Where wit is wanting it is not Fancy that is wanting, but discretion. Judgement therefore without fancy is Wit, but fancy without judgement not."[38] In other words, discretion is the key to the virtue of rationality as expressed in dexterity of the mind, and as such "Discretion is commended for it selfe."[39]

These passages immediately demonstrate that Hobbes is concerned with more than determined movement. He continues by talking of the "Trayne of thoughts," where he distinguished between thoughts unguided by design, and those of a more constant nature that he calls "regulated."[40] Hobbes would not have distinguished between the two forms of thought if he did not want to argue that the latter is preferable. The former he classes as wayward: "In which . . . the thoughts are said to wander, and seem impertinent to one another as in a dream. Such are commonly the thoughts of men . . . without care of any thing . . . their thoughts are . . . without harmony; as the sound which a Lute out of tune would yield."[41] The second type of thoughts are so regulated that they can often "hinder and break our sleep" and return to us constantly as a "guide to action."[42] This leads him to advise that "in all your actions, look often upon what you would have, as the thing that directs all your thoughts in the way to attain it."[43] This type of thinking has an even "higher" quality to it in that "when imagining any thing whatsoever, wee seek all the possible effects, that can by it be produced."[44] The capacity for such thinking separates us from animals that have "no other passion but sensuall, such as are hunger, thirst, lust, and anger."[45] So enamored is Hobbes with the notion of rationality that he states: "Man excelleth beasts only in making of rules to himself, that is to say, in remembering, and in reasoning aright upon that which he remembereth. They which do so, deserve an honour above brute beasts. But they which mistaking the use of words, deceive themselves and others, introducing error, and seducing men from the truth, are so much less to be honoured than brute beasts, as error is more vile than ignorance."[46] Here Hobbes shows his distaste for those who manipulate the use of reason and the correct science of language for their own purposes because by so doing they are undermining the criteria that makes human beings worthier than animals, which is "the knowledge that he acquires by meditation, and by the right use of reason in making good rules of his future actions."[47]

There is clearly a distinction here between acting according to desires in a determined or mechanical fashion (as with animals) and choosing the most desirable means to a given end (as with human beings). Hobbes makes a clear separation between desires and rational calculations to achieve those desires: "From desire, ariseth the Thought of some means . . . and from the thought of that, the thought of means to that mean."[48] He tells us that we have different methods of responding to the passions; these responses can vary from simply moving from one desire to another, to "the consideration of many of them together" and "from the alteration or succession it selfe."[49] Guided thoughts "run over all parts thereof, in the same manner, as one would sweep a room, to find a jewell,"[50] whereas madness "withdrawes a man by degrees from the intended way of his discourse."[51]

As far as Hobbes is concerned, the person without real passion is little more than a "dead man," just as to have weak passions is to suffer from "Dulnesse." To have "Passions indifferently for every thing" is to be in the grip of "Giddinesse," and to be under the influence of one overriding passion is "that which men call Madnesse."[52] Hobbes's discussion of madness continues when he says that to have "stronger, and more vehement Passions for any thing than is ordinarily seen in others, is that which men call Madnesse" and "all Passions that produce strange and unusuall behaviour are called by the general name, Madnesse."[53] Passions that are unguided and out of control are a form of madness. This means, as Hobbes says, that "there be almost as many kinds [of madness] as of the passions themselves"[54] for "if the excess be madness, there is no doubt but the passions themselves, when they tend to evil, are degrees of the same . . . madness is *nothing* else but too much appearing passion."[55] Supporters of the maximizing view of instrumental rationality are unwilling to make such value judgments about the pursuit of goals, and it is difficult to see how Hobbes can fit within this camp given these statements.

Even the incorrect use of language is classified by Hobbes as a form of madness:

> There is yet another fault in the discourses of some men which may also be numbered amongst the sorts of madness, namely, that abuse of words wherof I have spoken before in the fifth chapter, by the name of absurdity. And that is when men speak such words as, put together, have in them no signification at all, but are fallen upon by some through misunderstanding of the words they have received and repeat by rote, by others from intention to deceive by obscurity. And this is incident to none but those that converse in questions of matters incomprehensible, as the Schoolmen, or in questions of abstruse philosophy. The common sort of men seldom speak insignificantly, and are therefore, by those egregious persons counted idiots . . . what is the meaning of these words: "The first cause does not necessarily inflow any thing into the second by force of the essential subordination of the second causes, by which it may help it work." When men write whole volumes of such stuff, are they not mad, or intend to make others so? . . . this kind of absurdity may rightly be numbered amongst the many sorts of madness."[56]

Here his attack is addressed to the schoolmen who talk in incomprehensible terminology. In particular, the misuse of language is a sign of a defect of the intellect, and hence his critique is found in chapter 8 on the intellectual virtues and their defects. It is no wonder, then, that those in the universities should have disliked Hobbes so much. His attack went beyond a critique of their arguments and included the charge that they were all mad!

As mentioned earlier, to be vainglorious is also to suffer a sort of madness: "Excessive opinion of a mans own selfe, for divine inspiration, for wisdome, learning, forme, and the like, becomes Distraction and Giddinesse."[57] To be vainglorious is basically to lack self-awareness. It seems clear, therefore, that Hobbes does not think this is a natural state of mind for people. The normal condition is to think rationally and to control the natural passions because "the Passions themselves, when they tend to Evill, are degrees of the same [madness]."[58] This does not mean that we can all display great self-control at all times, but it does mean that most of us are rational enough to avoid the pitfalls of pride.

These passages all point to the conclusion that Hobbes thought that unguided and untempered passions are inconsistent with rational action. Hobbes concludes by comparing the behavior of the madman with the actions of drunkards who also act extravagantly: "some of them Raging, others Loving, others Laughing, all extravagantly, but according to their *domineering Passions* . . . without care and employment of the mind."[59] Clearly he thinks that rationality, that is "employment of the mind" should control the pursuit of the passions. This is why he distinguishes between desire and design; the latter gives order to our desires, not the other way round as most commentators have suggested.

Hobbes thought that the prudent person can make distinctions among the passions based upon evaluations of individual and collective good; we have passions that are good and bad for us as individuals and as members of a collective body. What Hobbes tries to show us is that we have to learn which is which, especially concerning those that are a threat to the commonwealth. Although Hobbes does not make a definitive list of the good and bad passions, I think they could be divided in the following way. Those to be promoted would include fear (but a qualified fear that lets us know the punishments for breaking the law, not a fear that keeps us in a condition of dread); hope; courage; benevolence; magnanimity; valor; kindness; liberality; curiosity;

joy (based on admiration); pity; and compassion. Those that need to be controlled are vainglory, contempt, diffidence, covetousness, melancholy, ambition, pusillanimity, revengefulness, impudence, cruelty, envy, joy (based on glory) and, of course, pride. The desire for riches, honor, and glory are good or bad depending on how they are pursued.

It is clear that passions and desires are not fixed and unchanging according to Hobbes. Or to be more accurate, the passions remain fixed, but the objects of our passions are malleable and can be shaped by either the constitution of the body (e.g., the appetite for food and exoneration) or by experience, particularly custom, and education. Hobbes wants to teach us the following: "I say the similitude of *passions* which are the same in all men, *desire*, ear, hope, etc, not the similitude of the *objects* of the passions, which are the things *desired, feared, hoped, etc;* for these the constitution individual and particular education do so vary."[60] It must be noted that Hobbes does not mean by passion that, for example, I wish for a bowl of ice cream. The passion is for food and the bowl of ice cream is then the object of the passion.

Given the extended nature of Hobbes's list of passions, it seems clear that pretty much anything that moves us is passion. They are the catalysts for many of our thoughts and actions and include terror, panic, curiosity, laughter, and joy to name but a few. He even describes religion as passion. The term, therefore is a catchall that includes emotions as well as desires, and the best way to judge the passions of an individual is simply to watch how he acts. As already noted, Hobbes says at one point that to claim that a person does not have desires can only mean that he is dead. Hence, for Hobbes to say that every human action has the tincture of the passions attached to it does not mean that we are incapable of reason; in fact reason itself can be thought of as a form of passion. Because everything that moves us is a form of desire, even the causes of the "difference of wits are in the passions; and the difference of passions proceedeth, partly from the different constitution of the body, and partly from different education . . . [difference] proceeds therefore from the passions, which are different, not only from the difference of men's complections, but also from their difference of customs and education."[61] Passions that have their source in the constitution of the body are not easily changed, but it is crucial to govern those that stem from education and custom:

> As for the passions of hate, lust, ambition, and covetousness, what crimes they are apt to produce is so obvious to every man's experience and understanding, as there needeth nothing to be said of them, saving that they are *infirmities* so annexed to the nature, both of man and all other living creatures, as that their effects cannot be hindered but by extraordinary use of reason. . . . Ambition and covetousness are passions also that are perpetually incumbent and pressing; whereas reason is not perpetually present to resist them.[62]

These quotes suggest that although it is not an easy thing to do, it is absolutely crucial that through education and the use of reason we can temper, control, and steer people away from passions that lead to instability and war and guide them to the passions and the objects of passions that foster stability and commodious living.

If passions are as malleable as this suggests, it seems that Hobbes gave a more sophisticated view of human psychology than he is usually given credit for. Passions can be shaped, formed, and controlled. It follows that it is admirable to have many and varied passions because "a man who has no great passion for any of these things, but is, as men term it, indifferent, though he may be so far a good man as to be free from giving offence, yet he cannot possibly have either a great fancy or much judgement."[63] It seems, therefore, that to live a contented life, one needs to achieve and maintain a balance among one's passions in order to make evaluations regarding the best course of action: "passions unguided, are for the most part meere Madnesse".[64] "All Actions and Speeches that proceed, or seem to proceed from much Experience, Science, Discretion, or Wit, are honourable"[65] because actions that demonstrate rationality are highly valued. The task is to utilize one's experience as a basis for determining the best action to be taken in light of previous events. This is a form of inductive reasoning in which we attempt to identify the best means to a desired end, based on a rational examination of our past experience: "Which kind of thought, is called *Foresight,* and *Prudence,,* or *Providence;* and sometimes *Wisdome?*"[66] Such is the "Discourse of the Mind when it is *governed by designe,*"[67] and "Of all *Discourse* governed by desire of Knowledge, there is at last an *End.*"[68] Hobbes's whole discussion of foresight, prudence, and wisdom, all under the umbrella of experience, adds weight to the claim that he is presenting something more than a theory of mechanistic movement.

To this point I have shown that Hobbes was concerned with rationality as the best means to a given end, although it has already been demonstrated that he was interested in motivations for actions that go considerably beyond mere mechanical movements. Hobbes summarizes this best himself when he writes that the "names *man* and *rationall,* are of equall extent, comprehending mutually one another."[69] This suggests that Hobbes thought that *all* humans were capable of rationality. Hobbes would not have felt it necessary to introduce the distinctions among the passions, or among prudence, foresight, wisdom, wit, deliberation, and reason if his concern was solely to describe mechanistic movement set in motion by external stimuli. Nor would he have made repeated references to action guided by an overarching design if his understanding of human behavior had been limited to the pursuit of immediate maximization. Finally, Hobbes would not have distinguished between children, fools, people governed by passion, and people ruled by wisdom, if he thought of all action as the same. Children, for example, should not be punished in the same manner as an adult: "[f]or the want of reason proceeding from want of age, does therefore take away the punishment, because it taketh away the crime, and makes them innocent;"[70] adults lacking in certain mental faculties should also be viewed differently: "Fools and madmen manifestly deliberate no less than the wisest men, though they make not so good a choice, the images of things being by diseases altered;"[71] and the person who follows his or her raw passions should be differentiated from the person of wisdom: "the will of a passionate and peevish fool doth no less follow the dictate of that little understanding he hath, than the will of the wisest man followeth his wisdom."[72]

The foregoing suggests that Hobbes promoted a theory of action considerably beyond determined movement. To add support to this suggestion it is worth examining Hobbes in relation to recent discussions of liberal autonomy. According to Benn and Richard Flathman, autonomous actions must be based on critical reflection. In this respect, autonomous behavior must be conduct that one can justify to oneself; autonomous actors are self-justifying actors. One has to be more than a chooser to be autonomous because, as Flathman points out, such choices may be the result of norms and principles that one holds uncritically.

One's belief system itself has to be the result of critical reflection and open to continual assessment through a process of substantive rationality. This is quite compatible with abiding by authoritative commands and rules of a sovereign as long as we have recognized the latter as legitimate after critical examination. The more rational and considered our thoughts, the more autonomous we become: "The autonomous person steadily thinks . . . autonomously in the important dimensions or aspects of her life."[73]

The condition of practical rationality takes us a considerable distance along the internal continuum of freedom because it requires self-directing behavior. It is, however, still short of the ideal of autonomy that requires greater control of the self. As I will demonstrate in chapter 5, Hobbes does take this extra step. His full theory of volition demands that ends as well as means can be rationally defended. Action for Hobbes is not simply to be attracted or repelled by external stimuli; in its fullest form it is dictated by reason, commitments, and obligations. Full freedom specifically demands that one's plans have to fit with one's *nomos,* that is, the decision maker must relate ends to some overarching norms and principles that take priority over more immediate interests. Before we reach this point, however, we need to complete the discussion of instrumental rationality by examining a further crucial condition of autonomy, the requirement that actions relate to one another coherently.

Rationality and Coherent Action: Good as Utile

In his introduction to *Leviathan,* Hobbes states that "life is but a motion of the limbs" toward or away from external stimuli. It is not surprising, therefore, that this is overwhelmingly interpreted as both a mechanistic theory of human nature and a minimal requirement of rationality. When this view is combined with the famous quote that "Felicity is a continuall progresse of the desire from one object to another," it is invariably suggested that Hobbes thinks that human beings are concerned only with immediate gratification. However, if we take the latter quote in its full context Hobbes's intent is clearly different: "Nor can a man any more live, whose Desires are at an end, than he, whose Senses and Imaginations are at a stand. Felicity is a continuall progresse of the desire, from one object to another. . . . The cause whereof is, *That the object of mans desire, is not to enjoy once onely, and for one instant in time; but to assure for ever, the way of his future desire.* And therefore the voluntary actions, and inclinations of all men, tend, not only to the procuring, *but also to the assuring of a contented life; and differ onely in the way.*"[74]

It now becomes apparent that the meaning of felicity is that we pursue goals according to a plan that guides our actions and that prevents us from following passions that we will *"enjoy once onely, and for one instant in time."* Felicity is not simply the never-ending movement from one immediate passion to the next; it is the reasoned pursuit of *integrated* goals over a whole lifetime. When Hobbes writes of felicity he means not only immediate success, but also continued prosperity in attaining the things we desire. He does suggest that human life is synonymous with desire, but this should not lead us to conclude that desires cannot be controlled. This perhaps is why he distinguishes between the felicity of humans and animals: "there is no other Felicity of beasts, but the enjoying of their quotidian food, ease and Lusts; as having little, *or no foresight of the time to come.*"[75] It is true that at times Hobbes linked felicity to the passions, but only, as he himself said, because "we have no name in our tongue"[76] that adequately describes what he had in mind with his discussion of felicity. The closest he can come to describing what he means is the Greek word *makarismos* that he interprets to mean a kind of profound happiness separate from the enjoyment that one derives from fleeting pleasure. Hobbes's discourse on prudence fits this interpretation: "When the thoughts of a man that has a *designe in hand, running over a multitude of things,* observes how they conduce to that *designe*; or what *designe* they may conduce unto . . . [t]his wit of his is called Prudence; and dependeth on much Experience, and memory of the like things, and their consequences heretofore."[77]

According to Hobbes, we think and act along the lines of *"What is it, when shall it, how is it done, and why so?"*[78] It is this capacity for rationality that is the distinguishing characteristic of human beings, in particular our desire to "know why and how . . . which is a lust of the mind, that by a perseverance of delight in the continuall and indefatigable generation of Knowledge, exceedeth the short vehemence of any carnall Pleasure."[79] Deliberation is precisely about pondering the causes of past events and the likely outcome of actions now and in the future. To be human is to be driven by "the Enquiry of the truth of *Past,* and *Future* . . . the whole chain of Opinions alternate, in the question of True or False."[80]

The more we engage in rational thought the more independent we become: "Want of science, that is, Ignorance of causes, disposeth, or rather constraineth a man to rely on the advise, and authority of others. . . . Ignorance of the signification of words . . . disposeth men to take on trust, not only the truth they know not; but also the errors; and which is more, the non-sense of them they trust."[81] One of the tasks of the text as a whole is to educate people in such a manner that they will no longer rely on the churchmen and on schoolmen and their tales of supernatural events in order to comprehend the world. Instead of dogma and superstition, Hobbes hopes that the introduction of a more scientific view of the world will produce people who are independently capable of "hunting out of the causes of some effect, present or past, or of the effects of some present or past cause."[82]

Hobbes felt that many people in his time did not engage in such mental acts to the extent he hoped for, but this does not mean he thought most were incapable of such activity. His belief that we are all basically equal in our faculties led him to state that "there is no other act of man's mind that I can remember, naturally planted in him so as to need no other thing to the exercise of it but to be born a man, and live with the use of his five senses. Those other faculties of which I shall speak by and by, and which seem proper to man only, are acquired and increased by study and industry, and of most men learned by instruction and discipline."[83] The prudent person is simply the one who has the discipline to learn, and all are capable of this. Hence Hobbes would have much preferred an educated and reflective populace than one that either relies upon the words of others or upon customary superstition for its guidance.

Once we understand that a person uses reason we can also comprehend that persons' actions that are "raised by foresight of good and evill consequences . . . the good or evill effect thereof dependeth on the foresight of *a long chaine of consequences* . . . so that he who hath by Experience, or Reason, the greatest and surest prospect of Consequences, Deliberates best himself" according to "the Felicity *of this life*."[84] Here Hobbes shows his concern with happiness over one's lifetime rather than the pleasure of the moment. This is a picture of life with a situated narrative, or "designe" in which we pursue ordered preferences according to reasoned deliberation: "there is required also an often application of his thoughts to their End."[85] Hobbes saw human beings as creatures in time who have a history, a memory, and a future. Fruitful deliberation must include a plan of life upon which to base one's decisions. In chapter 8 of *Leviathan* he says: "without Steddinesse and Direction to some End, a great Fancy is one kind of Madnesse; such as they have, that entering into any discourse, are snatched from their purpose by everything that comes in their thoughts. . . . Which kind of folly, I know no particular name for."[86] Perhaps lack of agency is an adequate name for such a condition.

Conclusion

These passages suggest that Hobbes believes we must rationally order our passions, thoughts, desires, and actions in order to live a fulfilling life. When people calculate in relation to good and evil, they do so according to "the opinion men have of the likelihood of attaining what they desire . . . from the object loved or hated . . . *from the consideration of many of them together.*"[87] The point is that we rationally examine the alternatives according to some form of dispositional long-term plan to give structure to our "inclinations to severall ends."[88] This textual evidence implies that Hobbes was concerned with deliberative action beyond the pursuit of immediate desires. We have to *choose* between our passions even if this means choosing the one we desire less in the short term. To act in this way an agent must display some of the attributes of autonomy, particularly the ability to deliberate over competing alternatives.

Hobbes's definition of a person supports this argument. He stressed the fact that we are not obliged to anybody other than through an act of our own will. A person is someone whose words and actions represent herself or another; when they are our own, we are a natural person, when representing another, artificial. When representing another person it is necessary to have placed oneself voluntarily in that position if one's words and behavior are to be binding. One has to be the author of one's actions, words, and deeds. No one is bound by contracts of which he or she is not the author, nor held responsible as the author of any action if incapable of reason. In other words, those who are incapable of rationality do not have the capacity for authority and hence are not capable of action. Clearly, however, Hobbes did think that most people were capable of acting authoritatively, otherwise he would not have been able to justify his arguments concerning contracts, promises, obligation, and justice.

One may reply that Hobbes was unconcerned about the innate value of human beings and support this criticism with his infamous statement that the worth of a man is his price. Careful reading of chapter 13 of *Leviathan*, however, reveals that Hobbes made a clear distinction between a person's worth and a person's worthiness. The former rests only upon reputation and popularity; the latter is determined by the character of the individual. It seems strange that Hobbes would make such a distinction if he did not also differentiate between movement and action, for if people are determined in their behavior there is little room for concepts such as worthiness of character.

It is helpful once again to examine the words of Hobbes in relation to the modern liberal theory of autonomy. Autonomy, we are told by Benn, is self-rule; one's thoughts and actions must be one's own and must be related together in a coherent fashion. If one believes that X is true and yet act according to not-X there is a clear discrepancy between thought and action. And of course, if one's beliefs change through rational reflection, one's actions must reflect this change. Autonomy, therefore, requires more than short-term rationality, although this is also a necessary condition. It also demands that we apply such rationality to a long-term life-plan. An autonomous agent needs to act according to a rationally conceived plan in which actions are integrated in such a manner that they correspond to long-term goals of life. In this sense, autonomy is significantly wrapped up in a more advanced form of rationality: "we approach it in part by extending the ambit and heightening the intensity of our rationality."[89] Rationality is not limited to a narrow instrumental pursuit of short-term interests, but is aimed at long-term goals that define who we are as persons. Hobbes's theory of rationality, therefore, is more complex than the one usually assigned to him and incorporates, but goes beyond, the instrumental theory of rational choice discussed at the beginning of the chapter.

To summarize we can say that Hobbes has taken the discussion concerning the internal requirements for voluntary action a long way from his original definition of freedom. We can encapsulate Hobbes's thoughts by comparing him with the following quote from Benn, where he suggests that autonomy demands a rational life-plan in which there is "continuity over time . . . corresponding to a single physically acting subject" whose "belief structure must yield a ranking of action commitments" in which "the immediacy of an expected gratification must not be sufficient . . . to confer lexical priority."[90]

5

❦

The Internal Conditions of Freedom:
Substantive Rationality and Autonomy

Introduction

Chapter 4 demonstrated that Hobbes distinguished between activities based on immediate urges and inclinations, and those rooted in a rational consideration of alternatives. This capacity for rational choice is a necessary requirement of a practical and reasonable life-plan. The next major requirement of a life-plan was that one's purposes fit together coherently. As John Finnis argues, this does not mean that life is to be lived according to a specific and rigid "blueprint," but neither is it reasonable to "live from moment to moment, following immediate cravings."[1] What is expected, according to Finnis, is a capacity for the "redirection of inclinations, the reformation of habits, the abandonment of old and adoption of new projects, as circumstances require . . . for which there is no blueprint, since basic aspects of human good are not like the definitive objectives of particular projects, but are *participated in.*"[2] Because of the unpredictable nature of human existence "to see our life as one whole is a rational effort only if it remains on the level of general commitments, and the harmonizing of them."[3]

In this chapter, I will discuss a third aspect of a life-plan, usually demanded by theorists of positive freedom, which extends the notion of a life-plan to include full harmony with an overarching law that one imposes upon oneself. Richard Flathman calls this freedom$_5$ and describes it as "Action attempted by an agent in the pursuit of a plan or project self-critically chosen to satisfy, and in fact satisfying, certifiably worthy norms and principles."[4] This takes us to the upper end of the freedom continuum. Action must be in line with the *nomos* of the decision-maker "which confers on the life of the autonomous person a coherence deriving from the consistency and coherence that he can achieve in the network of beliefs by which his actions are governed."[5] This concept of freedom suggests that rationality is an aid to attaining our goals but that it must also be used to judge the ends themselves. A further requirement is that we are usually successful in the task of integrating our beliefs and actions with rules we impose upon ourselves.

The more rational and considered our thoughts, the more autonomous we become. In this sense of autonomy we are individuals making decisions against the backdrop of our social condition. Full autonomy requires that we see ourselves as situated beings and that we act from a belief system that fits with our social circumstances. John Rawls argues that "we cannot realize ends the descriptions of which are meaningless, or contradict well-established truths."[6] Flathman takes a similar position when he states: "Those who have attained to autonomy employ their powers of rationality concerning the traditions and institutions, the conventions and rules, that provide the setting in which day-to-day activities occur."[7] As Stanley I. Benn argues, a person must subject her beliefs to the scrutiny of the public world in which evidence can be used to test the validity of those beliefs. If a person refuses to recognize a significant gap between her ends and reality, as established by public standards, then she fails one of the tests of autonomy: "The essential defect of the paranoiac is that, though his theory does provide him with a map of the world and is action guiding, it is not truth oriented."[8] Hence to be autonomous one must have a respect and concern for public standards of truth; what is important is not that one has arrived at a set of beliefs independently of authority, but that one holds the beliefs because one thinks them to be true after due reflection.

The fully free agent, according to this view, must display more than a capacity for instrumental rationality. In *Justification and Application,* Jurgen Habermas suggests that there are three domains of the rational, namely the pragmatic (instrumental, technical); the ethical (clinical, rationality in relation to one's life-plan); and the moral (other-regarding, substantive). Practical reason operates differently in each domain:

> the illocutionary meaning of "must" or "ought" changes with the practical relation and the kind of decision impending but also the *concept of the will* that is supposed to be open to determination by rationally grounded imperatives in each instance. The "ought" of pragmatic recommendations relativized to subjective ends and values is tailored to the *arbitrary choice* of a subject . . . the faculty of rational choice does not extend to the interests and value orientations themselves but presupposes them as given. The "ought" of clinical advice relativized to the telos of the good life is addressed to the striving of self-realization . . . [t]he categorical "ought" of moral injunctions, finally, is directed to the *free will* emphatically construed, of a person who acts in accordance with self-given laws. . . . Only a will that is guided by moral insight, and hence is completely rational, can be called autonomous.[9]

As this somewhat convoluted passage suggests, the claims made by those who support a strongly substantive concept of rationality, such as Habermas, do not deny that in many instances the description of instrumental rationality discussed in chapter 4 accurately describes many of the thoughts, motivations, and actions of human beings. They do deny, however, that this is all there is to be said about rational behavior. In particular, it has to be recognized that actions have to be judged rational or not in relation to norms of how one ought to behave. The "ought" here can be self-regarding or other-regarding. For example, one ought not to chop off one's own leg (even if it is a purely self-regarding action) no matter how efficiently one performs the task, because there is something inherently irrational about the goal. Here, the "ought" statement is of a *sensible* rather than a moral kind; one ought not to chop off one's leg because it literally *makes no sense* to do so from the ethically rational point of view of leading a meaningful life.

It is the moral "ought" aspect of rationality, however, which is particularly important for Habermas and he is especially worried by the separation of morality (other-regarding actions) from rationality in the instrumental view. He argues that rationality can tell us not only how best to pursue our ends, but also what motives we should have and what ends we should pursue. The normative terms *should* and *ought* have to be coupled to our understanding of rational behavior. As Jon Elster notes, the instrumental view also makes "ought" demands on agents, but it is only of the self-regarding kind, that is, one ought not to do act A if one has a preference for B where it is irrelevant whether B is a sensible, nonsensible, moral, or immoral act. Habermas disagrees; certain goals are irrational because they are immoral; they are irrational, firstly because they treat others as means to ends and this involves a form of performative contradiction because one is behaving in a manner that one would not accept as reasonable behavior from others. For example, for democratic deliberation to work we need to accept certain conditions and rules that apply equally to everyone; if I then break these rules I am in effect acting in a manner that suggests that the rules are necessary and universal but that they do not apply to me. I am, therefore, engaged in a logical contradiction along the lines of claiming that something is A and not A at the same time.

Secondly, it is irrational because rationality can guide us to moral truths and it is irrational to act in a manner that has been demonstrated by reason to be true. There is a universalizable aspect to rationality, therefore, which is lost with the instrumental concept of rationality. This can perhaps best be summarized by the claim that it is rational to be morally reasonable. Whereas rational choice theorists think that there is a tension between these two concepts, Habermas suggests that they are not in conflict once rationality is defined more broadly than the instrumental view. These claims place Habermas in the Kantian tradition that holds an "understanding of reason [that] already includes the moral dimension of impartiality."[10] Whereas the instrumental view suggests that rationality is always self-regarding, that is, related to the preferences of the acting agent, the *"universalistic* conception of rationality insists that what makes it rational to satisfy an interest does not depend on whose interest it is. Thus the rational person seeks to satisfy all interests. . . . If I have a direct interest in your welfare then on either conception I have reason to promote your welfare. But your interest in your welfare affords me such reason only given the universalistic conception."[11]

The test of whether an act is rational, for Habermas, is not whether one is successful in attaining one's goals but whether one can give good reasons, including moral reasons, for one's actions. Hence the concept of rationality is inherently intersubjective because only actions that can be coherently explained to others are rational. If actions cannot be explained, whether self-regarding (chopping one's leg off), or other-regarding (chopping off someone else's leg), then they cannot be classed as rational. Rationality therefore must rest upon norms that have been agreed upon through dialogue, and anyone who cannot explain actions "by appeal to standards of evaluation is not behaving rationally."[12] Simone Chambers summarizes Habermas's point well when she says that "At the center of Habermas's moral theory is a strong cognitivist claim. Moral statements are open to rational evaluation and are not mere statements of preference. Habermas maintains that what we mean when we say something is rational is that it could be defended with reasons. On this view, rationality is embedded in essentially public practices of communication. A statement or an action is rational to the extent that it could be *explained to others.*"[13]

This suggests that there is a two-tiered concept of universalism in Habermas's concept of rationality. The first is that there are societal norms that are universally valid within a particular context. If actions do not fit with these societal norms there is a good prima facie reason to question whether they are rational. The second is that there are certain necessary minimum conditions for free and equal speech to take place at all; these are not context specific and are hence universal in a fuller sense. If one accepts that such conditions are necessary for action and then proceed to act in a manner that contradicts them, one is again behaving irrationally. For example, when I enter into free and equal dialogue I am taking advantage of certain moral norms that regulate behavior; such norms allow me to participate without fear of coercion or violence. If I then proceed to act in a manner that violates these norms (perhaps preventing others from having their fair say, or rejecting first-order moral norms that have been agreed to in free and equal dialogue) then I am being irrational because I am contradicting my prior acceptance of the rules and outcomes of discourse. This is the sense in which it is irrational to be unreasonable.

Hence, for Habermas, moral constraints pose no problem for his concept of rationality because they are already a comprehensive part of the definition. As Chambers suggests: "For the Kantian, rationality is associated with reasoning in a world populated by other rational agents who are recognized as being worthy of the same consideration I am worthy of. Practical reason has an element of reciprocity built into it. Morality finds its underpinnings in a conception of practical reason that links the two (morality and reason) prior to the agreement. In the case of Scanlon (and Habermas), this Kantian idea is articulated in a notion of accountability or justification."[14] Chambers goes on to suggest that we distinguish between "rational-choice theory (the heirs of Hobbes) and rational-agreement theory (the heirs of Kant). Choice versus agreement adequately captures the individualistic versus intersubjective starting points of these two traditions."[15] The problem for theorists of this sort of substantive rationality is how to defend the definition of rationality itself; as David Gauthier notes "this assumption, of the impersonality or impartiality of reason, demands defense."[16]

I will now argue that Hobbes also thought actions had to be judged in substantive terms of reason-giving, but he did not think that dialogue was the best means of assessing the rationality of desires, means, and goals. Instead, one is more likely to comprehend the requirements for rational action while contemplating from the undisturbed peace of one's armchair. Hence, Chambers may be correct in noting the two strands of argument concerning rational behavior, but she is wrong to suggest, as almost all commentators have done, that Hobbes is only concerned with the instrumental rational-choice approach.

Substantive Rationality and Autonomy: Good as Jucundum

Hobbes's most complex discussion of rationality outlines similar criteria to those just discussed. Not only does he argue that there has to be a link between our rational train of thoughts and our actions, but he also requires that these thoughts and accompanying actions should be guided by *reason,* which in turn leads us to the moral dictates found in natural law. The laws of nature provide the guidance that allows us to promote the primary goods upon which we build our broad life-plans. These primary goods for Hobbes are peace, order, reduction of the fear of death, and commodious living. The key is to apply rationality, guided by reason, to attaining the most important social goods; once these are firmly in place it is possible to achieve the secondary goods. This two-step process has to have a lexical order; it is not possible to attain instrumental/individual goods until the primary goods are safeguarded and they can only be secured when everyone acts according to the dictates of reason prescribed by the laws of nature.

The laws of nature have often been summarized into the maxim Preserve Oneself, but Hobbes himself summed them up into the command, which he equates with the law of the Gospel: *"Do not that to another, which thou wouldest not have done to thy selfe."*[17] This, however, is not a command that necessarily sits well with a person's interests. We are not obliged to obey simply because it is rational to do so, but rather the reverse, that is, our rational capacity leads us to take on moral obligations. This is why contemporary applications of game theory to Hobbes's thoughts on rational behavior are misguided. The problem Hobbes tries to solve is not how we can maximize our preferences in a prisoner's dilemma situation, but instead, how to stop ourselves from ever getting into such a predicament. The way we prevent this is not by acting on prudential self-interest, but by following the moral code laid out in the laws of nature. In fact, if we think of Hobbes's problem as being how to maintain, rather than create a state, then it becomes apparent that maximizing behavior is the cause not the solution to the problem. The solution Hobbes suggests is to satisfice rather than to maximize, and we do the former when we let the laws of nature guide our actions. Goals that promote well-being, and bring preferences into a unified harmony are clearly more rational than those that bring war and disunity. The concept of satisficing fits well with Hobbes's view of human nature because he thinks that most will be content with a moderate amount of power as long as safety is not compromised.

The laws of nature are not good simply because we happen to agree that they are good; they are good independently of personal belief systems except in the broadest sense. What I mean is that they depend on the assumption that we prefer life over death and that we prefer conditions of civility over those of war and destruction; hence, they depend on a supposition that the preservation of human life is important. But these are assumptions that all moral codes share; the aim of morality is to make it possible for humans to live actively and productively together.

Notice that Hobbes makes a universal statement; he says that *all* humans who use correct reasoning agree that the laws of nature are the best means for preserving human society and hence that everyone agrees that the laws are the embodiment of moral virtue. Such laws are not dependent upon our particular preferences because they are "Immutable and Eternal" and the "Science of them is the true and onely Moral Philosophy."[18] Correct science necessarily leads us to true universal principles that can be known through deductive inference. Hobbes was willing to claim that only those actions that fit with his objective science are fully reasonable. The task Hobbes set for himself was to put people on the right path to discover these principles, for "all men by nature reason alike, and well, when they have good principles."[19] A man can be wrong in his reasoning, of course, but reason itself can never be wrong because it begins from first definitions "and preceed from one consequence to another"[20] until "all those Affirmations and Negations, on which it was grounded, are inferred."[21]

Discovering these life-guiding truths is not an easy task, but it is also not an impossible one as long as people are reasonable: "celerity of fancy makes the thoughts less steddy than is necessary to discern exactly between Right and Wrong. Again, in all Deliberations . . . the faculty of solid Reasoning, is necessary: for without it, the Resolutions of men are rash, and their Sentences unjust."[22] The task is not easy, but it is attainable because, as Hobbes says: "Man is distinguished . . . by his Reason."[23] This is not to say that it is an innate characteristic of humans; rather, it is something that we all acquire: "Though it be true that no man is born with the use of reason, yet all men may grow to it as well as lawyers: and when they have applied their reason to the laws, may be as fit for and capable of judicature, as Sir Edward Coke himself."[24]

Hobbes tells us that rules found through reason are "grounded upon principles of Truth" whereas those on "the Passions and Interests of men are different, and mutable,"[25] and the main truth that reason dictates is that we should follow the laws of nature to escape the condition of the war of all against all. It tells us that the wisest course of action is to live by those laws when they have been made positive in civil society. Because everyone, with very few exceptions, is capable of reason, those who choose to act against the law can be punished: "Seeing every man knoweth by his own reason what actions are against the law of reason, and knoweth what punishments are by this authority for ever evil action ordained; it is manifest reason, that for breaking the known laws he should suffer the known punishments."[26]

Hobbes claims that people commit crimes "by erroneous inferences from true principles, which happens commonly to men that are hasty and precipitate in concluding and resolving what to do, such as are they that have both a great opinion of their own understanding, and believe that things of this nature require not time and study, but only common experience and a good natural wit . . . whereas the knowledge of right and wrong, which is no less difficult, there is no man will pretend to without great and long study."[27] Hence "Ignorance of the laws of nature excuseth no man, because every man that hath attained to the use of reason is supposed to know, he ought not to do to another what he would not have done to himself. Therefore, onto what place soever a man shall come, if he do anything contrary to that law, it is a crime."[28]

Hobbes seems to suggest that whatever culture we come from, there are a few basic rational dictates that hold for everyone. This does not mean that rationality is not, in part, a social construct; it means that within all social constructs there are similar rules of behavior.

Through the use of reason and the putting aside of our individual preferences we can arrive at consensus. What this suggests, at the very least, is that Hobbes is concerned with providing a nonsubjectivist account of rational action. It is the difference between civil society and the state of nature, and hence between the right and laws of nature, which allows Hobbes to distinguish between substantive and instrumental behavior. Once we accept this distinction we also have to recognize that Hobbes did not mean that a rational action is one that is instrumentally valuable to the individual, as Jean Hampton suggests,[29] but that it involves acting according to certain principles discovered through reason.

The *nomos* for Hobbes's rational human being is over-whelmingly the path of peace. We will never be secure, Hobbes believed, until we impose upon ourselves the com-mitment to live by the laws of nature. Hobbes thought that it was as a consequence of the passions that we have a ten-dency to invade one another. But he must also have thought that we can control the passions through reason; otherwise, we would continue in a condition of perpetual war. That we do not is the result of reason dictating the laws of nature as the best means to the end of peace. As stated earlier, he was in no doubt that "these are indeed great difficulties but not impossibilities. For by education and discipline they may be, and are sometimes reconciled, Judgement and fancy may have place in the same man-but by turns, as the end which he aimeth at requireth."[30]

The key for Hobbes is that we restructure our lives in a manner that allows us to act peaceably according to our *conatus,* by which he means the continual movement in pursuit of our needs and desires. In particular, we have to give priority to primary goods because a long and coherent life is impossible without the prior conditions of peace and security. To follow such a path, to be guided by reason in the face of strong passion, is no easy task, as Hobbes shows in his description of the man, living in a society governed by laws, who still has to arm himself on his travels and who is required to lock his chests against family and ser-vants. But this is precisely why it is important to foster reason in the place of passion; we will never be secure, Hobbes believed, until humans have the capacity to live by the laws of nature.

I interpret Hobbes as having two distinct but related ideas about imposing laws upon ourselves. The first is that we give up our natural right so that we might live in peace under a sovereign. This is a form of rational self-limitation, but it is not what we would describe as direct self-rule. It is, however, only the necessary first stage in imposing the laws of the sovereign upon ourselves. Hobbes is concerned pri-marily with a more intricate relationship between the sov-ereign, law, and subjects than can be produced simply through fear of the sovereign's power. The fear of the sword is insufficient to create order; "essential rights . . . cannot be maintained by any Civill Law, or terrour of legal punishment."[31] Hobbes thinks that we must also *directly* impose the natural law upon ourselves. Self-government extends to the *rational acceptance* of the laws of nature when made positive by the sovereign. This in turn provides for a form of agency unrealizable when the rule of law rests solely upon fear.

Thus Hobbes provides us with the opportunity to live by universal principles that we directly, and through deliberation, impose upon ourselves. Reason enables us to discover the principles that help us to structure a civil society and our individual lives within that society, and it is obvious, Hobbes thought, that the rational person would act according to these principles. The laws of nature stand opposed to the idea of freedom as license and demonstrate the need for rational constraint rather than the gratification of passions. The laws are actually contrary to some of our natural passions. Nevertheless, the rational person will curb these passions: "the Lawes of Nature . . . are contrary to our naturall Passions, that carry us to Partiality, Pride, Revenge, and the like" yet an individual has "the will to keep them when he can do so safely."[32] The ability to act according to the laws of nature demands not only the external order of society but also the internal order of the individual. The person who is internally well-ordered will act in the correct manner externally. In a passage remarkably similar to modern liberal notions of rational, autonomous action, Hobbes demonstrates his concern that reason dominates passion: "he has no more to do in learning the Lawes of Nature, but, when weighing the actions of other men with his own, they seem too heavy, to put them into the other part of the ballance, and his own in their place, that his own passions, and self-love, may adde nothing to the weight; and then there is none of these Lawes of Nature that will not appear unto him very reasonable."[33]

Although Hobbes may not have thought that everyone could be virtuous in this sense he at least thought, according to Keith Thomas: "that the people at large were capable of learning political virtue, the poor no less than the rich."[34] And the point of all this for Hobbes? We impose the laws of nature and the sovereign upon ourselves in order to exchange the conditions of natural liberty for a social condition that gives us greater liberty to pursue our own conception of the good life. Once peace has been secured, we are able to live felicitous lives, pursuing long-term goals in a manner that augments our lives as a whole. Clearly Hobbes is concerned not with passion-driven movement, but with rational and reasonable action that is now governed by rational and reasonable deliberation.

A problem remains: How are we to make obligations self-imposed rather than imposed through fear of punishment? Hobbes lays out the method by which the sovereign can foster virtuous behavior in his subjects, particularly through civic education. As Alan Ryan argues, Hobbes had a concept of education based upon prudential toleration and hence: "Hobbes's sovereign cannot condition children as the Director in *Brave New World* can."[35] On simple grounds of expediency, the sovereign should not try to impose strict conformity because it will be rejected and lead to instability. What Hobbes wished for instead, is for the sovereign to foster the spirit of the laws of nature by means of civic education; this, in turn, will guarantee his own safety and public peace. Hence, in the fullest manifestation of human development, "generous souls" will be prevalent in whom reason effectively rules. These are no longer beings who are swayed by a random procession of passions, but persons who act according to the dictates of reason as expressed in moral law. Hobbes wanted more from humanity than fearful obedience to the sovereign; his goal was that over time we would impose the law upon ourselves. The more of these "generous souls" to be found in a civil society, the more stable that society will become.

Even if Hobbes does not provide a satisfactory answer to the problem of securing obedience and still has to rely upon fear to promote lawful behavior, his theory of autonomy is still persuasive; authority does not preclude autonomy; it makes it possible. As Rawls says, even in a well-ordered society: "a coercive sovereign is presumably always necessary . . . the existence of effective penal machinery serves as men's security to one another."[36] We criticize ourselves, therefore, to the extent that we criticize Hobbes on this issue.

People are also inclined to impose upon themselves the civil laws from a desire for commodious living. In the state of nature: "there is a dominion of passions, war, fear, poverty, slovenliness, solitude, barbarism, ignorance, cruelty"; in society: "the dominion of reason, peace, security, riches, decency, society, elegancy, sciences, and benevolence."[37] In other words, in the state of nature we live like beasts; in civil society we can live well, and improve ourselves. Hobbes argues that "Desire of Knowledge and Arts of Peace, enclineth men to obey a common power: For such desire, containeth a desire of leasure."[38] A political community is a necessary requirement for autonomous beings, and autonomy is the main aim of society, which is a step beyond peace and security. This is shown most clearly in what is perhaps Hobbes's most famous passage concerning the state of nature: "In such condition, there is no place for industry . . . no Culture of the Earth; no Navigation . . . no Knowledge of the face of the Earth; no account of Time; no Arts; no Letters; no society; and which is worst of all, continuall feare, and danger of violent death; And the life of man, solitary, poore, nasty, brutish, and short."[39]

Hobbes uses the state of nature in *Leviathan* in a variety of ways. It is a hypothetical contract, yet it also has to support his theory of justice. It is meant to have some historical reference, as with his example of American natives but it is also used as a heuristic device to demonstrate the necessity of government. As he argues, the state of nature probably never generally existed, but "Howsoever, it may be perceived what manner of life there would be where there were no common power."[40] Thus, Hobbes uses the idea of the state of nature as a thought-experiment in which we are asked to think of humans in a social vacuum, free from norms and the civil law. This does not mean that the behavior Hobbes envisioned occurring in such a condition is the true expression of human nature. In fact, it is the opposite because it is behavior that prevents us from living according to reason and peace.

Understood in this way, we can see how Hobbes uses his artificial construct to contrast a condition of license with one of rational action. It is a useful construct in part because it guides and warns people of *future* consequences should they disobey the sovereign. "Natural" human beings as described in the state of nature can be read as artificial constructs to justify obedience to the law. On this reading the description of "mechanistic" humans found in the early pages of *Leviathan* is never meant to represent humans as they exist in civil society; it is a description of humans stripped of their civility and manners who are unable to live in harmony with the laws of nature.

As Theodore Waldman argues, living by the laws of nature is not simply an act of self-interest: "It involves self-sacrifice, self-restraint, and dedication to peace as well as a heightened sense of civic virtue."[41] This is demonstrated by the fact that when we act in response to immediate passion we tend toward war and instability. It is only when we act rationally according to the dictates of reason that we live under government, and hence live as moral beings. This takes us beyond a morality imposed by fear. Rationality is no longer simply a guide to the passions; instead it becomes a means by which we control our passions in accord with self-imposed rules. The roles of rationality and passion are now reversed. This can be seen particularly when we remember that the purpose of creating a sovereign is to radically reduce our fear of death. The laws of nature allow us to control passions that may threaten peace, passions such as pride, partiality, revenge, and vainglory. Hence it is the laws, upheld by the sovereign we have appointed, which make us resist unsocial tendencies and act in favor of social reasonableness.

The full manifestation of a life lived by the laws of nature is the development of a particular rational character type, strikingly at odds with the usual view of humans attributed to Hobbes. Certain character traits are necessary so that we can live worthwhile lives because they allow us to utilize the full freedom available to us. We become equitable, reasonable, peace-seeking, just, other-regarding, even communal. Theorists such as Charles Taylor, who argue that Hobbes is the prime exponent of "Atomism,"[42] do not really get to the crux of his thought and method. It is precisely Hobbes's goal to show us that we cannot develop our human faculties without civil society and in all probability that we cannot even survive independently of a political community. For such a society to work, Hobbes's theory of action cannot simply be an ideal to be achieved by a select number of natural aristocrats. Rather, it calls for a substantial amount of self-direction from most members of Hobbes's commonwealth because the practice of making and keeping covenants requires the conformity to reason of almost everybody.

The upshot of the argument so far is that Hobbes presents a theory of rationality that is considerably different for the instrumentalism with which he is usually associated; it is a position that is, in fact, close to the strongly substantive positions of Kant/Habermas. Rational action is not simply judged in terms of how well ends are attained. Rather, for an act to be rational one must be able to give a good reason for the action—it must be explicable and comprehensible to others (rationality in terms of reason giving) and it must fit with the principles of reason found in the laws of nature (rationality in terms of moral reasonableness). I will now make a first cut at assessing this reformulated Hobbesian position.

Rationality and Self-regarding Actions

Problem case number 1: Is it irrational to perform an act that is both self-regarding and not self-defeating? Let us return to the example of chopping off my leg. Is it irrational to do so even if I can give reasons for the act and if I can show that it will not get in the way of my future preferences? If I can meet these two criteria then I think that I would have to say that it is rational to do so. But if we ponder the situation for a moment it seems to be extremely unlikely that this will actually be the case. First of all, there seems to be very little likelihood that I could give good reasons for the action; it is much more likely that if I could give reasons at all they would be shaped by irrational conscious or unconscious forces; even to desire to chop off one's leg is such an unlikely preference that we would suspect that something was brewing below the conscious surface.

It also seems to be next to impossible that I could demonstrate that chopping off my leg will not have unforeseen and undesired consequences in the future. Hence it will almost never be the case that such an act will not hinder my future preferences. But still one may say: "What if I really could give good reasons and could show that it would not be detrimental?" I think at this point, if all of these conditions of reason giving and future gazing are met, then we have to say that the action is rational. And it would have to be classed as rational because the reasons that were given would have to be very compelling in order to pass the tests set for them and because the reasons did not suggest that the person was contradicting any other preferences that were also deemed crucial to living a reasonable life. What this means is that for an act to be rational it has to be *judged* as rational and this means that rationality is intersubjective and contextual.

It seems to be counter to all our intuitions to state that the act is rational simply because the preference was pursued in a very vigorous and successful manner. If the measure of rationality is captured in the statement "I simply want to do the act," or "it makes me feel good," then almost every action is a *rational action* and the term loses any significance as a means of judging behavior. Similar criticisms can be applied to the idea that rationality is captured by the concept of maximization. This seems to be inadequate because I may have crazy preferences that when maximized would make my life unrecognizably human. Rational choice scholars are only willing to criticize the rationality of an act in terms of how well the goal is pursued, or whether preferences are transitively ordered. On this view Jeffrey Dahlmer is the very epitome of rationality. If the rational choice view is correct then we will need to purge our vocabulary of such terms as *mad, obsessive,* and *mentally ill,* terms that are often related to optimizing behavior. It is often better not to maximize; my health, for example, is promoted by only eating half the cake, even though I want more, and it may take an incredible amount of effort to attain that last 5 percent of my preference, when 95 percent is perfectly sufficient. Aversion to extremes can, therefore, be extremely rational. Efficiency also seems to be lacking as the benchmark for rational action because the ever more efficient attainment of ends that are bad for me seems to be hard to defend.

Simple transitivity in preference ordering is not enough to class an act as rational. Such conceptions of rationality also do not seem to fit well with how humans actually behave. No one would deny that on occasions we act in the manner predicted by the instrumental view, but we also make decisions based on concepts of fairness, cooperation, love, respect, delusion, mental illness, hate, and social norms, and often from habit, laziness, weakness of the will, and ignorance. The economic model also ignores the crucial question of where our preferences come from; even if the choices we make do reveal our core preferences, we still need to know what creates these preferences. Hobbes is well aware of this and, as will be seen later, he expends a great deal of time and effort suggesting ways in which preferences should be changed in order to promote peace and stability; he does not simply take preferences as given and stable, and suggests that human flourishing may well be at odds with preference maximization. What is needed, therefore, is a measure of the preferences themselves as the benchmark of rational behavior.

Unless someone could come up with a reason for the above mentioned self-mutilation, such as, "my leg is trapped under a burning car and this is necessary to save my life," I think we have to judge the act as irrational. Clearly unanimous agreement cannot be the criteria for judging rationality because almost nothing would be classed as rational (there will always be someone who disagrees, even if that person herself seems to be highly irrational). It seems that what measures up as rational action can only be judged in terms of very broad cultural norms regarding what counts as a meaningful human existence. This means that the very idea of rationality can only be understood as a very fuzzy concept that will change over time. I would argue, therefore, that Habermas and Hobbes are correct in suggesting that rationality has to be based at some level on reason giving.

Rationality and Other-regarding Actions

Problem case number 2: Sometimes a person can do an act that treats others in a terrible way. The question posed by such behavior is whether or not it is rational to be reasonable. Was Dahlmer, for instance, rational? The instrumental view would simply see if his preferences were well ordered and maximized; one could easily conclude that he was a paradigm of rationality on these terms. Can we say that there was something so wrong with his actions that they were irrational no matter what one could say about how well the goals were integrated and strategically pursued? Perhaps we can claim that his actions were irrational precisely because they were so unreasonable from the moral point of view.

Habermas would say, along Kantian (and, as we have seen, Hobbesian) lines, that it is irrational to treat people as means and not as ends. We ourselves demand to be treated as ends and hence we fall into a logical inconsistency if we do not at the same time allow the same courtesy to everyone else. Now clearly this means not treating people *solely* as means because every time we enter into a contract with someone, or employ them, or pay a wage, we are using others as means to our ends. So it seems that it is a particular form of treating people as means that is objectionable and that is when we are not treating them as *moral* ends in themselves. It follows that when Habermas says that rationality requires giving reasons, not just any reasons will be acceptable. To say that I killed someone because it gives me pleasure, or because it furnished me with material goods is not good enough to make the action rational. Similarly, Hobbes would say that the action was irrational because it stands in opposition to the dictates of morality in the laws of nature that tell us to treat others as we wish to be treated. It seems, therefore, that only acts that are morally reasonable in relation to the treatment of others or reasonable in the sense of being nonharmful to oneself can be classed as rational.

I do not think it is very persuasive to say that Dahlmer was irrational because he was immoral. Immoral actions, by definition are not irrational because for an act to be categorized as immoral the agent also has to be classed as a responsible agent. Morality and immorality are categories of *agency,* and agency has as part of its definition the claim that a person is rational. To say, therefore, that it is irrational to be unreasonable (in the moral sense) is to make a category mistake. It seems to be crucial given our intuitions about freedom and morality that we class the actions of most of those who break moral codes as rational but extremely unreasonable; otherwise, our categories of praise and blame, and accountability and responsibility no longer make much sense. But on another level our intuitions do suggest that we want to say that the goals of Dahlmer were so bizarre that we cannot call them "rational." They certainly cannot be defended on moral grounds, but, as we have just seen, this does not in and of itself make the actions irrational; the real test is whether or not they can be explained in such a manner that they make any sense to us. Hence, one could make a claim that actions that are extremely unreasonable in the moral sense are done by people who are mentally disturbed in some way that makes them irrational; this seems to me to be an accurate way in which to judge the actions of Dahlmer; the rationality of the behavior, as with the person who is about to chop off her leg, has to be judged not on the grounds of reasonableness in a moral sense but of reasonableness in the sense of *reason giving.* This is very different from the claim made by

Habermas who wants to suggest that it is irrational to *deliberately* be unreasonable.

I suggest, therefore, that Hobbes and Habermas are correct in arguing that the rational and the *reasonable* are linked when the term *reasonable* is used to suggest reason giving, but that they are wrong on the question of whether they are necessarily linked when the term *reasonable* is used in a moral sense. Just as the instrumental view of rationality is counterintuitive (because most people think that not all ends can be classed as rational), I also argue that the deeply substantive view of rationality also goes against the grain of our shared intuitions. Most people do want to claim that the vast majority of immoral persons are responsible for their actions and hence they also want to say that most immoral persons are rational. It is only when the immoral behavior reaches the level of incomprehensibility that it is judged irrational.

Conclusion

The arguments of this chapter and chapter 4 suggest a theory of autonomy and virtue in Hobbes; not virtue understood solely in terms of the moral worth of actions, but in the sense of being one's own person, controlling one's passions, and living according to a rational life-plan that relates actions to one another and to specific goals in a significantly meaningful way. Hobbes does not ignore the internal properties of agents when evaluating how free they are. One can agree with Gary Herbert that "Every thought and opinion, and therefore every action, carries the tincture of the passions."[43] This is not at odds with autonomy, as long as the passions are regulated by reason. One can also agree that according to Hobbes we are primarily driven by the desire for self-preservation. The crucial point for Hobbes is that we pursue self-preservation according to the dictates of reason, which means prioritizing desires and overcoming vainglory.

Hobbes did not think everyone could achieve this, but it was the standard that people should endeavor toward to achieve their best. The overall argument of this chapter and chapter 4, therefore, contests the almost universal view that Hobbes is a paradigmatic proponent of a narrow, instrumental, rational-choice view of politics and human behavior. Instead, Hobbes provides us with a nuanced understanding of rationality that examines the ends pursued as well as the means to those ends. Hobbes's theory of action leads to a conception of the self that resembles, in extensive ways, one strand of the modern liberal ideal.

In terms of the internal requirements for freedom, I have demonstrated that Hobbes is very concerned with the way in which people make *choices*. He does not simply ignore the internal conditions of agency as most commentators have suggested; instead he judges agency in terms of instrumentalism, rationality, reasonableness, coherency, and foresight. He is willing to say that the person who suffers from a variety of internal constraints that he labels under the term *madness* is not a full agent. Ultimately Hobbes's theory of rationality suggests that we can have different degrees of agency; a person who is gripped by vainglory is not capable of the same sort of self-control as the person who, through rational deliberation, decides to impose upon herself the laws of nature. To repeat the claim made at the beginning of the chapter, Hobbes's theory of agency takes us to an ideal that resembles what Flathman calls freedom$_5$, in which action is "attempted by an agent in the pursuit of a plan or project self-critically chosen to satisfy, and in fact satisfying, certifiably worthy norms or principles."[44] I also made the claim that Hobbes's theories of rationality and morality are inextricably linked. I have, however, only hinted at the claim that Hobbes has a robust moral theory and a stronger case needs to be argued that this is indeed so. If the case can be made, it will also add weight to the arguments in this chapter and in chapter 4. It is usually suggested, however, that one of Hobbes's claims to fame is his distinct lack of concern for moral principles. In chapter 6 I address this issue and argue that Hobbes can take his rightful place among the ranks of moral philosophers.

6

~

Voluntarism and Morality

Introduction

The reevaluation of Hobbes's theories of freedom, volition, and rationality, developed over chapters 3–5 has important consequences for many aspects of his political, philosophical, and psychological views. As Gregory S. Kavka has noted, Hobbes's theory of motion and volition is perhaps the single most important aspect of his philosophy. For Hobbes, everything ultimately boils down to motion. Patrick Riley agrees and argues that Hobbes's theory of volition has crucial implications for his ideas on covenanting, duty, justice, authority, and hence on the very legitimacy of the sovereign and the state.[1] In this chapter, I will focus in particular upon Hobbes's theory of psychological motivation and his theory of moral agency in order to assess the impact that his theory of volition has on his moral philosophy.

My interpretation will challenge the traditional view that Hobbes started from an egoistic understanding of human nature from which he derived a particular set of political institutions. The traditional interpretation presents Hobbes as a subjectivist who claims that what is good is based solely upon individual preference and that obligation only stems from self-interest (which means in effect that he does not have a theory of moral obligation at all because contracts are based purely on prudential reasons). Even current commentators who are more sympathetic to Hobbes tend to conclude that the laws of nature are a set of prudential maxims that help individuals preserve themselves and when it is not in one's self-interest there are no good reasons for keeping promises to fellow subjects or to the sovereign. We are, therefore, basically unmoved by moral concerns if morality is understood to mean acting in certain circumstances in a disinterested manner.

The traditional view is not surprising if one accepts that Hobbes has an egoistic account of human motivation that describes actions in terms of immediate desires that determine the things we class as good or evil. Such a seemingly deterministic view of human agency (or rather the lack of any form of agency) seems to preclude Hobbes from presenting a viable moral theory. This poses a problem because Hobbes also argues that consent is binding, not because it is necessary for our survival but because it stems from a willing agent who makes a voluntary moral commitment. A workable theory of consent demands that we assume that humans are capable of making choices and keeping promises. As Riley notes, almost everything for Hobbes, from the founding of a state to the relationship between parents and children is defined in terms of voluntary consent. Yet if Hobbes is presenting a deterministic and egoistic view of human behavior, how can he also seem to demand morally willing agents?

This problem has been addressed in three ways. The first is that taken by A. E. Taylor and Howard Warrender who claim that Hobbes's psychological and moral philosophies are simply incompatible.[2] Both find a moral theory in Hobbes's work, but they argue that this stems from a Christian theory of natural law that states that we are obliged because the law of nature is the law of God. The second alternative, suggested by David Gauthier, Thomas Nagel, Jean Hampton, and others is to argue that Hobbes does not have a *moral theory* at all in the conventional sense of the term and instead presents arguments that link "moral" behavior with prudential action.[3] The third response is that of Dana Chabot, who argues that Hobbes is not a moral skeptic but a skeptical moralist: "Hobbes uses skeptical argument as the foundation upon which to construct a challenging (if not terribly attractive) conception of moral life."[4]

The main interpretive dilemma for Warrender and Taylor is that they could not find a way to fit their understanding of Hobbes's objectivist morality with what they took to be his egoistic psychology. I intend to demonstrate that they can be linked together now that we can place a more voluntaristic notion of motivation at the heart of Hobbes's psychology. Hampton argues that we should take Hobbes at his word when he says that his morality can be derived from his psychology. However, because she interprets him as an egoist, she takes this to indicate that Hobbes must really mean that the laws of nature are only prudential maxims. It is thus argued that only the subjectivist interpretation can maintain consistency between Hobbes's ethics and psychology.

I attempt to turn the tables and suggest that his morality and psychology are compatible precisely because he is not an egoist. And with the theory of volition outlined here, we do not have to abandon his psychology to make such a claim, as Taylor suggests. At the same time, I argue that Hobbes has a moral theory that does not have to rest on a Christian theory of natural law as claimed by Warrender. In opposition to Chabot, who argues that Hobbes arrives at moral standards because of his skeptical view of human capabilities, I claim that Hobbes defends his moral theory from the standpoint of objective moral standards.

I wish, therefore, to suggest a fourth alternative, one that proposes a view of human volition in Hobbes's writings, a view that suggests that humans are capable of placing reason over passion, that they are capable of acting in a manner contrary to immediate self-interest and hence that they do not act simply as short-or long-term utility maximizers. The aim of this chapter is to demonstrate that Hobbes has a sophisticated view of human psychology and that this in turn suggests an adequate theory of human volition; if these claims are correct we can then make a strong case for Hobbes as a theorist of morality. We can, therefore, take Gauthier's approach of combining Hobbes's morality and psychology and yet still reach a conclusion that posits Hobbes as a theorist of *morality* in the conventional sense of the word.

Hobbes's Psychology

Hobbes is often accused of being a psychological egoist, that is, that every act is always and solely motivated by the selfish interest of the agent.[5] For example, Kavka, while not himself claiming that Hobbes promotes psychological egoism, suggests that the theory rules out certain motives for action such as "doing what is morally right, and promoting the well-being of others."[6] In other words, we cannot act from purposes that are "morally motivated, or altruistic."[7] Actions may actually lead to morally acceptable consequences, but these are not the motivational factors behind the decision to act. Instead, we are motivated in all our actions by the desire for personal gain that comes from such things as "wealth, power, security, liberty, glory, possession of particular objects, fame, health, status, self-assertion, reputation, honor."[8] What this amounts to is the claim that all acts are grounded in self-interest and, in fact, more than this, that we will always act selfishly.

Such an argument suggests that motion is only caused by the forethought of pleasure or pain as it relates to the particular agent. We find pleasure in certain things; hence we desire these things and move toward them in a determined manner. This view of Hobbes is shared by, among others, Richard S. Peters, Nagel, J. W. N. Watkins, and M. M. Goldsmith.[9] Hampton also leans toward a more sophisticated form of this interpretation, arguing that Hobbes only gives selfish reasons for obedience: "according to Hobbes, contractual obligations exist only insofar as it is in our interests to perform them."[10] She does not see this as a problem for Hobbes and argues that it is a virtue of his theory that self-interest and morality are in essence one and the same thing. Hobbes can now give a very strong answer to the question "why be moral?" by replying that "it is in my interest to be so." Gauthier claims that an unavoidable consequence of Hobbes's theory of motion is that "man is necessarily selfish."[11] In a similar vein, Kavka argues that Hobbes thought that morality and self-interest are compatible with one another: "[Hobbes], offering a novel view of the requirements of both morality and prudence, argues that the two are not really in conflict."[12] The difference between the work of earlier Hobbes scholars (Peters, Nagel, and Watkins) and later scholars (Gauthier, Hampton, and Kavka) is that the latter group provide a more sophisticated analysis of what Hobbes meant by prudence and recognize that for Hobbes, it can mean acting in a manner that promotes one's long-term over one's short-term interests. It is necessary, therefore, if one is to demonstrate that Hobbes is concerned with moral concepts, to show that his arguments go beyond sophisticated calculations of prudence and incorporate legitimate concern for the interests of others.

Hobbes clearly demands that individuals act in ways that do not seem to fit well with maximizing self-interest. Richard Flathman, while agreeing with these interpretations, also notes that Hobbes seems to condemn acts of cruelty and also provides strong support for the concept of equality. In effect, Hobbes seems to find himself in an impossible bind if he is a psychological egoist. On the one hand, he argues that we are determined in our movements by passion and selfishness. On the other hand, he also wants to argue that we are morally obliged when we make contracts and promises. This, however, seems to require a theory of the will that suggests that we do more than simply respond in a determined fashion to external stimuli. Riley summarizes the problem well when he says: "what is remarkable in Hobbes is that there seems to be a disjunction between his doctrine that wills make the essence of all covenants but also in the notion that there is 'no obligation on any man which ariseth not from some act of his own'—

and his account of the will and of the nature of voluntary actions in the rest of his system."[13]

What Riley is pointing to here is the gulf that exists between Hobbes's idea that the will is determined in the pursuit of appetite and self-interest and his arguments that suggest that humans are capable of moral agency when making contracts, and hence are morally obliged to keep their promises. As Riley says, a theory of consent "that suggests that wills make the essence of all covenants might be expected to develop a notion of will as a moral faculty whose free choice gives rise to authority and to obligation."[14] But what Hobbes seems to leave us with is "a rather stark contrast between a moral and political theory that requires a family of voluntarist concepts as its foundation, and a theory of volition as appetite and aversion which is ill suited to account for the moral importance of consenting, promising, and agreeing."[15]

As Riley also suggests, commentators have been left with little recourse except to assert that one passage is more important than another, or that an argument should or should not be taken literally. The result is that one often cannot determine "whether one is satisfying Hobbes or oneself"[16] with these interpretations. What I wish to suggest is that we can better address this tension now that we have a better understanding of what Hobbes meant by freedom and voluntary movement. If one accepts his pure negative theory of freedom (see chap. 3), one is more likely to favor the interpretation that Hobbes does not have anything more in mind than the fact that humans are determined in their pursuit of appetite and self-interest. One cannot be confident about the accuracy of such a claim once we have reformulated the theory of freedom and examined his psychology in greater detail. The arguments presented in this chapter intimate a solution to this puzzle because they suggest that Hobbes is not in fact a psychological egoist, that he does have a more adequate theory of volition than has been thought, and consequently that his psychology is compatible with moral conduct.

It is crucially important to recognize another feature of psychological egoism at this point, namely that the theory does not state that we will *sometimes* act in a selfish manner but that we will *always* do so and that everyone will do so. It is not enough, therefore, for those who think that Hobbes falls into this category to simply point to textual evidence that suggests that he thinks we will act selfishly on occasion. They must also answer for the many places where he seems to claim that we can act morally and altruistically. The task is easier for those wishing to deny that Hobbes is a psychological egoist because they can make use of most of this evidence and also need not be worried at the places where Hobbes hints that we will act in a self-interested manner. One can argue that humans are motivated some of the time by the things on Kavka's list without embracing egoism. In fact, it is sometimes necessary to act in a self-interested manner in order for justice to be served, because self-interest ensures that each is treated fairly. It is only the sections of *Leviathan* that state that we will always under all conditions act in this manner that pose problems, and we will find that such examples are very rare in the text and can be explained by the distinction Hobbes makes between the right and the laws of nature.

Psychological Egoism

At times Hobbes does seem to lean toward the theory of psychological egoism, as for instance when he claims that the terms good and evil are used solely in relation to the preferences of the person who uses the terms: "But whatsoever is the object of any man's Appetite or Desire; that it is, which he for his part calleth *Good.*"[17] This statement, on its own, is not enough to characterize Hobbes as a supporter of egoism because people may call many things good, including actions that do not advance their interests. But he continues by making the stronger claim in chapter 14 of *Leviathan* that the result of every action is deemed good solely in terms of the benefit to the agent: "and of the voluntary acts of every man, the object is some *Good to himselfe.*"[18] Hobbes repeats this sentiment in a couple of other places, particularly in chapter 15 of *Leviathan* where he says the following concerning gift giving: "For no man giveth, but with intention of Goode to himselfe; because Gift is Voluntary; and of all Voluntary Acts, the Object is to every man his own good."[19] These are the major instances in *Leviathan* where Hobbes seems to be presenting strongly egoistic motivations for behavior. Is this enough evidence to suggest that this is his view of human motivation?

When deciding whether Hobbes favors the theory of psychological egoism, much depends on what he means by claiming that an action is always in the agent's own good; does he mean short-term or long-term, or real or perceived good? It is not clear that Hobbes means by the word *good* that we will always act to promote our own self-interest. When he defines good he does not specifically mention self-interest at all: "of Good there be three kinds; Good in the Promise . . . Good in Effect . . . and Good as the Means."[20] What he does not say is that each of these is to be judged solely in terms of the perceptions of a particular agent. If we interpret Hobbes to mean something the agent would *call* good as opposed to always being good *for himself* then this is not egoism. And sometimes he does suggest this: "But whatsoever is the object of any man's Appetite or Desire; that is which he for his part *calleth* good."[21]

In many places he talks of good without it specifically relating to the interest of the agent and actually suggests that we can behave in an altruistic manner. For example, he talks of the "*Desire* of good to another, BENEVOLENCE, GOOD WILL, CHARITY. If to men generally, GOOD NATURE."[22] Hobbes seems to use the term in both senses (i.e., good for oneself and for others) as, for example, when he differentiates between command and counsel: "Therefore between Counsell and Command, one great difference is, that Command is directed to a mans own benefit; and counsell to the benefit of another man."[23] It is clear from this statement that Hobbes thinks we are capable of acting in response to the interest of others. His general discussion of the role of counselors, while too extensive to discuss here, leaves one with the impression that Hobbes clearly thought people were capable of giving disinterested advice.

It is interesting to note the context in which the most egoistic statements are made in *Leviathan*. Hobbes is preoccupied in chapters 14 and 15 of *Leviathan* with the right of nature and hence with conditions that are potentially harmful to an individual's self-preservation, particularly in conditions such as the state of nature. Because Hobbes is concerned primarily with self-preservation in these chapters, he doesn't argue that in conditions under which we are threatened we will act in an egoistic manner. In other words, when Hobbes seems to discuss humans in egoistic terms, he is not really describing them as they are in a commonwealth, but as they might be when they have to act as if the right of nature is the primary motivator of action. A view of humans acting as egoists in such aberrant conditions is not unusual; as Michael Oakeshott notes, to talk of morality in a meaningful sense requires that humans live under conditions of at least minimal security and subsistence.[24] It is too demanding to expect moral behavior from individuals living under the conditions of Hobbes's state of nature.

Hobbes gives a very different impression of human behavior when he turns his attention to the laws of nature. Now Hobbes talks of accommodating oneself to the rest, of acting upon gratitude, of keeping promises irrespective of whether one gains from such behavior (even in the state of nature Hobbes says we are morally obliged to keep a promise if the other party has performed his part of the contract), and of not trying to reserve rights to oneself that are not available to everyone else. We need to be willing to forgive others, express gratitude, rid ourselves of arrogant pride, and be willing to act on the principles of mutuality and cooperation. As Flathman argues, Hobbes's philosophy promotes such virtues as "justice and fidelity, moderation and self-control, magnanimity, and even a certain rare but distinctively admirable nobility."[25] In fact, one can interpret the laws of nature as prescribing behavior that is the opposite of egoism, and that in fact changes the definition of good from an individualistic notion to one of collective benefit: "And the science of them [the laws], as the true and onely Moral Philosophy. For Moral Philosophy is nothing else but *the Science of what is Good and Evill in the conversation, and Society of mankind* . . . and consequently all men agree on this, that Peace is Good, and therefore also the way, or means of Peace, which . . . are *Justice, Gratitude, Modesty, Equity, Mercy,* and the rest of the Laws of Nature are good; that is to say, *Morall Vertues;* and their contrarie *Vices,* Evil."[26] As discussed in chapter 4, the laws of nature allow the members of the commonwealth to pursue the "primary goods" that benefit everyone, goods such as peace, order, the reduction of the fear of violent death, a sense of worth, the controlled pursuit of power, and commodious living. These are the key ingredients to a collective existence but they are only attainable if we do not act in an egoistic manner and, in particular, they can only be achieved if reason dominates the passions. When Hobbes says, therefore, that what an individual calls good and evil is what she either desires or is averse to, he is simply stating a tautology; he is basically saying that an individual claims her desires are good precisely because they are what she desires. But this does not mean that she cannot be wrong about what she desires. Hobbes would not be troubled to say that an individual who desired war over peace was simply wrong and that her real good was being undermined by his false desire. The laws of nature tell us that there are certain things that are good and evil regardless of the preferences of particular individuals.

I argue, therefore, that we can best make sense of the manner in which Hobbes sometimes thinks we have egoistic tendencies and other times when he thinks that we do not by drawing a distinction between the right and the laws of nature. When he talks of the former he is more inclined to think that we will behave egotistically. However, given that it is in the state of nature that the right takes precedence, this is not too strong a condemnation of human behavior. But once we can live by the laws of nature, that is, almost all the time we live within the safety of a commonwealth, Hobbes expects very different motivations for action. I think that this is a better explanation than the two major commentaries that challenge the view that Hobbes presents a theory of psychological egoism. The first of these is offered by Bernhard Gert, who argues that we can simply discount the more egoistic passages as overexuberance on the part of Hobbes, and the second is that of F. S. McNeilly who claims that Hobbes is simply careless in conveying his thoughts on egoism from earlier works.[27]

Rather than having to depend upon a theory of egoism to make his political philosophy work, as some have suggested (because only egoists will make the state of nature unbearable and only calculations of self-interest can get us out of it) Hobbes's theory actually requires a nonegoistic conception of human motivation because he recognizes that pure self-interest alone is not enough to promote the survival of the commonwealth. What is needed is communal action, a certain nobility of character and a willingness to take into account the interests of others. In other words, his theory depends on the rational and autonomous character type discussed in chapters 4 and 5. However, demonstrating that Hobbes's psychology is compatible with morality does not also demonstrate that he actually presents a theory of moral conduct; it could still be the case that Gauthier, Hampton, and Kavka are correct in claiming that Hobbes is still presenting a theory of prudence, albeit of a sophisticated kind.

Morality

As Nagel has argued, we are not really talking about morality at all if we simply equate it solely with self-interest: "genuine moral obligation plays no part at all in *Leviathan* [because] what Hobbes calls moral obligation is based exclusively on considerations of rational self-interest."[28] Self-interest may be a very good reason for following rules of conduct, but it is not a moral reason for doing so. One of the main functions of a moral theory is to give us rules suggesting that we ought to act one way or another regardless of whether we stand to gain an advantage. Thus, Nagel concludes that Hobbes cannot have a theory of morality because of his "egoistic theory of motivation."[29]

Hence, if one interprets Hobbes as a psychological egoist it is difficult to piece together his views into a coherent whole. If Hobbes thinks we act on our own immediate self-interest at all times then he does not really have a workable theory of moral and political obligation; the most he can offer is a theory of obedience through coercion. Morality has no motivational power over the individual, and even worse, we are psychologically incapable of doing duty for duty's sake. In fact, the term *moral agent* does not apply at all because it suggests the ability to make choices and to perform our duties, whereas the egoistic view of human behavior is based on a more brute form of determined movement.

We have already addressed one obstacle preventing us from interpreting Hobbes as a theorist of morality by suggesting he does not support the theory of psychological egoism. A further clue that suggests Hobbes thinks that we are capable of moral action can be found in his distinction (that must be based on a perception of human beings as willing agents) between coerced acts and authoritative acts in civil society. Hobbes argues that we cannot be obliged to another person except through an act of the will; for a statement or an action to be authoritative it has to have been done voluntarily. Only if one is the author of a contract is it binding: "so the Right of doing any Action, is called AUTHORITY. So that by Authority, is alwayes understood a Right of doing any act: and *done by Authority,* done by Commission, or license from him whose right it is . . . no man is obliged by a Covenant, whereof he is not Author; not consequently by a Covenant made against, or beside the Authority he gave."[30]

This is how Hobbes talks of contracts in civil society; but it does not fit well with an egoistic, nonmoral view of human behavior because authority requires that the agent is responsible for the action. In order to locate authority one has to be able to identify those who are responsible for actions, but this is only possible when Hobbes begins to make distinctions between movements. As Riley says, a voluntary act "cannot be just any act: it cannot be, say, the mere feeling of an appetite such as lust, because in a world of appetites and aversions the notions of obligation and authority could not exist at all . . . Hobbes needs not just any act but a free act on the part of a free agent."[31] Hobbes is not describing a creature determined by passion but is arguing instead in favor of a rational willing self able to make free choices and control behavior according to moral principles. True freedom is linked to promising, covenanting, and acting justly because here we can demonstrate that we are the authors of our actions.

A claim that is often made by contemporary interpreters of Hobbes is that because he links the laws of nature to our long-term interests, he is only presenting a prudential rather than a moral theory. He clearly thinks that acting in conformity with the laws is in our best interest in the long run as the following quote from *Behemoth or the Long Parliament* makes clear: "Likewise, to obey the laws, is the prudence of a subject; for without such obedience the commonwealth (which is every subject's safety and protection) cannot subsist. And though it be prudence also in private men, justly and moderately to enrich themselves, yet craftily to withhold from the public or defraud it of such part of their wealth, as is by law required, is no sign of prudence, but want of knowledge or what is necessary for their own defense."[32] Here Hobbes clearly states that acting upon one's immediate self-interest is a foolish thing to do and that one should not free ride even if the opportunity presents itself. But he nevertheless still links long term self-interest with doing the right thing. These sorts of claims lead Hampton to argue that for Hobbes "contractual obligations exist only insofar as it is in our interests to perform them."[33]

It is clear, as for instance with the famous advice to the fool, that Hobbes thinks it can be compatible with one's interest to keep promises in society: "The fool hath said in his heart: 'there is no such thing as justice' . . . and therefore also to make or not make, keep or not keep, covenants was

not against reason, when it conduced to one's benefit. . . .
[T]his specious reasoning is nevertheless false . . . I say it is
not against reason . . . [for] he which declares he thinks it
reason to deceive those that help him can in reason expect
no other means of safety than what can be had from his
single power."[34] It is against one's self-interest to break
covenants, therefore, because others will no longer trust
one's word and could quite possibly cast one out of society.
This is the advice he gives to the fool; it is of a prudential
rather than moral nature. But there is a very good reason
why this should be so and it is because the fool has already
denied that moral reasons will persuade him to keep his
contracts; there is no point using arguments that have already been ruled out as persuasive by one's interlocutor.
Hence, Hobbes tries to persuade the fool on his own terms
that he should still act according to the principles of justice.
But ultimately self-interest is not the primary reason why
Hobbes thinks we ought to keep our promises. If Hobbes
had thought this was the right way to behave, he would
hardly have described the person as a fool. And if he had really thought that it was legitimate to break a promise
whenever it was in one's interest to do so, he would not
have started his enterprise of civil philosophy in the first
place.

Hobbes provides many arguments for keeping promises
even if doing so is contrary to one's interests. He makes it
clear that I am obliged, especially if I am expected to act
after the other contractor has already performed: "In
Contracts, the right passeth, not onely where the words are
of the time Present, or Past; but also where they are of the
future . . . and therefore he that promiseth onely, because he
hath already the benefit for which he promiseth is to be understood as if he intended the Right should passe."[35] Such a
requirement holds even in the state of nature because even
here the promise can only be broken upon "reasonable suspicion."[36] Hobbes actually takes the principle of keeping
covenants to ridiculous extremes: "if I Covenant to pay a
randsome, or service for my life, to an enemy; I am bound by
it. For it is a Contract, wherein one receiveth the benefit of

life; the other is to receive mony, or services for it."[37] I am even obliged to keep a promise to a criminal: "if I be forced to redeem my selfe from a Theefe by promising him mony, I am bound to pay it, till the Civill Law discharge me."[38] It is difficult to see how such an act can be in my self-interest.

The upshot of his arguments is that if I enter into an arrangement with another person to buy a car, for example, I may do so purely from a consideration of my own interest; consequently the covenant I enter into is based on this motivation. But I am then obliged to pay for the car; it may not be in my interest, short- or long-term, to do so after I have received the vehicle, but Hobbes would clearly argue that I still have to pay because I have promised to do so. The promise holds independently of my self-interest: "And when a man hath . . . abandoned, or granted away his Right: then is he said to be OBLIGED, or BOUND, not to hinder those, to whom such a Right is granted, or abandoned, from the benefit of it; and that he *Ought,* and it is his Duty, not to make voyd that voluntary act of his own."[39] The "ought" in this statement is clearly the language of morality, not of self-interest.

The reason why we ought to honor our obligations is simply because we have promised to do so; a promise brings with it an obligation. Through the act of promising, a person gives away the right to act in any way she wishes. Consequently she is bound not to hinder the exercise of the right of the other to the thing promised. Hobbes says that the "bonds of words"[40] are not enough on their own to keep everyone to their promises; but note that our words, that is, our promises, bind us, even if we do not always act upon our obligations. Hobbes attempts to demonstrate that it is rational to be reasonable and this adds to the persuasiveness of his claims, he thinks, because he is now giving good reasons why the moral and the immoral person should act in the same manner. But he never says that if it is possible to be unreasonable without any costs attached that one should be so. Hobbes, in fact, clearly distinguishes between prudence and injustice: "To prudence, if you adde the use of unjust and dishonest means, such as usually are promoted to men by fear or want, you have that crooked wisdom which is called CRAFT, which is a sign of pusillanimity. For magnanimity is contempt for unjust and dishonest helps."[41] He continues in the same vein in *Behemoth:* "The end of moral philosophy is, to teach men of all sorts, their duty, both to the public and to one another . . . it is not the Much or Little that makes an action virtuous, but the cause; nor Much or Little that makes an action vicious, but its being unconformable to the laws in such men as are subject to the law or it being unconformable to equity or charity in all men whatsoever."[42]

There is a difference between acting justly for moral as opposed to prudential reasons. I think it worth quoting Hobbes at length on what he has to say concerning this distinction:

> The names of just and unjust, when they are attributed to men, signify one thing; and when they are attributed to actions another. When they are attributed to men, they signify conformity and inconformity of manners to reason. But when they are attributed to actions, they signify the conformity or inconformity to reason, not of manners or manner of life, but of particular actions. A just man, therefore, is he that taketh all the care he can that his actions may be all just; and an unjust man is he that neglecteth it. And such men are more often in our language styled by the names of righteous and unrighteous, than just and unjust, though the meaning be the same. Therefore, a righteous man does not lose that title by one or a few unjust actions that proceed from sudden passion or mistake or things or persons; not does an unrighteous man lose his character for such actions as he does or forebears to do for fear, because his will is not framed by the justice, *but by the apparent benefit of what he is to do.* That which gives to human actions the relish of justice is a certain nobleness or gallantness of courage (rarely found) by which a man scorns to be beholden for the contentments of his life to fraud or breach of promise. This justice of the manners is that which is meant where justice is called a virtue, and injustice a vice. But the justice of actions denominates men, not just, but *guiltless;* and

the injustice of the same (which is called injury) gives them but the name of *guilty*.[43]

Strange comments, indeed, if Hobbes really thinks people only, and ought only, to act on prudence!

What Hobbes really hopes for is the sort of gallant person he describes in *Behemoth:*

> B. You make the members of that Parliament very simple men; and yet the people chose them for the wisest of the land.
>
> A. If craft be wisdom, they were wise enough. But *wise,* as I define it, is he that knows how to bring his business to pass (without the assistance of knavery and ignoble shifts) by the sole strength of his good contrivance. A fool may win from a better gamester, by the advantage of false dice and packing of cards.
>
> B. According to your definition, there be few wise men now-a-days. Such wisdom is a kind of gallantry, that few are brought up to, and most think folly. Fine clothes, great feathers, civility towards men that will not swallow injuries, and injury towards them that will, is the present gallantry.[44]

This text is full of strong moral language as Hobbes charges the people he blames for the civil war as being hypocrites, dishonest, uncharitable, fraudulent, spiteful, carnal, swearers in vain, and malicious. One may justifiably classify *Behemoth* as a text about morality every bit as much as it is about the specifics of the civil war: "it is not want of wit, but want of the science of justice, that brought them into these troubles [of war]."[45] Part of Hobbes's wrath is caused by the fact that people are often too blind to see that their interests are not promoted by the behavior just described. If we were more prudent we would also live better lives. But there is also a strong moral tone to his complaints. Hobbes would not endorse uncharitable and fraudulent behavior even if it did pay off in the long run.

Preachers, in particular get in the way of the creation of a virtuous citizenry: "I have observed in history, and in other writings of heathens, Greek and Latin, that those heathens were not at all behind us in point of virtue and moral duties, notwithstanding that we have had much preaching and they none at all."[46] If the influence of such men could be eradicated Hobbes sees no reason why people

> may not . . . be taught their duty, that is, the science of *just* and *unjust* as divers other sciences have been taught, from true principles and evident demonstration; and much more easily than any of those preachers and democratical gentlemen could teach rebellion and treason? . . . The rules of *just* and *unjust* sufficiently demonstrated, and from principles evident to the meanest capacity, have not been wanting; and not withstanding the obscurity of their author, have shined not only in this, but also in foreign countries, to men of good education.[47]

Brian Barry is correct, therefore, in arguing that the sovereign is not installed in order to create obligations but rather as an added incentive to make us keep our promises and to fulfill our obligations.[48] Hobbes says this himself more clearly in *De Cive* where he writes that "Contracts oblige us; laws tie us fast being obliged."[49] Hobbes is clearly presenting a theory of moral obligation, but he is also giving us a persuasive reason why we should abide by his moral code; the fear of sanction. He does not doubt that we can have a moral obligation; his doubt is that precisely because morality and self-interest conflict, that the former may be insufficient to motivate us over the latter. This is why we need the power of the sovereign to make us keep our promises. In other words, society is a precondition for moral action. It is in fact a defect of reasoning to assume, as does the fool, that there is no such thing as justice. Such foolish individuals have "thereupon taken for principles, and grounds of their reasoning, *That justice is but a vain word; that whatsoever a man can get by his own industry, and hazard is his own; that examples of former times are good arguments of doing the like again.*"[50] Not so says

Hobbes; justice is not simply another way of saying that every person should act to promote her interests regardless of promises and obligations.

Nagel argues that Hobbes does not present a moral theory because he gives a subjectivist view of what is right and wrong. At the pinnacle of his system, we are told, is nothing other than the preference of each individual. Richard Tuck also argues that a relativism of the "grimmest vision . . . is the only moral vision"[51] to be found in Hobbes's writings. A moral theory, however, demands that there is some more objective standard independent of the preferences of the individual; in particular a moral theory requires precepts for treating others fairly irrespective of our own preferences.

Again, the views expressed by Nagel and Tuck hold some validity as a reading of Hobbes's view of the state of nature in which the right of nature is dominant and private judgment is the only form of opinion. But it is equally clear that Hobbes does not favor this form of subjective condition in civil society and demands instead that we have an objective standard of fair treatment for everyone. This standard is found in the laws of nature and will be discussed in more detail in chapter 7, where I argue that it is precisely Hobbes's aim to create a society in which the fundamental goal is that of equity.

Hobbes says that it will be in our interest to follow such laws, but he means interest here in a very broad sense of being able to make life-plans, of living a contented life, and having long-term security; ultimately it is in our interest to follow the laws of nature because they are the most rational way of preserving human life. He does not mean the type of self-interest that is associated with short-term instrumental behavior. It is very difficult to see how Hobbes can be an egoist in light of the following statement (quoted in chap. 5, but worth noting again) in which the laws of nature are summed up by the maxim: *"Do not that to another, which thou wouldest not have done to thy selfe;* which sheweth him, that he has no more to do in learning the Lawes of Nature, but, when weighing the actions of other men with his own, they seem to heavy, to put them into the other part of the ballance, and his own into their place, that his own passions, and self-love, may adde nothing to the weight."[52] This suggests the very opposite of egoism: self-ishness is to count for nothing in motivating our behavior. One can still say that morality is linked to self-interest but now everyone's self-interest is the same and is found in the laws of nature rather than in personal preference. But it is not self-interest in terms of calculations of either short- or long-term individual prudence. I should obey the law of nature even if I gain nothing from such obedience other than the most basic form of security. Watkins is wrong, therefore, in suggesting that Hobbes cannot be classed as a theorist of morality because he does not provide an adequate account of impartiality.[53] The laws of nature, perhaps more than anything else are precisely an account of impartiality. Hobbes makes this point in several of his works. In *Of Liberty and Necessity,* for example, he claims that "[t]hings may be therefore necessary and yet praiseworthy, as also necessary and yet dispraised, and neither of both in vain, because praise and dispraise, and likewise reward and punishment, do by example make and conform the will to good and evil."[54] Hence good and evil are not purely subjective. In *Liberty, Necessity and Chance,* he states: "The true reason we admonish men and not children is because admonition is nothing else but telling a man the good and evil consequences of his actions."[55] Now why would Hobbes say this if good and evil are solely to be decided by each individual agent? The fact is they are not, and are instead given to us by natural law: "Children are ignorant, and madmen *in an error,* concerning what is good or evil for themselves."[56]

David Boonin-Vail has recently noted that when Hobbes says that there is no absolute good, he means it in the sense that we cannot find good in the nature of objects independent of the value we place on the object.[57] But this does not entail the conclusion that good can only be discussed in terms of individual preference. If we act upon reason, everyone will ultimately give value to the same thing—the laws of nature. The role of the laws of nature is precisely to give an objective description of virtue and vice regardless of the views each individual may hold on such issues. In this respect, Hobbes's argument concerning the laws of nature predates Rousseau's concept of the General Will, Kant's Categorical Imperative, and John Rawls's Original Position. A precept that cannot be universalized cannot also be consistent with the law of nature. Like Rousseau, Kant, and Rawls, Hobbes believed that we can arrive at moral principles solely through the correct use of reason. Morality, therefore, is whatever is discovered in the laws of nature.

This is not a subjectivist position; rather it is a universalistic one in which the ultimate good is that of peaceful and commodious living. It is a good which, as Hobbes says: *"every man . . . has hope of obtaining"*[58] for *"all men agree on this,* that peace is Good, and therefore also the way, or means of Peace."[59] The core of morality, therefore, is peace and the means of attaining it are *"Justice, Gratitude, Modesty, Equity, Mercy,* and the rest of the Laws of Nature."[60] As stated earlier, the laws of nature cannot really have individual self-interest as their primary aim because Hobbes specifically states that they are about promoting the collective good. The state of nature is Hobbes's description of the human condition when we forget this and let private judgment dictate actions. In this sense, as Tuck has noted, Hobbes was probably the first philosopher to note the full implications of subjectivism. Unlike Tuck, I conclude that Hobbes would not support a subjectivist view of morality given his awareness of these implications.

The laws of nature represent moral truth even though we may only be able to live by such laws when they are turned into a legal code by the sovereign. And it is clear that morality stretches beyond human convention and contracts because, as Hobbes says: "The laws of nature are immutable and eternal . . . and he that fulfilleth the Law is just."[61] Justice, that is, the keeping of promises is, however, only a subsection of his broader theory of morality that also includes notions of equity, the promotion of certain civic virtues such as tolerance, and the ability to act disinterestedly in accordance with equity and reason. Those who identify Hobbes as a virtue theorist are correct, but this is only a part of his overall moral project. The virtues are necessary because without them we would not have the character types discussed in chapters 4 and 5 who are capable of acting in the disinterested and universalizable manner demanded by the laws of nature.

Hobbes is often taken to be a subjectivist because he claims the following:

> For seeing all names are imposed to signify our conceptions, and all our affections are but conceptions, when we conceive the same things differently, we can hardly avoid different naming of them [because] our reception of it, in respect of different constitutions of body and prejudices of opinion gives everything a tincture of our different passions . . . for one man calleth *wisdom,* what another calleth fear; and one *cruelty,* what another *justice;* one *prodigality,* what another *magnanimity;* and one *gravity,* what another *stupidity.*"[62]

The reason why Hobbes points this out, however, is precisely to show that this is a problem, that it does not have to be the way of things, and to offer a solution through the use of reason. In a sense, what Hobbes is pointing to here is a dilemma of the human condition. Because of the way in which we receive and process information, we are not all going to agree on the same things. What I see as red, someone else will perceive as orange; what I think of as a wise decision will be seen by another as rash or foolish. But Hobbes does think that there are certain things, discovered through the use of reason as opposed to sensory imagination, which we can all agree upon, and these are the laws of nature.

Another cause of misjudging right and wrong is relying on custom as opposed to reason to arrive at the true meaning of moral terms:

> Ignorance of the causes and original constitution of right, equity, law, and justice disposeth a man to make custom and example the rule of his action . . . like little children,

> that have no other rule of good and evil manners but the
> correction they receive from their parents and masters;
> save that children are constant to their rule, whereas
> men are not so, because, grown strong and stubborn, they
> appeal from custom to reason and from reason to custom,
> as it serves their turn . . . which is the cause that the doc-
> trine of right and wrong is perpetually disputed . . .
> whereas the doctrine of lines and figures is not so, be-
> cause men care not, in that subject, what be truth, as a
> thing that crosses no man's ambition, profit or lust."[63]

This is an important passage because it demonstrates
that Hobbes thinks that right and wrong are disputed, not
because there cannot be a correct answer as to what they
are, but because people let custom, passion, and greed get
in the way of truth. If we address the question of morality
in the same disinterested way that we approach geometry,
we will find the same level of agreement in both.

Morality is primarily a social phenomena for Hobbes
because outside of society there is very little possibility for
acting according to anything other than the second clause
of the first law of nature, that is, the right of nature. Hence
sin also does not exist unless it is a transgression of a law:
"Where law ceaseth, sin ceaseth."[64] This refers to natural as
well as to civil law: "But because the law of nature is eternal, violation of covenants, ingratitude, arrogance and all
facts contrary to any moral virtue can never cease to be
sin."[65] This is not contradictory, because although Hobbes
talks of the state of nature he also says that in fact there
has never been a time when humans did not live without
some rule of law. This means that for all intents and purposes, the law of nature has always been a code applicable
to the judgment of human actions. Basically a sin is an act
against the law of nature, and a crime is more narrowly defined as a breach of civil law "So that every crime is a sin;
but not every sin a crime."[66] This is the case for two reasons; firstly because not every law of nature is written
down in civil law; secondly, because it is a sin to intend to
break the natural or civil law and it is a crime only when
one breaks the latter through action or speech.

I hope that these arguments have demonstrated that Hobbes is concerned with more than self-interest as the benchmark for human behavior. He links prudence in the very broadest sense of human survival to morality, but I would argue that this is a necessary requirement for any viable moral code. Having established that Hobbes is concerned with moral issues, a question arises: Does Hobbes's moral theory cause a problem for his subjects? Chabot suggests that Hobbes's subjects have to struggle with a divided self in which there is tension between, on the one hand, the requirement to obey the sovereign's commands (the external) and, on the other hand, the realm of conscience (the internal). There will often be tension, according to Chabot, between the inner and outer lives of the subjects, that is, between the subject's beliefs, and what the sovereign allows her to do and say: "we are obliged to submit our wills and our judgements to the will and judgement of the sovereign. . . . To be a subject, then, is to find oneself in a difficult predicament. . . . Cognitive dissonance seems to have been part of Hobbes's design."[67] Is this really a problem for Hobbes's subjects? I would say no more so than for any other moral and political theorist. There are four possible scenarios that need to be dealt with: (1) the sovereign and the subject both act according to the laws of nature; (2) neither the sovereign or the subject act according to the laws of nature; (3) the sovereign acts according to the laws of nature and the subject does not; and (4) the subject acts according to the laws of nature and the sovereign does not.

If the first scenario holds then there is no tension between the internal and external demands on the subject. This is Hobbes's preferred outcome, so clearly cognitive dissonance is not "built in" to Hobbes's design as Chabot suggests. To maintain a peaceful commonwealth, the sovereign will treat everyone equally: "The *End* of this institution is the Peace and Defense of them *all*. . . . For in this consisteth Equity; to which as being a Precept of the Law of Nature, a sovereign is as much subject, as any of the meanest of his people. All breaches of the Law, are offences against the Common-wealth."[68]

If the second scenario holds the result will be the collapse of civil society and a return to the state of nature and hence we will no longer have to worry about morality. The subject again will not have a divided self because now she acts solely according to her own private judgment. If the third scenario holds then there is tension between what the sovereign demands and what the subject wants to do, but as what the subject wants to do is against the moral code this also is not a problem for Hobbes. If this is cognitive dissonance then it is built into every theory of sovereignty because every subject or citizen is expected to obey just laws. Finally, we have the possibility that the subjects but not the sovereign obey the laws of nature. This is the nub of the problem because Hobbes seems to suggest that we are still obliged to obey the sovereign. If this happens then the problem is much more serious than tension between the two selves of the subject because it means that Hobbes's project is in danger of collapse.

The problem of the tension between the two selves, however, is not clear-cut even in this case because if the sovereign's abuses become life threatening then one is entitled to abandon one's promise to obey and to revert back to one's own conscience. As Hobbes himself notes, a sovereign who abuses his subjects will become the victim of "natural rebellion." Every citizen of every country has to face these issues (should one disobey the law to protest nuclear weapons?) and it seems to be somewhat misleading to portray this as a form of cognitive dissonance. The upshot seems to be that there can at times be tension within the self but that this does not pose a serious problem for Hobbes's moral theory and it does not seem to be a "difficult predicament" for Hobbes's subject. In a well-governed commonwealth there will not be strong tension between the rule of law and individual moral conscience.

A question remains: Exactly what type of moral theory does Hobbes support? At times he sounds somewhat like a deontologist and could perhaps be classed as a proto-Kantian; the laws of nature are presented as eternal and immutable truths; we are told that we should always act in accordance with such laws (even the right of nature is a subclause of the first law of nature); he talks of doing one's duty for the sake of duty; we are supposedly freer when we act according to reason; the moral law has to be internalized; moral acts are done because of a respect for the moral law; and one could perhaps sum up the laws of nature as a moral code for treating persons as ends not means. I have also argued that Hobbes presents a theory of autonomy that has similarities with the Kantian model.

Having said this, I think that an examination of the goals of the laws of nature rule Hobbes out as a proto-Kantian moral theorist (Taylor's position) and instead suggest that he is a consequentialist. The laws do not give strict moral orders such as "never tell a lie" or "never steal." Instead they are general rules of conduct that promote peace, order, and more importantly, a certain form of "commodious living." Instead of commanding "never lie" the laws of nature tell us "do not lie unless self-preservation is threatened," or "do not lie unless doing so is a threat to peace and the survival of the commonwealth." Hobbes is presenting rules of thumb that promote the long-term interests of everyone. The more deontological-sounding passages should be understood as an attempt by Hobbes to introduce a certain linguistic rigor into the discussion of morality. For example, Hobbes's description of promising is meant to demonstrate that such a speech act has behavioral expectations attached to it—it is a descriptive statement that tells us that promising entails acting in such a way as to keep the promise. In this sense Hobbes is like Kant because at the moment of the speech act it is a contradiction to will to break a promise: he is unlike Kant in that it is justifiable to break the promise at a later date if circumstances dictate that such an action is appropriate to the spirit of the laws of nature.

The laws of nature that promote equality, justice, gratitude, mutual accommodation, and impartial judgment can be seen in the same light. Such laws tell each person how best to preserve life, but the main task is to foster rules as "a means of the conservation of men in multitudes." The laws "only concern the doctrine of civil society. There be other things tending to the destruction of particular men ... which may therefore also be reckoned amongst those things which the laws of nature hath forbidden; but are not necessary to be mentioned, nor are pertinent enough to this place."[69] These laws, therefore, have as their goal the "conservation and society of mankind." This point is important; it is not simply survival that the laws promote but also a certain form of society that treats people as equals and promotes their well-being. The goal is to promote the collective good and by doing so the good of each individual will be enhanced. Unlike the schoolmen, who want to claim, using Aristotle as their authority, that things are in and of themselves good, Hobbes wants to suggest that good can only be judged in reference to our understanding of consequences. Like later supporters of utilitarianism, Hobbes wants to argue that there is nothing *necessarily* good about a specific action; its goodness depends on how it effects us: "if all things were absolutely good, we should be all pleased with their *being,* which we are not, when the actions that depend upon their being are hurtful to us. And therefore, to speak properly, nothing is good or evil but in regard to the action that proceedeth from it ... and as for natural goodness and evilness, that also is but the goodness and evilness of actions."[70]

Hence, when Hobbes states that we pursue our own good he means that in civil society we will do so not through selfish behavior but through following the moral code set down in the laws of nature: "It is the law from whence proceeds the difference between the moral and the natural goodness; so that it is well enough said by him [Bramhall] that moral goodness is the conformity of an action with right reason."[71] The law is the best guide for moral action because "There is no man living that seeth all the consequences of an action from the beginning to the end, whereby to weigh the whole sum of the good with the whole sum of the evil consequences. We choose no further than we can weigh. That is good to every man, which is so far good as he can see. All real good, which we call honest and morally virtuous, is that which is not repugnant

to the law, civil or natural; for the law is all the right reason we have, and, is the infallible rule of moral goodness."[72] Such a form of rule consequentialism fits well
with Hobbes's view of how humans think: "When we reason, we imagine the consequence of affirmations and
negations joined together."[73]

The consequence of not following such rules is spelled
out all too clearly in Hobbes's discussion of the state of nature. It is important to remember that the laws *always*
bind *in foro interno*. This gives a clear indication that
Hobbes did not think we would simply act "morally" when
forced to do so by the sovereign. In civil society there are
many aspects of life untouched by civil law (especially in
Hobbes's ideal commonwealth where he says that laws will
be few) and it is crucial that in these pockets of freedom
people still behave civilly to one another. Hobbes argues
that we are always *morally* obliged to act according to the
laws of nature, even when we are not *politically* obliged to
do so. By arguing that we are always internally obliged to
obey, Hobbes suggests that we are both rationally and
morally obliged, but this is not a problem because morality
and *long-term* rationality are very compatible with one another. It may of course happen that the civil law, which is
set up for the good of the people, may not fully realize this
goal, but again Hobbes shows himself to be a rule consequentialist by stating that even if the laws do not promote
the good of the people because of error, "yet the actions of
subjects, if they be conformable to the law, are morally
good."[74]

In Hobbes's chart concerning the several subjects of
knowledge, he states that ethics is knowledge of the consequences of our passions. This means that ethics is linked,
not to the objects of our passions, but to the passions themselves, and to the passions that we all share. Given that
people have the same fundamental passions, they can all
agree that certain rules of conduct, namely the laws of nature, are conducive to allowing the felicitous pursuit of the
passions. But it is not just any passions from which his ethical code is derived because as Hobbes says, the laws of

nature are against those passions that lead us to war, pride, partiality, and revenge. The ethical code must be traced to those passions that are linked to peace and well-being because these are the ones that all can agree upon as good. This adds weight to the claim that Hobbes is not a deontologist as Taylor suggests because his concept of the right depends on prioritizing a view of the good. Hobbes means, perhaps, something similar to Jeremy Bentham's claim that "Nature has placed mankind under the governance of two sovereign masters, *pain* and *pleasure*. It is for them alone to point out what we ought to do, as well as determine what we shall do. One the one hand the standard of right and wrong, on the other the chain of causes and effects, are fastened to their throne."[75] In the place of pain and pleasure, Hobbes would put the desire for peace and security (which Bentham would tell us are reducible to pleasure) as the foundation for morality.

Hobbes's consequentialism has some similarities with the later utilitarianism of John Stuart Mill; both are willing to rank desires, both defend a bounded liberty in terms of benefits rather than rights, both argue that consequences should be calculated from the disinterested point of view, and both agree that peace and order are seen as the necessary requisites for human flourishing. Both also return to the Greeks for an adequate conception of human happiness (Hobbes refers to what the Greeks called *makarismos*) that suggests that human flourishing over a lifetime is preferable to the pursuit of immediate gratification. None of Hobbes's arguments necessarily depends on a Christian concept of natural law; it certainly does not hurt if the members of the commonwealth are Christians but one can remove God from the argument and reach the same moral conclusions.

One could of course argue that consequentialism itself is simply a theory of prudence and, therefore, Hobbes is ultimately not rescued from the claim that he boils morality down to long-term self-interest. I do not think that this claim holds. If we take the utilitarianism brand of consequentialism it suggests that the greatest good should be promoted, but it also demands that this should be for the greatest number and hence my own interests are to count for one, and no more than one. As a good utilitarian, therefore, I should calculate in a manner that does not discount my own interests, because I count for as much as everyone else, but I should not weigh my own preferences above those of others, and I have to be willing to sacrifice my own preferences should this be necessary for the greater good. Hence, utilitarianism is only prudential in the sense that it takes account of outcomes, and in this regard I would state (but do not have space to provide an argument in its favor) that this is a requirement for any viable moral theory. It is not prudential in the sense of demanding that people calculate based on their own long-term interests. In fact, the more compelling criticism of consequentialism as a moral theory is that it demands a type of rigid and disinterested form of calculation that is beyond the reach of most mortals.

In sum, Hobbes does not posit individual preference as the criteria for determining right and wrong, but rather a moral code he thinks all can aspire to and understand through the use of reason. In *De Cive* he criticizes Aristotle for trying to find the morality in the mean between extremes because such an enterprise is "wholly estranged from the moral law, and unconstant with itself."[76] Although Hobbes does say that there is no *summum bonum,* he comes very close to arguing that the laws of nature do actually show us an ultimate good that all can agree on, and that good is peace. Our conclusion has to be that Gauthier is wrong in claiming that Hobbes argues from the premise of our nonmoral nature to the conclusion that from this nature we arrive at moral conventions. Hobbes actually assumes that we are capable of moral conduct and that a commonwealth cannot exist without people who can put aside selfish considerations. Hobbes makes this clear in *De Cive* when he says: "to be unjust is to neglect righteous dealing, or to think it is to be measured *not according to my contract, but some present benefit.*"[77]

Conclusion

My argument so far has demonstrated that Oakeshott is incorrect in stating that Hobbes "never had a satisfactory or coherent theory of volition."[78] It also illustrates why Kavka is wrong in suggesting that Hobbes's theory of action is insufficient because it does not cover premeditated acts, the cumulative consideration of consequences and reasons, or the weighing of different alternatives open to the agent.[79] The theory of rational, autonomous action developed in chapters 4 and 5 also suggests that Oakeshott is wrong in concluding that "A writer so completely devoid of a satisfactory philosophy of volition lacks something vital to modern political thought."[80] It is my contention that Hobbes has a complex theory of volition concerning internal influences upon the agent and this is precisely why he is so important to modern liberal philosophy.

If humans are capable of reason, volition, and hence choice, then they are also capable of moral action. The extended theory of freedom points to a view of the self as capable of making moral choices and hence of being morally obliged. The will is no longer explained in terms of appetite but instead in terms of reason. Hence, Hobbes also distinguishes between movement and rational *action*. Once we discover this theory of voluntary action in *Leviathan,* we no longer have to separate his psychological theory from his ethical theory because his theory of human psychology is more complicated than traditional interpretations have held; agency involves reason, rationality, deliberation, and acting in a disinterested manner; all the things required for moral autonomy. The result is a fairly thick theory of the good (discovered in the laws of nature) in which peace, equity, commodious living, and certain protections from harm are promoted over the pursuit of more personal and self-interested goals. Hobbes is telling us that freedom, when it is unhinged from reason and moral obligation, is very dangerous; freedom and virtue have to go hand in hand if we are to have peace and the good life. Chapters 3–5 have hopefully demonstrated that Hobbes did not think that the rational and the reasonable are in conflict with one another. The fully free agent, he thought, will recognize that it is also rational to be moral because the laws of nature, which are the benchmarks for rational behavior, are also the standards by which morality is measured.

We can see, therefore, that the extended theory of freedom and rationality leads us to reevaluate his theories of movement, freedom, agency, psychology, morality, and his concept of the self. Such a reevaluation, however, places some of Hobbes's other concepts under threat. In chapter 8 I will highlight how my interpretation affects other pivotal concepts in Hobbes's political and philosophical system. Before discussing these issues, however, it is necessary to deal with what Hobbes has to say about the external conditions of freedom. If I am correct in finding a more complex theory of the self in Hobbes's work, it also becomes necessary to square this with his political philosophy—a liberal theory of the self requires a liberal political society to accompany it.

Part III

External Freedom

7

~

Freedom, Equality, and the Laws of Nature

Introduction

In chapters 4, 5, and 6, I argued that the laws of nature serve not only as a prudential guide to self-preservation, but also promote morally reasonable behavior. In this chapter, I extend my analysis and claim that the natural laws also establish the conditions most advantageous for freedom within a commonwealth, that is, that they also give guidelines for promoting the most advantageous form of external freedom. My intention is to demonstrate that Hobbes was concerned mainly with creating a society characterized by civil freedom. Only under certain conditions are human beings able to live in peace, order, and security, features of civil society that considerably extend the freedom of all subjects.

This concern for freedom is expressed in Hobbes's hope for a society founded on manners, by which he meant not simply manners in terms of small politenesses, but "those qualities of mankind that concern their living together in Peace and Unity."[1] The ultimate goal for Hobbes is a society organized according to the principles of equality found in the laws of nature. Only then can we have a *civil* society and hence only then can we have industry, private property, arts, sciences, the accumulation of knowledge, cultivation of the earth, and so forth; all the things Hobbes thought were necessary requirements for a free society. The notion of civility becomes a moral ideal for Hobbes and is linked to the idea of the "generous souls" discussed in chapters 5 and 6. The more "civil" a society becomes, the more of these generous types there will be.

Freedom in the liberal tradition is justifiable only to the extent that it is compatible with the rights of others. In particular, equality of opportunity in the pursuit of ends is crucial for promoting equal freedom for everyone. When we examine *Leviathan,* we find that the laws of nature act as a guide for individuals and for the sovereign with regard to these concerns. The laws of nature link together freedom and formal *equality* in a manner Hobbes thought most conducive to the rational pursuit of ends. Hobbes was one of the first political theorists to state that we are all equal, first in nature, and then before the law. He tends to use the term *equality* differently depending on whether he is focusing on the state of nature or on civil society. When he discusses the former he directs attention to our equal vulnerability. However, he has to concentrate on the more positive aspects of equality when he writes of civil society, because one of the primary justifications of the state is that it protects us from this equal likelihood of violent death. In the state of nature, freedom and equality combine to make our lives miserable, but when they are controlled in civil society they create the conditions for all to live a good life.

Such security is gained through the equal protection we have via the sovereign, whose task is to enforce and make into positive law the equality we have under the laws of nature. Civil society transforms our natural but somewhat dangerous equality into an equality made safe because of the rule of law. In civil society, Hobbes wants action to be constrained by law; freedom exists where the law is silent. This does not mean that he thinks we have less capacity for action; in civil society our ability to comport ourselves in a reasonable manner is enhanced because we are able to act on rational decisions, whereas under conditions of war we are unable to do so. Life without law is "solitary, poore, nasty, brutish and short,"[2] which results in a de facto loss of liberty. This is why Hobbes tells us that the laws of nature he identifies are those that can be translated into positive law and hence "which only concern the doctrine of Civill Society."[3] *Leviathan* is a particularly interesting book because Hobbes recognizes the tension that exists between theories of freedom and equality. At the same time, he presents us with the first liberal solution for reconciling these potentially competing ideals.

One of Hobbes's major concerns, therefore, which is expressed in his discussion of the laws of nature, is the requirement for equity among people living within a commonwealth. Only when equality exists in the commonwealth can each individual exercise freedom. I intend to draw out this concern through an examination of the laws of nature. Although not expressed in these terms, the laws can be viewed collectively as an embryonic set of liberal "harm principles" that prescribe the boundaries for human interaction and the external conditions necessary for freedom. I use the term *harm principle* in the Millian sense of a principle that places limits upon actions that affect other people. As John Stuart Mill said: "All that makes existence valuable to anyone depends on the enforcement of restraints upon the actions of other people. Some rules of conduct, therefore, must be imposed."[4] Hobbes and Mill grapple with the same problem, which is: "where to place the limit—how to make the fitting adjustment between individual independence and social control. What these rules should be is the principle question of human affairs."[5]

Hobbes presents the laws of nature as the primary guidelines for freedom and equality and consequently as the most favorable rules by which we can all safely pursue our individual ends. More specifically, the natural laws that Hobbes discusses in *Leviathan* prescribe the boundaries for other-regarding actions. I do not wish to claim that Hobbes had the same thoughts in mind concerning the extent of state authority as did Mill in his book *On Liberty;* what I do wish to argue is that we can find in *Leviathan* a defense of a political state that is the forerunner of later liberal polities, particularly ones that emphasize the equal protection of interests. Hence I use the term *harm principle* as a heuristic device to suggest that Hobbes does not support an intolerant and tyrannical government. Instead, he argues for a sovereign who allows the necessary freedom for competing conceptions of the good life as long as they do not recommend harm to other individuals or to the commonwealth.

The traditional interpretation of Hobbes has not questioned the individualistic aspect of his methodology, but it is argued that this method leads to political authoritarianism not individualism. This interpretation has been attacked in recent years by Alan Ryan and Richard Flathman, who have shown some of the liberal strands in Hobbes's political thought.[6] In line with, but moving beyond the claims of these commentators, I will argue that the Hobbesian state is liberal in character, and allows for a substantial amount of personal freedom. I will spell out in detail how the laws of nature, when made into positive laws in civil society, shape civil equality, freedom, toleration, religion, and education in Hobbes's ideal commonwealth. The continuum of external freedom takes us beyond an examination of physical external impediments to motion. Hobbes obviously takes into account how physical impediments affect freedom (as was demonstrated in chapter 3) but he also discusses external freedom in terms of rights, laws, equality, education, and economics. The general aim of this chapter is to persuade the reader that Hobbes thinks political authority is used legitimately when it helps to promote and maintain a free and peaceful society.

The Harm Principle and the Protection of Freedom and Equality

The fundamental law of nature states *"That every man, ought to endeavour Peace, as farre as he has a hope of obtaining it."*[7] This is only a very general statement and does not spell out the specific actions required to promote peace. The rest of the laws of nature, however, give more detail to this general demand for peace. The major requirement of all members of the commonwealth is to lay down the natural right to act toward others in any way deemed suitable for self-preservation. This is what the second law of nature advises. This means that in civil society the laws of nature take priority over the right of nature because only then is peace at all possible. We have to create definable boundaries that allow for the legitimate interference by one person with another. As Hobbes says: "To lay *downe* a mans *Right* to any thing, is to *devest* himselfe of the *Liberty,* of hindering another."[8]

Having given us these broad principles, Hobbes begins to prescribe specific content to these limits. These limitations on liberty are linked to his ideas on justice and injustice. When a man gives up the right of nature to certain things "then he is said to be Obliged, or Bound, not to hinder ... he *Ought,* and it is his DUTY, not to make voyd that voluntary act of his own: and that such hinderance is INJUSTICE."[9] This leads Hobbes to the third law of nature, which links actions and justice. Hobbes demands *"That men performe their Covenants made."*[10] Ignoring this law of nature can lead to harm in two senses. First, it results in an act of injustice to particular individuals. Secondly, and more importantly for Hobbes, ignoring this law will lead us back to a condition of war. Once promise keeping can no longer be relied upon, we revert back to the conditions of uncertainty found in the state of nature, and consequently such acts harm everyone. According to Hobbes, peace cannot last for long unless we act justly. This is why we need "some coercive power to compel men *equally* to the performance of their covenants;"[11] without a sovereign, justice would not be possible at all. The third law of nature is therefore the most crucial component of Hobbes's political theory, for without adherence to contracts there can be no peace and as a result very little freedom.

The fifth law of nature is particularly crucial in creating conditions conducive to liberty and is one of the first liberal calls for toleration. The law demands *"That every man strive to accommodate himselfe to the rest."*[12] Toleration is necessary because of the diversity of our natures and our affections. It is interesting to note that rather than have the sovereign dictate a shared view of the good life, or attempt to quell our individual passions, Hobbes instead suggests that individuals accommodate themselves to one another. Hobbes is, of course, famous for telling us that there is no summum bonum, and it would seem that he wants people to pursue their own visions of the good. Only when views of the good life threaten the safety of others and/or the peace of the community does Hobbes suggest that intervention is necessary. The person who observes this fifth law is to be called "sociable" and praised accordingly, whereas the person who "for the stubbornness of his passions, cannot be corrected, is to be left, or cast out of Society, as cumbersome thereunto."[13]

The fifth law also makes the strong claim that the sovereign can redistribute certain goods if they are superfluous to one person and necessary to another. Unlike John Locke, who argues that government is set up to protect what people already possess, Hobbes argues that the sovereign ultimately has control over economic distribution and property relationships (although one could argue that Locke's position ultimately suggests the same thing). The reason why Hobbes does this is important to understand. Hobbes does not provide such powers simply as a means of promoting the interests of the sovereign, but rather because he sees clearly that large discrepancies in wealth and an underprivileged class of subjects are great threats to peace and security: "There is nothing more afflicts the mind of man than poverty."[14] The laws of nature demand a life above mere subsistence and as the sovereign is supposed to act according to these laws he needs to legislate accordingly.

To allow some members of a commonwealth to live in abject poverty while at the same time allowing unlimited appropriation for others is one of the root causes of war. Also, some minimal form of property is necessary for survival and for the opportunity to make free decisions. The sovereign can therefore distribute land "to *every* man"[15] according to the two principles of "equity and the common good."[16] In fact, Hobbes thought that too much wealth in the hands of monopolies or in a few private individuals would lead to disease within the body politic and "breedeth there an Inflammation, accompanied with a Fever."[17] Hobbes placed limits on the liberty of accumulation for the sake of equality and commodious living; instead of a free-for-all competitive market, he preferred a condition of civility. Rather than being a theorist of possessive individualism as C. B Macpherson suggests, Hobbes wished to limit accumulation in return for the greater good of civility between the classes.[18] This can be traced back to the requirement that everyone benefit from living in civil society, in this case through limited social welfarism. The twelfth and thirteenth laws also focus on the question of distribution; Hobbes states that "equall distribution is of the Law of Nature."[19] We should not make the unjustified leap from these sorts of claims made by Hobbes to the conclusion that he is suggesting that the sovereign should have arbitrary access to one's possessions; he is really making these suggestions in opposition to the view that a man should be thought "to be so much master of whatsoever he possessed, that it could not be taken from him upon *any* pretense of common safety without his own consent."[20]

The sixth law suggests that we pardon those who repent and who do not represent a threat to peace. The seventh law, which defends the interests of those charged with crimes, suggests that those who cannot be pardoned should only be punished as a means of rehabilitation. The seventh law also prevents acts of revenge, for "Revenge without respect to the Example, and profit to come, is a triumph, or glorying in the hurt of another . . . and contrary to reason; and to hurt without reason, tendeth to the introduction of Warre."[21]

The eighth law is also crucial for a doctrine limiting harm to others, and restricts speech that may lead to war. Hobbes councils *"That no man by deed, word, countenance, or gesture, declare Hatred, or Contempt of another."*[22] This again is a liberal notion; note that Hobbes does not think that speech should be limited according to the whims of the sovereign. Rather, he argues that such limits are justifiable when it can be demonstrated that speech will lead to a breakdown in peace. When peace is not threatened, Hobbes demonstrates his tolerance for freedom of conscience and free speech by saying that it is a "very Evill act, for any man to speak against his *Conscience:* or to corrupt or force another to do so."[23] What he means here in particular, is that we should not be forced to say things that we know are contrary to the facts.

It is true that Hobbes says it is up to the sovereign to decide what the boundaries of free speech will be, but this is no different than what we expect from the modern liberal state. The sovereign makes laws that have a moral content and as such they also set the boundaries for freedom of expression. What Hobbes does not tell us in specific detail is what is to be allowed and disallowed; his criteria for free speech seems to be that we draw the boundaries according to the principle of preventing direct harm to individuals and the community and that only speech that threatens peace is to be disallowed. This clearly does not add up to as strong a defense of free speech as the one supplied by Mill (more on this later), but I think it is fair to say that it can be characterized as a protoliberal position.

The ninth law, which states that we should regard each other as naturally equal is perhaps the first clear statement of a major premise of liberal egalitarian political thought. As Hobbes says: "there are very few so foolish that had not rather governe themselves."[24] Hobbes recognizes that self-governance is desirable for reasons of personal well-being, peace and security, and that people will not stand for a lot of interference in their personal lives. The fact that we will only enter into society on equal terms shows that we see each other as equals, and that we ought to do so for the sake of peace. As the law states: *"That every man acknowledge the other for his Equall by Nature.* The breach of this Precept is *Pride."*[25] Hobbes takes equality seriously: "The safety of the People, requireth . . . from him that have the Sovereign Power, that Justice be equally administered to all degrees of People; that is, that as well as the rich, and mighty, as poor and obscure persons might be righted of the injuries done them. . . . For in this consisteth

Equity; to which, as being a Precept of the Law of Nature, a Sovereign is as much subject as any of the meanest of his people."[26] All of Hobbes's works are sprinkled with his concern for equality: "The common law itself is nothing else but reason" and that "Equity is a certain perfect reason . . . and consisting in nothing else but right reason."[27] "[I]njustice is the transgression of a stature-law, and iniquity the transgression of the law of reason."[28] "Equity, which I take to be the same with the law of nature."[29]

Following from the ninth law, the tenth reinforces equality and provides another crucial component of liberal philosophy. It states that we do not try to claim rights that are not reserved for everyone else: *"That at the entrance into conditions of Peace, no man require to reserve to himselfe any right, which he is not content should be reserved to every one of the rest."*[30] In particular, this law suggests that modesty should take priority over the unreasonable pursuit of power; to demand more than one's share is to go against the dictates of nature. This means that actions have to be limited according to the interests of others and each has "to lay down certaine Rights of Nature; that is to say, not to have libertie to do all they list: so it is necessarie for mans life to retaine some; as right to governe their owne bodies; enjoy aire, water, motion, waies to go from place to place; and all things else without which a man cannot live, or not live well."[31] Hobbes understands well the crucial link between equality and the necessary conditions for action. Without equality before the law, equality in the satisfaction of basic needs, equality in laying down the right of nature (which basically means equality of constraints) then there is no chance of at least a rough equality in choices and opportunities for all members of the commonwealth. When we lay down our right to all things we also acknowledge an *equality of constraint* that prevents us from harming others for our own benefit. Hobbes tells us that the purpose of law "is no other . . . but to limit the naturall liberty of particular men, in such a manner, as they might not hurt but assist one another."[32] The eleventh law stresses equal treatment before the law: "if *a man be trusted to judge between man and man,* it is a precept of the Law of Nature, *that he deale Equally between them.* The observance of this law, from the equall distribution to each man, of that which in reason belongeth to him, is called EQUITY."³³ This equality is protected by the sixteenth, seventeenth and eighteenth laws that demand that controversies are submitted to the judgment of an impartial arbiter whose decisions are based on questions of right rather than favoritism or self-interest.

What Hobbes is developing in this discussion of the laws of nature is a reasonably strict code of conduct to protect and maintain external conditions for freedom. Hobbes summarizes the laws of nature in the following manner: *"Do not that to another, which thou wouldest not have done to thy selfe."*³⁴ The laws of nature allow us to use our liberty to the extent we do not harm others and the right of nature is only to be invoked as a final justification for self-defense. This means that the right of nature is still held by inhabitants of civil society but it is less forceful because in the state of nature it allows for preemptive strikes, whereas this is not justified in civil society. Justifiable self-defense has more limited parameters once we have a sovereign to defend us.

We have seen how the laws of nature, promoting the principle of equality, create a space in civil society that allows for all to pursue personal freedom. Not only do they make negative demands on people (including the sovereign) to refrain from certain types of behavior, but they also prescribe certain behavior in the form of positive moral commands. However, as critics of Hobbes have been quick to point out, the sovereign still seems to have the potential to tyrannize the inhabitants of the commonwealth. In the next section I argue that such fears are unfounded because the laws of nature also place additional limits upon the sovereign.

The Laws of Nature and the Sovereign

It is an old criticism of Hobbes that his sovereign is too powerful to allow any meaningful exercise of freedom. It was articulated by his contemporaries and continues to be a current theme. For example, in the collection of essays in the book *Liberalism and the Moral Life,* several of the authors conclude that Hobbes cannot be classed as a proponent of liberalism because of his supposed tyrannical sovereign.[35] Hence Judith Shklar argues that the "convoluted genealogy of liberalism that insists on seeing its origins in a theory of absolutism" is incorrect.[36] Susan Moller Okin, while not denying that Hobbes has had a deep impact on liberal ideas of freedom and equality concludes that "Hobbes was no liberal in his conclusions, advocating an absolute rather than restrained state."[37] Okin's comments are a good example of the ambiguous feelings many liberals hold about Hobbes. They are drawn to many of his ideas but they almost always conclude that his politics (as opposed to his understanding of the self) is fundamentally illiberal in character. In the same volume, Benjamin Barber claims that despite the same liberal trends that Okin and many others identify: "Liberals rightly pall at the idea of Hobbes as a liberal predecessor because his fear of anarchy leads him to embrace an authoritarian conception of the state incompatible with limited government."[38]

More recent works by David Gauthier and Michael Ridge takes a similar stance.[39] The latter makes the following argument: Hobbes sees conflict as a necessary consequence of fallible human beings utilizing private (natural) reason. His solution to this problem is to replace the natural reason of all with the public reason of the one (expressed in the will of the sovereign). Ridge (and Gauthier) see a major problem with Hobbes's approach, primarily because they claim that the public figure of reason has to have absolute power. The problem with setting up such a pubic authority, according to Ridge (and Gauthier), is that it runs the "serious risk of creating a monster."[40] Gauthier's solution is to maintain the idea of reason residing in a public figure, but to limit the scope and power of such an authority. Ridge abandons the Hobbesian model and argues instead for a set of public principles that have legitimate authority. In this section, I argue that Ridge, Gauthier, and most other commentators are incorrect in suggesting that

Hobbes's sovereign will display the sorts of monstrous qualities they identify. I also claim that Hobbes is more sophisticated than he is presented to be by Ridge; conflict resolution, according to Hobbes, is not only attained through the coercive power of the sovereign but also comes from the development of a certain form of civic culture. Given this, Ridge has not demonstrated that his system of authoritative principles is a step forward from Hobbes's concept of sovereignty. I suggest that a close reading of *Leviathan* leads one to the conclusion that the sovereign is limited by both morality and prudence. He is also limited by the very task he is set by Hobbes, which is to pass between the points of liberty and authority "unwounded."[41] I argue that the sovereign's exercise of rights is limited fairly stringently by natural law. Should the sovereign threaten the right of self-preservation that each individual still retains in society, the subject has legitimate grounds for disobedience. Hobbes also made it quite clear that self-preservation does not mean only a base form of survival. By safety of the subjects "is not meant a bare preservation, but also all other contentments of life, which every man by lawfull Industry, without danger, or hurt to the Commonwealth, shall acquire to himselfe."[42]

The fourth law of nature, stating that those who bestow a free gift do not later come to regret the action, has usually been interpreted in terms of contracts between individuals. It takes on special significance, however, when it is applied to the sovereign. In particular, the sovereign is not entitled to make the lives of his subjects miserable: *"That a man which receiveth Benefit from another of meer Grace, Endeavor that he which giveth it, have no reasonable cause to repent him of his good will."*[43] The importance of this requirement is suggested by the fact that Hobbes places it fourth on his list of the laws of nature. This law applies particularly to the sovereign because he has received a gift, namely the transfer of natural right, from every member of the commonwealth.

Hobbes hints that the liberty granted to subjects will be quite broad and includes the "Liberty to buy, and sell, and otherwise contract with one another; to choose their own aboad, their own diet, their own trade of life, and institute their children as they themselves think fit; and the like."⁴⁴ He continues by claiming that individuals have the liberty to get "food, ayre, medecine, or *any* other thing without which he cannot live."⁴⁵ All of this is rather vague but this is to be expected of a theory that allows as much freedom as is compatible with peace. Hobbes wanted us to be left alone to take care of our own business: "A plain husbandman is more prudent in the affairs of his own house than a privy councillor in the affairs of another man."⁴⁶ In essence, the sovereign provides us with protection from attack and robbery, grants equal protection under the law, and allows freedom within the family and among professions.

To maintain a peaceful commonwealth, the sovereign will treat everyone as the laws of nature demand, that is to say equally: "The *End* of this institution is the Peace and Defense of them *all* . . . For in this consisteth Equity; to which as being a Precept of the Law of Nature, a sovereign is as much subject, as any of the meanest of his people. All breaches of the Law, are offences against the Commonwealth."⁴⁷ It is important to recognize that such behavior coincides with the sovereign's own interests because Hobbes makes it clear that the material riches of the sovereign come from his subjects. Hobbes says: "It is a weak Soveraign, that has weak Subjects; and a weak People, whose Soveraign wanteth Power to rule them at his will."⁴⁸ Hobbes continues the same theme in *A Dialogue Between a Philosopher and a Student* where, in answer to the criticism that the sovereign will harm the people he says:

> but they have no reason to think he will, unless it be for his own profit; which cannot be, for he loves his own power; and what becomes of his power when his subjects are destroyed or weakened, by whose multitude and strength he enjoys his power and every one of his subjects his fortune? And lastly, whereas they sometimes say the King is bound, not only to cause his laws to be observed, but also to observe them himself; I think the King causing them to be observed is the same thing as observing them himself.⁴⁹

In fact, this whole text is based on the premise of the rule of law and not on the arbitrary rule of monarchs. He is basically defending the English legal system of the time, which Hobbes himself certainly did not think allowed for tyranny. This notion of mutual benefit is well demonstrated by the frontispiece of *Leviathan* that shows the sovereign's body made up of his subjects. As he makes clear in the introduction: "The *wealth* and *riches* of all the particular members are the *strength; salus populi* (the people's safety) its business."[50] If the sovereign injures his subjects he injures himself: "Governours, proceedeth not from any delight, or profit they can expect in the dammage, or weakening of their Subjects, in whose vigor, consisteth their own strength and glory."[51] Hobbes maintains this view throughout his writings, and in *Behemoth or the Long Parliament* he states: "Nor any other fundamental law to a King, but *salus populi,* the safety and well-being of his people."[52] "For that law of *salus populi* is directed only to those that have power enough to defend the people; that is, to them that have the supreme power."[53]

The laws of nature provide a combination of self-interest and moral rules that protect individuals from abuse by the sovereign. The reason why Hobbes prefers a monarchy over an assembly is precisely because he thinks that we have a tendency to promote our own interests over those of others. With a monarchy, however: "the publique and private interest are most closely united."[54] In fact he goes as far as to say that "in Monarchy, the private interest is the same with the publique."[55] As Deborah Baumgold notes, if the sovereign rules well and makes good laws, his power will not diminish: "right makes might"[56] and right action is aimed at "the people's safety."[57]

It should also be remembered that the natural right that the sovereign alone keeps, is only a right to its own self-preservation (this is all a natural right is as far as Hobbes is concerned) not a right to do anything it likes to those under its political rule. As a point of definition the sovereign cannot treat its subjects unjustly because it has not entered into a contract and only the breaking of a contract counts as injustice. But Hobbes is quite willing to say that it "may commit iniquity"[58] and be justifiably condemned for the act. This is made more explicit in the Latin version of *Leviathan* where Hobbes says "That he who has the supreme power can act inequitably, I have not denied. For what is done contrary to the laws of nature is called inequitable."[59] It also needs to be noted that each individual always retains the right to disobey if she feels directly threatened by the actions of the sovereign. The whole point of giving up the right of nature is that by doing so we secure our person; consequently our obligation lasts only as long as the sovereign provides security, and security in such a manner that we do not become weary of our existence.

In one sense, Hobbes actually gives a stronger right of resistance than Locke. For the latter, one can only rebel after a long train of abuses, and serious abuses at that. For Hobbes, one is removed from the obligation to obey if the sovereign uses force: "A covenant not to defend myself from force by force is always void. For (as I have showed before) no man can transfer or lay down his right to save himself from death, wounds, and imprisonment . . . and therefore the promise of not resisting force in no covenant transferreth any right nor is obliging . . . notwithstanding that such Criminals have consented to the law, by which they are condemned."[60] This is a very startling statement for Hobbes to make because it means that we are not obliged even when the sovereign is using force in the form of legitimate punishment. If I break the law and the police come to take me away, all bets are off as far as Hobbes is concerned. This claim by Hobbes leads him to the ridiculous conclusion that as soon as the sovereign attempts to implement the law (which must rest on the use of force) our obligation ends. The whole of his civil philosophy disintegrates at this point because the very reason for introducing a sovereign is undermined. It is legitimate for the sovereign to try and impose the law, of course, but it is equally legitimate for subjects to oppose this use of force. The prudent subject will avoid such confrontations given the imbalance of power between himself and the sovereign, and hence Hobbes's system is still safe on a practical level, but theoretically it collapses. His theory of resistance is less strong than Locke's in the sense that if the sovereign is not using force then one should obey, even if it does engage in a long string of abuses.

It is difficult to find a passage in *Leviathan* where Hobbes argues for an extension of sovereign power beyond what he thinks is minimally necessary for the preservation of peace. I argued earlier that there is no ultimate good for Hobbes, but at times he comes close to suggesting that there is certainly one good that should have the highest priority with everyone: "The Finall Cause, End or Designe of men . . . is the foresight of their own preservation, and a more contented life thereby."[61] If this is everyone's goal, it would seem very strange for Hobbes to argue for a sovereign who does not foster such a good. Hobbes places so much emphasis on "doing well" that his argument leads to the second startling conclusion that rebellion is justified if the sovereign does not provide the necessary conditions for subjects to live well. The motivation to seek peace goes beyond the fear of violent death and includes "the Desire of such things as are necessary to commodious living: and a Hope by their Industry to obtain them,"[62] although he does think that no matter how bad the sovereign, the condition of the state of nature is always worse.

While Hobbes leaves us in no doubt as to the requirement of an absolute sovereign, this stems from a desire for peace and not from any authoritarian leanings on its part. Hobbes's argument for absolutism also represents a view shared by many of his contemporaries that there had to be some ultimate source of authority; for Hobbes, Jean Bodin, and others, the buck has to stop somewhere. As Baumgold shows, Hobbes's argument for his sovereign is a "statement about the constitution of sovereignty, as opposed to the exercise of power. Only after 1640 . . . did absolutism take on the further, pejorative connotation of arbitrary government outside the law."[63]

Baumgold notes that the sovereign is more limited than many commentators have suggested. She argues that chapter 30 of *Leviathan* "enjoins concern for the people's safety and prosperity, political education, promulgation of good laws, equal justice" [and] "fair execution of punishments and rewards."[64] As Hobbes notes, his concern is for "The *Wealth* and *Riches* of all the particular members."[65] A good law for Hobbes is one that fosters the interests of the subject as well as the monarch; "A good Law is that, which is *Needfull,* for the *Good of the People,* and withall *Perspicuous.*"[66] Hobbes questions whether "a law may be . . . good, when it is for the benefit of the soveraign; though it be not necessary for the people; but it is not so. For the good of the Soveraign and the people cannot be separated."[67] This suggests that Hobbes's concern is to promote the very opposite of arbitrary and tyrannical rule.

Hobbes seems to argue at times that even though the sovereign is not obliged to its subjects it is still obliged to God and will pay a heavy price in the next life if it abuses its position. In chapter 26, Hobbes even suggests that dictates of the sovereign that offend against the laws of nature cannot be made into civil law: "for whatsoever is not against the Law of Nature, may be made law."[68] This is a strange claim for Hobbes to make because the sovereign has the de facto authority to make such laws. What he means, I think, is that the sovereign is only behaving in a manner consonant with the rationale for civil laws when it makes laws that do not conflict with the laws of nature. Hobbes makes the same sorts of claims in most of his works. In *A Dialogue Between a Philosopher and a Student,* he states the following: "I am one of the common people, and one of that almost infinite number of men, for whose welfare Kings and other sovereigns were by God ordained: for God and Kings for the people, and not the people for Kings."[69] "The king, who is to answer to God Almighty for the safety of the people."[70] "Also the King, as is on all hands confessed, hath the charge lying upon him to protect his people against foreign enemies, and to keep the peace betwixt them within the kingdom: if he do not his upmost endeavor to discharge himself thereof, he commiteth a sin, which neither King nor Parliament can lawfully commit."[71] Hobbes also makes the philosopher agree with the lawyer that if the king "will not consult with the Lords or Parliament . . . he sinneth against God . . . we agreed upon that already."[72] In *The Questions Concerning LIBERTY, NECESSITY AND CHANCE,* Hobbes goes even further and seems to distinguish the justice of a law in relation to a particular people and to God. He says that in relation to a polity, what the sovereign decides cannot be unjust but that:

> in relation to God, if God have by a law forbidden it, the making of such a law is injustice. Which law of God was to those heathen princes no other but *salus populi,* that is to say, the properest use of their natural reason for the preservation of their subjects. If therefore, those laws were ordained out of wantonness, or cruelty, or envy, or for the pleasing of a favorite, or out of any other sinister end, as it seems they were, the making of those laws was unjust. And for the Pharisees, who had the same written law of God that we have their excommunication of the Christians, proceeding, as it did, from envy, was an act of malicious injustice. Nevertheless, as it was a law to their subjects the law was not unjust. But the making of it was an unjust action, of which they were to give account to none but God. I fear the Bishop will think this discourse too subtle; but the judgement is the reader's.[73]

Here, despite his repeated claims about justice only relating to the law of the sovereign, he is giving two concepts of justice, one relating to sovereigns (lawgivers) and subjects, and another relating to human beings and God (who is himself a lawgiver). This means that injustice is not only related to breaking civil law, but the law of any legitimate lawgiver, which can mean a civil sovereign's laws but can also mean God's laws expressed in the laws of nature. Hence, a sovereign who does break natural law, on this argument at least, can behave unjustly. This is perhaps why Hobbes, on the one hand, states that before the introduction of civil law there can be no concept of just or unjust, but then, on the other hand, immediately qualifies this by saying this only applies when "I speak of human justice."[74]

These statements by Hobbes fit with his claim that "Injustice, Ingratitude, Arrogance, pride, Iniquity, Acception of persons, and the rest, can never be made lawfull. For it can never be that Warre shall preserve life, and Peace destroy it."[75] What this means in effect is that because "The Law of Nature, and the Civill Law, contain each other, and are of equall extent,"[76] the laws the sovereign makes will foster "Equity, Justice, Gratitude, and other morall Vertues."[77] This is a long way from the Hobbes who is sometimes presented as favoring tyrannical rule. As Mary Dietz argues: "The Hobbesian commonwealth, to paraphrase Plato, is a luxurious city, not a city of pigs (or state police). Fear . . . does not adequately capture the lively and prosperous polity Hobbes imagined."[78]

The only real difference between the natural and civil law is that the latter are promulgated *by Word, Writing, or other sufficient Sign of the Will*[79] of the sovereign. Such laws should be made as plain and clear as possible: "It belongeth therefore to the Office of the Legislator . . . to make the reason Perspicuous, why the Law was made; and the Body of the Law it selfe, as short, but in as proper, and significant termes as may be."[80] It is worth noting that in *Behemoth,* Hobbes gives a list of virtues that one would hope to find in a sovereign. These include fortitude, frugality, and liberality, and "In sum, all actions and habits [of the sovereign] are to be esteemed good or evil by their causes and usefulness in reference to the commonwealth and not by their mediocrity, nor by their being commanded."[81]

Hobbes's arguments concerning punishment are particularly relevant to the claim that his sovereign is not a tyrant. Any form of punishment is only justified if it is inflicted because of the breach of a known law. If the sovereign does not make the laws sufficiently known then one is excused from obedience: "if the civil law of a man's own country be not so sufficiently declared as he may know it if he will . . . the ignorance is a good excuse."[82] Overall, Hobbes is very careful to suggest that only the sovereign body can punish, that punishment should be inflicted only for making the person follow the law in future, that the punishment should fit the crime and not be too excessive, that crimes cannot be grandfathered in, and that "no man is supposed to be punished before he be judicially heard and declared guilty: "And therefore, whatsoever hurt a man is made to suffer by bonds or restraint before his cause be heard, over and above that which is necessary to assure his custody, is against the law of nature."[83] In *LIBERTY, NE-CESSITY AND CHANCE*, he continues the same theme and suggests that punishment is "for nothing else but for a correction, or for an example, which hath for end the *framing* and *necessitating of the will* to virtue; and that he is no good man, that upon any provocation useth his power, though a power lawfully obtained, to afflict another man without this end, to reform the will of him or others."[84]

Hobbes continues in the same tone by declaring that "All punishments of innocent subjects, be they great or little, are against the laws of nature."[85] The reason for this has a utilitarian flavor to it because the laws of nature "forbiddeth all men, in their revenges, to look at anything but some future good. For there can arrive no good to the commonwealth, by punishing the innocent."[86] Such punishment also goes against equity, which the law also suggests is the correct principle for punishment. Hobbes never suggests that the sovereign should harm anyone who is not guilty of an offense; what is to count as an offense is decided by the sovereign but his choices should be dictated by the laws of nature. He goes as far as to argue that the sovereign should not punish the people harshly, even if they are threatening peace: "The punishment of the leaders and teachers in a commotion, not the poor seduced people, when they are punished, can profit the commonwealth by their example. To be severe to the people is to punish that ignorance which may in great part be imputed to the sovereign, whose fault it was they were no better instructed."[87] In all punishments the sovereign should have an eye to clemency when it is safe to do so because "lenity, when there is such a place for it, is required by the laws of nature."[88] In the following dialogue from *Behemoth,* Hobbes makes it clear that he is interested in the rule of law rather than arbitrary rule:

B. Must tyrants also be obeyed in everything actively? What if he should command me with my own hands to execute my father, in case he should be condemned to die by the law?

A. This is a case that need not be put. We never have read or heard of any King or tyrant so inhuman as to command it. If any did, we are to consider whether that command were one of his laws. For by disobeying Kings, we mean the disobeying of his laws, those his laws that were made before they were applied to any particular person . . . he commands the people in general never but by a precedent law, and as a politic, not a natural person . . . if such a command was made into a general law, then we are bound to obey it [because the logic of his arguments necessitates this, but such a law] never was, nor never will be [made].[89]

Hobbes prefers the rule of law because it creates a uniform standard of conduct. Arbitrary rule on the other hand ultimately loses its power to create and maintain a stable arena for action because individuals can no longer predict the consequences of their own actions or those of the sovereign. As Hobbes says, the ultimate fate of such an arbitrary government is to suffer the "naturell punishment" of open rebellion. At one point he even claims that the sovereign "is obliged by the laws of nature" to procure *the safety of the people.*[90] There is much debate in the literature as to exactly what Hobbes means by obligation in this sense, but whether he means morally or prudentially is unimportant for the current discussion because either way the point remains that Hobbes expects the sovereign to act in accordance with the laws of nature. If the sovereign does not provide safety we "may nevertheless, without injustice, refuse [to obey], as every subject has liberty in all those things, the right whereof cannot by Covenant be transferred."[91] He reiterates this point when he states: "When, therefore, our refusal to obey frustrates the end for which the sovereignty was ordained [peace, security and commodious living], then there is no liberty to refuse; otherwise there is."[92] This is quite a caveat allowed for by Hobbes.

In essence, Hobbes's enterprise is not to set up a power to quash individuals in their endeavors but rather to restrain them from harming others. It is crucial to recognize that the sovereign is necessary not so much to force a person to perform a contract as to make it so that a person can actually perform a contract safely. Like Mill's harm principle, the laws of nature, when enforced by the sovereign, provide a protective barrier from the unjustified interference of others. Rather than political authority being a threat to individual liberty, Hobbes thought that freedom could only be guaranteed by the type of sovereign he proposed. While Hobbes clearly sees the need for political *authority*, therefore, he cannot be accurately described as *authoritarian*.

Hobbes seems to think that the best form of government is a noninterventionist one. His writings are sprinkled with suggestions that the fewer laws there are the better: "For the use of Lawes . . . is not to bind the People from all Voluntary actions; but to direct and keep them in such a motion, as not to hurt themselves by their own impetuous desires, rashnesse, or indiscretion, as hedges are set, not to stop Travellers, but to keep them in the way. And therefore a Law that is not Needfull, having not the true End of a Law, is not good."[93] Laws that are needed are ones that focus on the similarities of human passions such as partiality and vanity because these can be controlled; but Hobbes is very clear that laws cannot be aimed at determining the *objects* of human passions that will differ quite dramatically. Hence a good law is one that limits certain harmful acts, not one that promotes the interests of the sovereign at the expense of the subjects or that tries to promote unanimity in the pursuit of ends.

Hobbes continues by claiming that "Unnecessary Lawes are not good Lawes; but trapps for mony: which where the right of Soveraign Power is acknowledged, are superfluous; and where it is not acknowledged, unsufficient to defend the People."[94] In other words, an excess of laws is not beneficial to the sovereign and the subjects. As Hobbes argues that civil freedom resides where the law is silent, this means that we can expect a large degree of freedom (probably more than we exercise in the modern state), in his commonwealth. He makes this even more explicit in *De Cive* where he hopes "there be few laws, few prohibitions, and those too such, that except there were forbidden, there could be no peace."[95]

Sovereignty and Democracy

In the last section, evidence was marshalled to suggest that Hobbes's sovereign allows enough external freedom to promote the autonomous persons described in chapter 6. Ridge and Gauthier may reply that even if all of this is accurate, Hobbes's sovereign is still too powerful because when all is said and done, these are only moral and prudential limitations on the sovereign and hence he is still too powerful because there are no formal checks on his use of power. Such a claim can be made all the stronger when it is linked to the criticism that Hobbes's sovereign is too dangerous because it is not democratic. Absolute power in the hands of one person is especially dangerous. In this section I examine what Hobbes has to say about sovereigntly and democracy and argue that his sovereign is again a lot less dangerous than it seems to be at first glance.

There is, however, clearly tension between the need to evaluate one's government critically, and the fundamental demand by Hobbes that the sovereign be virtually above criticism. Perhaps the boundaries for self-expression in *Leviathan* are still too narrow. But we can forgive Hobbes for being overly pessimistic and overzealous on behalf of the authority of the sovereign, given the situation in which he lived. And as Michael Oakeshott and others have noted, the sovereign may decide to permit all sorts of criticisms of the desirability of the law, as long as its authority remains unimpugned. Hobbes's main concern was that the criticism of a particular law should be divorced from the question of the authority of the law. As long as this distinction is maintained, a wide range of criticism is still compatible with a "civilized" society and political stability.

Criticism of Hobbes's pessimism about political participation and support for absolute sovereignty does not invalidate the argument that he was concerned with producing
self-disciplined, moderate, and autonomous beings; the
most it can show is that he may not have uncovered the
best conditions for achieving such a high ideal. His demand
for an absolute sovereign does not threaten the argument
presented here because neither Hobbes nor the modern liberal demands political participation as a *necessary* condition of autonomy.

Hobbes was concerned that we be political only to
the extent of recognizing our obligations to the sovereign
and to each other. He wished for a clear distinction between public and private spheres and clearly thought the
latter was sufficient for self-realizing action. In fact,
democracy is dangerous in Hobbes's eyes because of its
tendency to undermine peace, and hence to limit the possibility of rational action. The quest for glory in public
life, where the private judgment of the individual can
sometimes dominate, has a tendency to lead to war,
Hobbes believed. As Stephen Holmes points out, Hobbes
thought that politically ambitious individuals participated not out of a sense of extending their freedom, but
because of a narcissistic and "foolish desire to consume
the envy of nonparticipants."[96]

Mark Warren's recent outline of modern liberal theory
demonstrates how liberal societies have tended to follow
Hobbes. According to Warren, liberalism posits the idea
that "Institutions should be designed to separate political
judgements from those of individuals. . . . Standard liberal
democracy holds, in effect, that it is desirable to depoliticize
as many spheres of society as possible. . . . Although standard liberal-democratic theory places a high value on autonomy, it conceives autonomy as a prepolitical capacity,
maximized by clear separations of public and private life."[97]
What needs to be emphasized is that Hobbes wanted to
demonstrate that a stable form of liberty is unlikely without the rule of law. If we have to exchange natural liberty
for autonomy then it is a bargain well made because, as

Hobbes repeatedly makes clear, natural liberty is counter-productive to the promotion of agency.

Hobbes clearly distrusted the sort of mob rule that can stem from democracy. Flathman argues that Hobbes was worried about democracy precisely because of his love of individuality; the mob always threatens to ride roughshod over the individual.[98] And the mob will be dominated by an elite of orators who will pursue their own agenda. Such elites can harm the individual and the community. Stirred by such orators, pride and passion can lead to a form of collective madness: "For what argument of madness can there be greater, than to clamour, strike, and throw stones at our best friends? Yet this is somewhat lesse than such a multitude will do."[99] The reason why Hobbes prefers monarchy over democracy is precisely because he thinks the former is more modest in behavior. As liberty is promoted where laws are few, Hobbes did not think there was any more freedom in a democracy; there is no "more liberty in democracy than monarchy; for the one as truly consisteth with such a liberty as the other."[100] In fact there is probably more freedom in the latter because democratic government tends to be more active.

A monarch is also more likely to take advice from "men versed in the matter about which he deliberates, of what rank or quality soever."[101] This statement suggests that Hobbes thought that people would be able to have a say in decisions, but in a controlled manner. We certainly have the right to petition the sovereign: "If a subject have a controversie with his soveraign. . . . He hath the same liberty to sue for his right . . . and consequently . . . the liberty to demand the hearing of his cause."[102] If there is a disagreement between a judge and the judged man, then the matter goes to the sovereign to decide. Hobbes thought the English system of appeal was adequate for the purpose: "These properties of just and rational judicature considered, I cannot forbear to observe the excellent constitution of the court of justice established both for common and also for Pubic Pleas in *England*."[103] There should be as much public appeal to Hobbes's sovereign as there is to the English courts. This is to be preferred to a democratic assembly that is more likely to be swayed by the wealthy rather than by the knowledgeable. This is why Hobbes favored political authority "but neither an active nor very powerful government."[104]

Despite all the negative things that Hobbes has to say regarding democracy, I wish to argue that his sovereign could in fact be a fully participatory democratic assembly of the type outlined by Rousseau. Hobbes says the following: "the sovereign is either in one man or in an assembly of more than one, and into that assembly either every man hath right to enter or not every one (but certain men distinguished from the rest), it is manifest there can be but three kinds of commonwealth."[105] The three kinds are monarchy, aristocracy, and democracy. It is interesting to note, therefore, that Hobbes does not rule out democracy as a legitimate form of sovereign power. He thinks it is dangerous and inefficient, but it is not logically ruled out by his system of thought: "the difference between these three kinds of commonwealth consisteth not in the difference of power, but in the difference of convenience or aptitude to produce the peace and security of the people."[106] In fact, Hobbes claims that he has proven all his claims in *Leviathan* except his arguments in favor of monarchy, which he says are not truths but only his opinion.

Surely one reason why Hobbes is opposed to democracy is because he thinks of the "democratical men" as being one of the main perpetrators of the civil war. If such individuals had gone about their claims in a nonviolent way, Hobbes might well have been less antagonistic. This shows, perhaps, in the following passage from *Behemoth* where Hobbes puts aside his rhetorical flourishes for the moment to state that "the supreme authority must needs be in one man or in more. If the authority were in more than one, it was in all, or in fewer than all. When in all, it is a democracy; for every man may enter into the assembly which makes the Sovereign Court. If they have but one voice, though they be many men, yet are they one person; and therefore they might govern well enough, if they had honesty and wit enough."[107]

We should not let the fact that Hobbes repeatedly calls the sovereign a person lead us to the conclusion that it can be only one individual: "The person to whom this authority of defining punishments is given, can be no other, in any place of the world, but the same person that hath the sovereign power, be it one man or one assembly of men."[108] The key to understanding Hobbes's use of the term *person* lies in chapter 16 of *Leviathan;* "*A person is he whose words or actions are considered, either as his own, or as representing the words or actions of an other man, or of any other thing to whom they are attributed . . . .*When they are considered as his own, then he is called a *Naturall Person:* And when they are considered as representing the words and actions of an other, then is he a *feigned* or *Artificiall person.*"[109] The sovereign, therefore, is an artificial person because it performs as the representative of those who have given it authority to act. Personhood in this respect has nothing to do with whether the sovereign is a single individual or made up of a great many people: "A multitude of men, are made *One* person, when they are by one man, or one Person, Represented; so that it be done with the consent of every one of that Multitude in particular. For it is the *Unity* of the Representer, not the *Unity* of the Represented that maketh the Person *One* . . . [a]nd if the Representative consist of many men, the voyce of the greater number, must be considered as the voyce of them all."[110]

Rousseau's sovereign body therefore is as justified by Hobbes's philosophy (i.e., civil science) as is an hereditary sovereign. They become even more similar when we note that both Hobbes's and Rousseau's sovereigns are supposed to be ruled by impartial reason. Hobbes's sovereign, whether a monarch or a collective body should put aside considerations of interest and use reason to access the truths found in the laws of nature. For Rousseau, the sovereign body should act in a like manner, using impartial reason to remove the pluses and minuses of the will of all until what is purely general is discovered. This suggests that Hobbes's notion of reason is more universal than Rousseau's. For the latter, the general will that is the product of reason is particular to a society and is shaped by the demands of a community, whereas for Hobbes, reason leads us to universal laws of nature that are then applied in a particularistic manner. For both authors, it is rational to accept the consequences of such reasoning and irrational to go against the will of the sovereign. It is also why both suggest that sovereignty cannot be divided or alienated.

The difference between the two is that Hobbes is not as optimistic as Rousseau that human beings in a democracy will be able to put aside their particular wills. This is not so much because they are driven by self-interest but because the multitude is always susceptible to the persuasive powers of vainglorious men. Hobbes also seems to think that sown into the very nature of democracy is faction: "If the sovereign power be in a great assembly, and a number of men (part of the assembly without authority) consult apart to contrive the guidance of the rest, this is a faction, or conspiracy unlawful, as being a fraudulent seducing of the assembly for their particular interest."[111] Rousseau is also aware of this problem but thinks it can be avoided if people ponder the collective good in a nondeliberative fashion:

> If, when a sufficiently informed populace deliberates, the citizens were to have no communication among themselves, the general will would always result from the large number of small differences, and the deliberation would always be good. But when intrigues and partial associations come into being at the expense of the large association, the will of each of these associates becomes general in relation to its members and particular in relation to the state.[112]

The disagreement between the two authors is again not one of philosophical principle concerning sovereignty, but rests on a difference of opinion concerning the practical consequences of democratic participation.

Hobbes also argues that "that king whose power is limited is not superior to him or them that have the power to limit it; and he that is not superior is not supreme, that is to say not sovereign. The sovereignty therefore was always in that assembly which had the right to limit him; and by consequence the government not monarchy, but either democracy or aristocracy."[113] This suggests that representative democracy is also not ruled out by Hobbes's system. Ultimately, whichever body, whether government institutions or the population at large, which has the power to say who can and cannot exercise the rights outlined in chapter 18 of *Leviathan* is the sovereign power. Hence: "elective kings are not sovereigns, but ministers of the sovereign; nor limited kings sovereign, but ministers of them that have the sovereign power."[114]

These considerations are important when weighing the claim that Hobbes's sovereign is too powerful. In particular, the claim that the sovereign is above the law has worried commentators from Hobbes's time to our own and it is often suggested that such a claim by Hobbes opens the door for a tyrannical sovereign to act with impunity. Now that we have fleshed out his concept of sovereignty we can see that this is not the case. For example, if the sovereign body is a democracy, it means that everyone is a member of the sovereign. This does not mean that everyone can break the law and go unpunished simply because the sovereign is "above" the law. What Hobbes means when he says that the sovereign is beyond the law is simply that there has to be some governing body that can legislate. Hobbes thought that this logically entailed the fact that if a body can make laws, it can also change laws, and because it can change laws it must be above any particular set of laws. If we think of the British Parliament we get a more concrete example of what Hobbes had in mind. The British legislature can pass any law it wishes, and because of this it is above any particular set of laws because it can change any law that it no longer favors. This does not mean that the members of Parliament are beyond the reach of the laws currently on the statute books; they are as subject to them as everybody else. In *A Dialogue,* Hobbes is actually very careful to distinguish between natural and political capacities: "If the sovereign power be in an assembly of men, that assembly, whether it be *aristocratical* or *democratical* may possess lands; but it is in their politic capacity: because no natural man has any right to those lands, or any part of them. In the same manner, they can command an act by plurality of commands; but the command of any one of them is of no effect."[115] The fact of the matter is that Hobbes's sovereign can take on many different forms depending on the preferences of rational consenting adults, and it is incorrect to make a blanket statement that his concept of public reason necessarily has the threat of a monstrous sovereign attached to it.

It remains the case that Hobbes does suggest that the sovereign should have a wide range of powers. Most of these are largely uncontroversial, such as the power to raise taxes, have a militia, coin money, and make laws. There are however, some powers that are seen as a cause for concern, particularly given the way that Hobbes describes how they are to be used. They include the powers of censorship, of dictating civil education, of deciding matters of freedom of association, and of dictating a civil religion. Despite the fact that Hobbes is often accused of limiting freedom in all of these areas, a discussion on these issues in the secondary literature is somewhat sparse and I wish to suggest that a closer examination reveals that Hobbes is not guilty of some of the abuses suggested by his critics.

Education, Censorship, Religion, Free Association, and the Preservation of Peace and Freedom

Education and Order

Hobbes's solution to the problem of maintaining a stable political order depends on fostering reason and rationality. Without these characteristics we are incapable of acting in accordance with the laws of nature. This is why education becomes such a vital tool in Hobbes's work; without it we are likely to continue to fight and place the commonwealth in danger. We have to be schooled to overcome such passions as partiality, pride, revenge, and vainglory. We also have to be capable of making contracts with each other and Hobbes tells us repeatedly that without reason we cannot be the authors of our deeds and hence cannot be held responsible for our actions and promises.

We have to acquire opinions that do not threaten the very existence of the commonwealth and we must be taught that the laws of nature relating specifically to civil society dictate that we do unto others as we would have them do unto ourselves. As Hobbes says: "the actions of men proceed from their opinions: and in the well governing of opinions, consisteth the well governing of mens actions, in order to their peace and concord."[116] Hobbes is usually interpreted to mean here that the sovereign can control our thoughts. William E. Connolly, for example, argues that Hobbesian education disciplines us in a way that makes us tame: "The Hobbesian individual is a domesticated human,"[117] and Hobbes's strategy for achieving this goal, we are told, is one of "regulation and control."[118] One way of attaining this end is through the fiction of the state of nature, which tells "imperfectly domesticated subjects that they, in their present state, should consent to remain there."[119] The tale of the natural condition is "shock therapy,"[120] and presumably, once humans are completely domesticated there will be no need for such tall tales.

I argue that when Hobbes talks of well-regulated thoughts he is really talking of self-regulation, in particular that reason controls the passions. As Holmes notes: "Hobbes stressed the self-defeating character of attempts to change people's minds by brutal means."[121] When individuals can control passion they can also control their actions "in order to their peace and concord." Peace, comfort, progress, and science, all of which Hobbes supports, are impossible without "the well governing of opinions." As Hobbes says in *De Cive*, "Man is made fit for society not by nature, but by education."[122] The passions seem to have two wellsprings for Hobbes; one is from "the Constitution of the body"[123] and the other is from education. Those springing from the latter are more easily structured toward peace and can be tempered, but the sovereign should not try to eradicate passions in his subjects. Hobbes starts from the assumption that we are free thinkers; he does not want to beat this out of us, nor does he think it is possible to do so. His task is the same as the one that Mill set himself, namely to find the proper limits, not to thoughts but to actions.

Hobbes was convinced that his task was bound to fail without some form of tutelary sovereign. But with the correct environment, beliefs and opinions can be guided in the direction of peaceful actions and mutual accommodation. This does not mean that the sovereign should try and brainwash its subjects. As Ryan has suggested: "Hobbes's sovereign cannot condition children as the Director in *Brave New World* can."[124] Such tactics are a greater threat to peace than is freedom of thought. The sovereign has to teach respect for the government and acceptance of one's fellow subjects because without obedience to the law and harmony among people the state cannot exist. As Ryan also notes, Hobbes recognized that peace, control of nature, and human comfort are all dependent on expanding human knowledge that is not possible if indoctrination takes the place of freedom of thought and expression.

The first thing the sovereign has to do, however, is to make sure that the subjects are educated to know what their rights are and to explain the "grounds and reasons"[125] for these rights. This is what every American child is taught in civics class. It is the general principle that should underpin the sovereign's teachings and there is nothing here that is necessarily antiliberal. But what of the particular teachings? Perhaps Hobbes goes too far in the specifics of what is necessary to guarantee peace and to make sure that the sovereign's rights are known. Hobbes suggest that the people should be taught to love their own form of government above that of others. This could perhaps be seen as objectionable, but it seems reasonable, for example, to suggest that a democracy should promote the idea that democracy is best. Note that Hobbes does not suggest that other forms of government cannot be taught; he only suggests that the sovereign body itself should promote the view that it is the best form of government.

The populous is also to be taught that no one person should be so honored as to be deemed the equal of the sovereign in terms of obedience. Again, this seems to be quite reasonable and in line with liberal politics; it would be a strange argument to suggest that a particular individual had the same legitimate use of force, for example, as the state. Hobbes also suggests that the people be taught that they should not speak evil of the sovereign nor talk irreverently of the body. This clearly is too severe a restriction for a liberal to endorse, but note that Hobbes immediately tones down this statement. The solution to the problem of fostering respect for the institution of sovereignty is not to enforce a strict speech code, but rather to set aside periodic times when people are to be told simply and clearly what the rights and duties of being a subject entail. This may still worry the modern liberal, but it is hardly indoctrination, especially when we consider what the sovereign is supposed to teach. In particular, the sovereign has to uphold the precepts of justice that dictate that people ought "not to deprive their neighbors, by violance, or fraud, of anything which by the Sovereign Authority is theirs."[126] The sum of the teachings that the sovereign imparts is not "I am all mighty" or "I am a tyrant, so beware." Hobbes tells us instead, that the message "is reduced to this one commandment of mutual charity: *Thou shalt love thy neighbour as thyself.*"[127]

The key is to safeguard peace "and this is intended should be done, not by care applied to individuals, further than their protection from injuries when they shall complain, but by a general providence, contained in public instruction, both of doctrine and example, and in the making and executing of good laws, to which individuals may apply their own cases."[128] Hence the task for the sovereign is to set a good example, make laws that individuals will apply to themselves, and educate them into certain doctrines. This is certainly not a prescription to terrify and indoctrinate the subjects into obedience: "these rights have to be diligently and truly taught, because they cannot be maintained by any civil law or terror of legal punishment."[129]

Hobbes's concept of education is clearly not one that attempts to be value neutral. On the few occasions when Hobbes is recognized as a liberal it is always of the modus vivendi type in which institutions are constructed to arbitrate between individuals (about whose moral character the state is indifferent), in a neutral manner. As Amy Gutmann and many others have noted, this is an impossible position to hold because even the claim to neutrality is a moral argument. I think, therefore that Hobbes would agree with her when she states that "Any defensible understanding of education depends on some conception of a good society, and every conception worth defending threatens some conception (or conceptions) of a good life."[130]

The type of Hobbesian education that supports the good life is not the Platonic form of "horticultural imagery [of] pruning and weeding children's desires, carefully shaping their character."[131] In some respects it is like the one supported by Gutmann herself in which the state should be interventionist but nonrepressive and should attempt to inculcate the virtues of veracity, toleration, nonviolence, respect for others, and respect for reasonable difference. In a liberal society "we do have a right, even a duty, to shape the character and bias the choices of children for the sake of cultural coherence."[132]

Hobbes's ideas also have some similarity with those of William Galston who claims that civic education, which he argues is crucial for any liberal polity to flourish, differs from a purely philosophical education because "Its purpose is not the pursuit of and acquisition of truth, but rather the formation of individuals who can effectively conduct their lives within, and support, their political community . . . [n]or is civic education homogeneous and universal. It is by definition education within, and on behalf of, a particular political order."[133] In fact Galston, who is clearly a liberal, goes as far as to make the very republican-sounding suggestion that

> On the practical level, very few individuals will come to
> embrace the core commitments of liberal society through

a process of rational inquiry. If children are to be brought to accept these commitments as valid and binding, it can only be through a pedagogy that is far more rhetorical than rational. For example, rigorous historical research will almost certainly vindicate complex "revisionist" accounts of key figures in American history. Civic education, however, requires a more noble, moralizing history: a pantheon of heroes who confer legitimacy on central institutions and constitute worthy objects of emulation.[134]

There are at least some similarities, therefore between Hobbes and contemporary liberals, such as Gutmann and Galston, who accept the fact that liberalism cannot sustain itself without a moral core, and whose "liberalism allows, supports, inculcates, and preserves a defensible view of the moral life."[135]

It is also worth noting that Hobbes is not suggesting that the sovereign should go out table thumping and browbeating; he thinks that the best arenas for such teachings are in the universities, that is, Oxford and Cambridge. The real key to success is not to brainwash the common people but to make the political elite recognize their responsibilities. Given that the universities were in fact teaching doctrine, Hobbes thinks that they should at least teach one that promotes peace, equality, and stability. As he says in *Behemoth:* "The core of rebellion, as you have seen by this, and read of other rebellions, are the Universities; which nevertheless are not to be cast away, but to be better disciplined."[136] What should be taught at the universities instead of the doctrine of the schoolmen, is that one should obey the law of the land; that Christianity recognizes the second coming in the future; that no one should injure another person; that everyone should act charitably to all others persons, rich and poor alike; and that all should try to live soberly. As Flathman notes, given Hobbes's epistemology he cannot expect the sovereign to inculcate more than a few basic values and the fact that Hobbes thinks that the sovereign should *teach* rather than use coercive power tells a lot about how he hopes peace will be realized.[137] If Hobbes has simply been interested in the use of force he would not have worried about education. The form of education Hobbes has in mind is the type that fosters the rational and autonomous characters discussed in chapter 6 who are capable of living an examined life.

Censorship

A related topic to education is the seemingly worrisome power of censorship that Hobbes places in the hands of the sovereign. Hobbes claims that the sovereign should decide "how far, and what men are to be trusted withal, in speaking to multitudes of people, and who shall examine the doctrines of all books before they are published."[138] This has often led to the claim that Hobbes's sovereign would tend to censor too much information and interfere too much with freedom of association. Connolly for example, claims that the sovereign provides "a form of public discourse that keeps its lustful, aggressive, and prideful passions under wraps. The sovereign must cleanse the public environment of debates and texts that inflame the passions . . . and must foster a public discourse that cools the passions, concentrates the mind upon the laws of nature, [and] discourages feelings of pride, hatred and revenge."[139] Connolly is right to a point, although I would argue that it is actually commendable to try and control for hatred and revenge in public discourse. Connolly, however, suggests that Hobbes's "texts anticipate the rule-bound character of bureaucratic society and the experience people have of increasing the weight of power bearing down on them as they enlarge the sphere of consent . . . [i]n the hands of the analyst and the sovereign it constitutes an apparatus of order and regularity; it operates to delegitimize irregularity, disruptive thoughts, and actions flowing outside the channel of Hobbesian reason."[140]

It should be noted that Hobbes makes it clear that the sovereign should only exercise these powers in relation to preserving peace. Such power is "annexed to the sovereignty to be judge of what opinions and doctrines are averse, and what conducing, to peace. . . . It belongeth therefore to him that hath the sovereign power to be judge (or constitute all judges) of opinions and doctrines, as a thing necessary to peace, thereby to prevent discord and civil war."[141] Hobbes does not suggest that we cannot publish on many and varied topics or associate for many reasons that do not directly threaten the commonwealth. The sovereign has to be able to judge all opinions and doctrines, but it is not suggested that they should all be banned. It is worth noting again that the British Parliament has the same power and, only occasionally, does it misuse it! It is also worth reiterating the point that Hobbes does not extend this power beyond the preservation of peace—for example, he does not suggest that the government should ban books because they are morally unsavory. In fact, given that civil society is prized over the state of nature precisely because it is a realm of arts, science, and letters, I think Hobbes would have preferred a public arena of lively debate.

It has yet to be demonstrated, therefore, that because the sovereign has the power to censor that it will do so in a heavy-handed manner. It should use this power only to censor those texts that threaten the peace. In practice this may mean that very few books will be denied to the public—less so than today, perhaps, where books are censored for reasons concerning public sensibilities rather than for reasons concerning peace. Where things get more tricky for those wishing to defend Hobbes is when he writes passages that seem to suggest that he would like to ban certain histories of the Greeks and Romans—this because their content suggests that it is acceptable to kill monarchs. On close reading, however, Hobbes does not say that such texts should be banned, even though they are listed as things that are likely to weaken a commonwealth. Instead, he says that "I cannot imagine how anything can be more prejudicial to a monarchy than the allowing of such books to be publicly read without present applying such correctives of discreet masters as are fit to take away their venom."[142] They are not to be banned, even though the venom is described by Hobbes as comparable to the biting of a rabid dog; quite to the contrary, they are allowed but they are to be challenged by other works of "discreet masters." We can guess that one such masterful corrective would be his own work. If the sovereign is not a monarch, as is quite possible, such books are even less of a threat because they do not supply any threat to public peace. I suggest, therefore, that Hobbes will be very sparing in what is to be banned, and only books that really do threaten the peace (and presumably even the advocacy of killing the monarch does not do this) should be prohibited. In *Behemoth* the following exchange on censorship takes place:

> B. It is a strange thing, that scholars, obscure men, and such as could receive no clarity but from the flame of the state, should be suffered to bring their unnecessary disputes, and together with them their quarrels, out of the universities into the commonwealth; and more strange, that the state should engage in their parties, and not rather put them both to silence.

> A. A state can constrain obedience, but convince no error, or alter the minds of them that believe they have the better reason. Suppression of doctrine does but unite and exasperate, that is, increase both the malice and power of them that have already believed them.[143]

Finally, it is also claimed that freedom of speech is crushed in Hobbes's *Leviathan* because he states that the sovereign is to be the judge of good and evil actions, or in other words, Hobbes demands that each individual has to give up private judgment if he or she wishes to live in a peaceful commonwealth. First, as already noted, we never actually do fully give up this right, because if the sovereign ever attempts to use force against us, we are entitled to fight back. Secondly no society, liberal or otherwise, could survive if it does not demand that its citizens do not lay down the right of private judgment on certain issues. I will soon find the long arm of the law grasping for my collar if I conclude that I should decide whether or not I can abuse the life, liberty, property, and well-being of other members of society, no matter how much my own private judgment suggest that it is "good" to do so. Finally, it is worth remembering that when Hobbes suggests that we need public principles of good and evil he is mainly suggesting that the laws of nature should be made into positive law. As he also tells us that the laws will be few, the bulk of the decisions concerning what is necessary for an ethical life will be determined individually and extralegally. Put these three considerations together and I suggest that there is every bit as much private judgment in Hobbes's commonwealth as there is in any well-ordered liberal polity.

Freedom of Association

Hobbes tells us that when any number of individuals join together to promote their interests, it is called a "system." Of systems there are two types; the first is called "regular," and is identified by the fact that it has a representative body that promotes the interests of its members. Of the regular associations, some are absolute and independent, by which Hobbes means that the members answer to no other body other than their own representative. These are commonwealths. All other regular systems are dependent. Of these, some are private; some are political. Of the private, they are lawful or unlawful depending on whether they are allowed by the commonwealth. A family is a lawful private system, in which the father is the head of the family. Unlawful private regular systems would be "those that unite themselves into one person representative, without any public authority at all, such as are the corporations of beggars, thieves and gypsies . . . and the corporations of men that by authority from any foreign person unite themselves on another's dominion, for the easier propagation of doctrines, and for making a party against the power of the commonwealth."[144]

All other types of systems, and the ones we are most interested in in terms of free association, are called "irregular" and consist of people gathering together informally. Such gatherings are to be allowed unless the intention is evil, or the number is very large and the intention is unknown. This suggests that there will be considerable freedom to assemble; the basic requirement is that such gatherings stay within the law:

concourse of people is an irregular system the lawfulness or unlawfulness whereof dependeth on the occasion and on the number of them that are assembled. If the occasion be lawful and manifest, the concourse is lawful (as the usual meeting of men at church, or at a public show) in usual numbers; for if the numbers be extraordinarily great, the occasion is not evident, and consequently he that cannot render a particular and good account of his being amongst them is to be judged conscious of an unlawful and tumultuous design. It may be lawful for a thousand men to join in a petition to be delivered to a judge or magistrate; yet if a thousand men come to present it, it is a tumultuous assembly, because there needs but one or two for that purpose. But in such cases as these, it is not a set number that makes the assembly unlawful, but such a number as the present officers are not able to suppress and bring to justice.[145]

It is worth bearing in mind one of the things that Hobbes particularly wanted to prevent; freedom of association should not stretch to having a private army. Nor should it be expanded to allow religious factions to gain political control. These were the two biggest threats to peace and security and the sovereign should be on the alert. Hobbes summarizes these statements in the following colorful way: "And this is all I shall say concerning *systems* and assemblies of people, which may be compared (as I said) to the similar parts of man's body; such as be lawful, to the muscles; such as are unlawful to wens, biles, apostems, engendered by the unnatural conflux of evil humours."[146] Once again, Hobbes is very consistent; freedom of association should be limited but only those gatherings and groups that actively threaten the commonwealth should be disallowed.

Religion and Order

At least half of *Leviathan* is devoted to the question of religion and many have accused Hobbes of being intolerant toward freedom of religious expression. Hobbes was not *necessarily* against religious speech but he did think it necessary to regulate public expressions of faith if they undermine peace. According to S. A. Lloyd, Hobbes saw religious transcendental interests as the major threat to peace and security.[147] The proper regulation of religious expression is crucial, because the major cause of disorder for Hobbes is the tension between having to obey one's sovereign and one's God. Here, in particular, we cannot expect the fear of punishment to overcome our ultimate duty to God.

Hobbes's solution is in the governing of opinions concerning beliefs that we hold most dearly. As he says in chapter 18: "It belongeth therefore to him that hath the Sovereign Power, to be Judge, or constitute all Judges of Opinions and Doctrines, as the thing necessary to Peace; thereby to prevent Discord and Civill Warre."[148] This passage does not suggest that the sovereign should limit all forms of speech, but only those that are particularly prone to creating discord and war. Nor does it suggest that the sovereign has to indoctrinate subjects into a particular belief system; what Hobbes is calling for is a basic but uniform civil religion that is broad enough for all to embrace. As Ryan says, the "effect is to make uniform public worship a political good and not a religious issue in the usual sense, while strongly suggesting that private opinion can be left unfettered."[149] Hence, the sovereign basically gives broad guidelines for the public interpretation of Scripture, but does not try to enforce this in private. The sovereign does this in part by interpreting the Kingdom of God in Scripture in such a way that it cannot be identified with the beliefs of a particular religious sect.

The task is to control rather than suppress belief systems. The sovereign does this primarily through creating a civic religion, accessible to all, which does not rest for its validity upon religious elites. In particular, it is the role of the sovereign to make sure that the civic religion fits well with the laws of nature, which means that to practice religion publicly one has to "accommodate oneselfe to the rest." It is the task of the sovereign to make good laws, for if he makes good laws he will not suffer disobedience because subjects are obliged to obey all commands "not repugnant to the laws of God."[150] As Hobbes says in *Behemoth*: "I confess I know very few controversies amongst Christians, of points necessary to salvation. They are the questions of authority and power over the Church, or of profit, or of honour to churchmen, that for the most part raise all the controversies."[151]

The major component of the civil religion is that we should believe in Christ and God. More or less everything else is left to the individuals' own conscience. As Ryan says, such a basic public belief allows for "a large measure of speculative freedom."[152] The sovereign "who understands Hobbes's philosophy will remember the injunction of *de Corporo Politico* to leave his subjects as much natural liberty as he can. He will not stretch their willingness to obey him to things necessary to peace by enquiring minutely into their private opinions."[153]

If the sovereign can manage in this task, it will have succeeded in conscripting the strongest passions of human beings to work for rather than against order. This is the task Hobbes sets himself in the latter half of *Leviathan*. I would argue, therefore, that the role of the sovereign is to be tolerant toward religious beliefs that do not threaten the survival of the state. Hobbes realized that any attempt to ban religious practices will have a very destabilizing effect; as long as these belief systems do not infringe upon the practices of others and do not directly threaten the commonwealth, the sovereign's task is to promote religious freedom. As Timothy Fuller puts it: "Hobbes's proposals for seeking religious and civil peace conjointly are such, he thinks, as to enhance the capacity of individuals to take personal responsibility for civic and spiritual virtue, consistent both with their inevitable dependence on their own understanding and judgement, and with their admitted need for reliable and unambiguous political authority, leading to a new level of liberty and dignity, and to a sophisticated appreciation for the importance of civil law."[154] In particular, the sovereign reveals to us the attributes of

God as discovered through reason. According to Fuller, Hobbes tells us that we can know God exists, that he is the cause of the world and hence not identical to the world, that he cares for the world which is an act demanding our respect, that he is infinite, and that as such there can only be one God. The basis of the sovereign's public doctrine is very general and leaves considerable room for private belief: "care of public doctrine is preservative, not revelatory. Subjects retain the ability to read the Scriptures for themselves and to assess the consistency of the sovereign's laws with the Scriptures. The subject is obliged to obey the sovereign unless there is a contradiction between Scripture and his commands."[155]

Liberalism supposes a separation between religion and the state. One may wish to argue that despite these arguments, Hobbes's state is still overly intrusive in religious practices. Clearly Hobbes does seem to be limiting freedom of religious speech; but one has also to take into account his circumstances. In seventeenth-century England there was little freedom of religious thought; the church dictated belief. Hobbes at least tries to have religious belief controlled in a manner that preserves the peace, and it is obviously better, he thinks, to do this through the sovereign rather than through the church. He asks whether it is better to let the church or the sovereign make demands concerning civil obedience. Obviously for Hobbes, the sovereign is the safest and most reasonable choice; it is less likely to be overly dogmatic because the source of its authority does not come from Scripture but from authorization. Hence, even when its solutions to problems are not fully liberal, they are still motivated by the desire to promote an arena where people can have the peace and freedom to worship unmolested. The sovereign can be magnanimous and allow a broad freedom of conscience as long as peace is not threatened. In this way, religious practice serves the individual rather than the church. This is why Hobbes was so concerned with fastening religious and civil power in the same hands; he did not believe that peace was possible until "Kings were Pastors, or Pastors Kings."[156]

Conclusion

In this chapter, I have argued that freedom is protected in a variety of ways by the laws of nature. In particular, Hobbes's deep commitment to equality demonstrates that he wished everyone would have the opportunity for considerable freedom. Hobbes provides us with a theory of politics that in large part manages to overcome the tension many liberals find between liberty and equality. Whereas freedom and equality lead to war in the state of nature, they foster peace and the good life when they are promoted in accord with the laws of nature. When such natural laws are made positive by the sovereign they provide a solid bulwark against abuse by one's fellow human beings. The sovereign is not checked in the same manner as subjects, but I have argued that the moral prescriptions within the laws, which are also tied to the sovereign's self-interest, provide protection from the abuse of political authority. Such moral demands on the sovereign may ultimately prove to be insufficient in quelling the actions of a tyrant, but if the sovereign of any political state acts in a brutal fashion, written constitutions and bills of rights will also prove to be inadequate. Such documents ultimately gain their force from moral persuasion. But if each person abides by the laws of nature, everyone can be guaranteed protection in the pursuit of a wide variety of ends. Only when such ends threaten the peace and security of the commonwealth should the sovereign interfere. It is my suggestion, therefore, that Hobbes means what he says when he tells us that "in all kinds of actions, by the laws praetermitted, men have the liberty of doing what their own reasons shall suggest."[157] In the introduction to *Leviathan,* Hobbes declares that his task (as Mill later claims is his own) is to find a middle ground between "too great Liberty" and "too much Authority." I have argued that the laws of nature operate much as Mill's harm proviso does in protecting freedom and as such Hobbes should be seen as one of the founding authors of liberal political philosophy.

The laws of nature promote freedom by securing a condition of equality before civil law. At a minimal level they create a formalistic/legalistic equality of opportunity. But, as the discussions of wealth distribution and public education suggest, Hobbes also displays an interest in a more substantive notion of equality. He makes it clear throughout *Leviathan* that he is concerned with the interests of *all* who live within the commonwealth. This requirement seems to extend to the public expression of religious beliefs; each belief system is to be allowed and its supporters left unmolested as long as the safety of the commonwealth is not jeopardized.

Connolly is wrong, therefore, in suggesting that Hobbes is trying to create normalized, passive, domesticated subjects. He is right in noting that "The Hobbesian individual is thus in part a product of the civil society which is to regulate it, and the Hobbesian problem is how to form it so that it will be able and willing to abide by the natural law and contracts appropriate to civil society."[158] Connolly's error is in concluding that Hobbes achieves this goal by producing automatons that have had the passions knocked out of them through the socializing force of rules and policies. The fifth law of nature, which demands that we accommodate ourselves to the rest, is interpreted by Connolly as an attempt to make the "individual to be an artifice formed by rubbing off irregular features that do not "fit" neatly into the form of civil society."[159] We start off as diverse individuals and are then "sculpted to fit into the edifice under construction."[160] The end result, we are told, is that "[t]o become a Hobbesian individual one must give up much of one's own individuality. Those too stubborn to accept correction of refinement are on warning."[161]

Connolly suggests, therefore, that the Hobbesian project undermines otherness through regulatory methods that shave off anything that makes people distinctive: "The way a theory defines and copes with otherness—with the things, actions, beings and events that fall outside the range of normality it accepts—illuminates its ideas about the character and stability of the normal individual."[162] When the sovereign gets it right it "converts a being dominated by unruly, lustful, unguided passions into the suspicious, calculating, prudent, sober, self-interested subject who is to populate the Hobbesian world."[163] This interpretation just will not fit the text. Part of the problem with this view of Hobbes is that it places too much emphasis, as many other interpretations have done, on what he says about the fear of death. Connolly claims that the theory "domesticates by eliciting the vicarious fear of violent death in those who have not had to confront it directly. And when one confronts the fear of early and violent death, one becomes willing to regulate oneself and to accept external regulations that will secure life against its dangers. The fear of death pulls the self together. It induces subjects to accept civil society and it becomes an instrumentality of sovereign control."[164] Actually, the fear of death can never do this amount of work in Hobbes's theory, nor is it meant to. Hobbes is much more interested in promoting the many benefits of society, such as arts, letters, commodious living, and fraternity, than producing cringing and cramped individuals who scurry around in constant fear. The Hobbesian state is not the panopticon state. None of this, of course, will persuade the opponent of liberalism that the liberal state promotes freedom. But I hope that it will at least persuade the reader that Hobbes's political philosophy approximates to that of liberalism.

Carol Patemen offers a different criticism of Hobbes and suggests that his theories of freedom and equality are inadequate because they do not deal sufficiently with half of the members of a commonwealth: "The social contract presupposed the sexual contract, and civil freedom presupposed patriarchal right." She argues that at best, Hobbes is only giving freedom and equality to all men. The very contract to form the *Leviathan* comes at the price of female subjugation and the freedom that men enjoy once the contract has been made depends on female subservience. The consequence of the victory of contract theory is that "In modern society all men are deemed good enough to be women's masters; civil freedom depends on patriarchal right."[165] Hobbes is not as bad as some of the other contract theorists when he discusses freedom in the natural condition, because he posits women as equal to men, and suggests that parental right lies with the mother. But he assumes that women will eventually be enslaved by men in the state of nature and hence when it comes time for the contract, only men have full property ownership in themselves and hence only they are full *individuals* who can enter into the contract. The upshot is that "sexual difference is the difference between freedom and subjection."[166]

Pateman offers a severe test of Hobbes's proclaimed desire to promote equality. Does his theory stand up to the test? It seems clear, as Preston King and Gabriella Slomp argue, that in the natural condition women are deemed the equal of men.[167] All human beings have certain natural faculties of the mind and body and each functions in approximately the same manner. We all move and respond to external stimuli in the same way, and we all have passions, reason, and the deliberative faculties. As Pateman notes, Hobbes actually grants maternal rights over children in the natural condition. Added to this that all humans think that they are equal to one another and the differences that exist from one individual to the next are never so great to give a person an overwhelming advantage. Men would actually have to expend a large amount of energy and place themselves in the face of extreme danger to subjugate either men or women in the state of nature and hence each sex is as vulnerable as the other without the rule of law. I do not think Pateman is right, therefore, in arguing that Hobbes assumes that women will be taken prisoner by men in the natural condition (although some of them might) and hence it does not follow that only men are full individuals at the time of contract. And if we remember that the contract argument is largely hypothetical, there is no reason to believe that women should not be treated equally. Even if women are taken prisoner in the natural condition, this would be invalidated by the social contract because men would not have authority to act on their behalf. As Hobbes says, such authority "has no place but in a State Civill, because before such estate, there is no Dominion of Persons."[168]

Does Hobbes's argument fare as well in civil society? The ruling principles of the state can be found in the laws of nature and these certainly prescribe that everyone should be treated equally. But Hobbes seems to be guilty as charged by Pateman because he argues that men are the heads of households and that children belong to fathers. But as Slomp notes, Hobbes does not argue for this as a necessary consequence of his political science, but instead claims that it occurs from convention and custom. The inequality we find, therefore, is not a necessary inequality but is the result of social factors that can be remedied. One way to do this is to make sure that the equality that lies at the heart of the laws of nature should be promoted regardless of sex because nowhere do the laws state that inequality between men and women is justified. We can legitimately claim, therefore, that although Hobbes did allow for inequalities between men and women, this was because of sociological and not philosophical reasons, and consequently his civil science is compatible, and in fact recommends the equal treatment of all members of the commonwealth. In his defense we can perhaps claim that Hobbes would indeed have been a man ahead of his time if he had thought out all the implications of his own arguments concerning the status of women. One can argue, of course, that a fully fleshed out Hobbesian equality along the lines of contemporary liberal equality is still inadequate for true equality between the sexes. If a modern liberal can rebuff this argument then a proponent of Hobbesian equality should be able to do the same.

I hope that I have demonstrated that Hobbes wanted to create an arena in which people can make most of their decisions for themselves. It is true that he places limits on actions to preserve the peace, but these are fairly minimal in Hobbes's state and the fifth law of nature is really concerned with promoting tolerance at a minimum and hopefully the more worthy end of acceptance, and hence of reinforcing otherness. Hobbes himself was too quirky an individual not to realize the value of difference. This takes us back to Ridge's view of Hobbes's concept of public reason.

On one level Hobbes does place the preservation of peace in the hands of the sovereign. But as noted, he did not think that peace could be maintained by an absolute sovereign wielding a sword. Nor would he have thought that Ridge's alternative is any better. Threats cannot guarantee peace, and neither can pieces of paper with principles written upon them. We should not forget that since the Constitution was drawn up the United States has seen slavery, Jim Crow laws, Prohibition, women denied the franchise until the twentieth century, the internment of Japanese Americans in World War II, and McCarthyism. All of these took place with the kind of authoritative public principles in place advocated by Ridge. As Shklar notes: "liberalism has been very rare both in theory and in practice in the last two hundred odd years . . . let us not forget that the United States was not a liberal state until after the Civil War, and even then often in name only . . . [it was powerful in the United States only if black people are not counted as members of its society."[169] Such abuses also took place under a system of divided government and separation of powers, which Hobbes is also heavily criticized for rejecting. One can also look at the old constitution of the Soviet Union to see an even starker discrepancy between principles of public reason and political reality.

It is one of the great paradoxes of politics that if the state is powerful enough to provide adequate protection to its citizens, then it is also powerful enough to cause them great harm. Therefore, the real key to safety, stability, and ultimately to what Hobbes refers to as commodious living, is through the development of civic-minded members of a commonwealth. This is why Hobbes is concerned with educating rather than coercing. What Ridge and others miss about Hobbes is that he recognizes that the problems of peace and conflict resolution have to be approached from a variety of angles. One of them is through the use of political power; a second is to educate citizens into a civic culture; and a third is to educate them into the moral philosophy embedded in the laws of nature. This last approach is actually quite close to Ridge's own position because the laws of nature can be viewed as the embodiment of a public philosophy of reasonableness.

If we think of liberalism as a doctrine that is concerned with liberty, equality (and the tension that can exist between these two ideals), autonomy, a diversity of human goods, the rule of law, due process, a conception of a particular form of the moral life (which modern liberals now tend to endorse), a distinction between public and private life, religious toleration, a desire to contain passions with rational constraints, a belief in progress, and at least a minimal safety net for all persons, then we can say, at least, that these are features of Hobbes's political philosophy. Schklar distances herself from the Hobbesian project, but her major concern, expressed in "The Liberalism of Fear" is perhaps also that of Hobbes: "Liberalism has only one overriding aim: to secure the political conditions that are necessary for the exercise of personal freedom."[170] What better title could we use for Hobbes's liberalism that the liberalism of fear? Hobbes was a psychologist as well as a philosopher and he recognized (as did Shklar) that cruelty, pain, torture, and undiluted fear greatly impede agency. Hobbes, therefore, would also surely agree with Shklar that "Systematic fear is the condition that makes freedom impossible."[171] For both theorists there is no difficulty identifying a *summum malum*.

Part IV

Conclusion

8

⮌

Hobbes's Dualism

Introduction

It has been a point of contention for many years as to
exactly how well Hobbes's arguments fit together into a coherent whole. It is usually concluded that it is not possible
to tie all the strands of his thought into a neat package. For
example, as seen in chapter 7, those who believe that
Hobbes presents a theory of morality also argue that one
simply has to abandon his theory of psychological motivation. Another example is Hobbes's description of human nature that seems to vary widely depending on the passages
one reads in *Leviathan;* sometimes humans are described
as always pursuing immediate self-interest, while at other
times Hobbes makes it a necessary condition of following
the laws of nature that we cast aside considerations of our
own interests. The discussions of determinism, freedom,
and consent are also confusing, not only because of how
Hobbes defines his terms but also because of the value he
places on such philosophical concepts.

How then should one deal with this apparent confusion? Should one simply argue that Hobbes was sloppy and
inconsistent in his work? Or should one be more generous
and argue that while there are parts of his system that do
not fit well together, Hobbes still does a pretty good job of
providing a coherent program of thought? I think the correct

reply is that neither of these answers is sufficient. I think it is futile to try and find a coherent thread that links everything Hobbes said into a unified system of thought. This is because there are two separate arguments presented to us by Hobbes.

On many issues Hobbes seems to present a minimal and simplified argument about a particular topic. On further reading, however, there seems to be a more compelling and sophisticated argument to be found, although it is usually less clearly stated and is certainly not presented in the loud tones of his more forceful diatribes. We should not simply write off this dichotomy as incoherence on the part of Hobbes but instead try and find a way to explain both sets of arguments.

I suggest that Hobbes is presenting a dualism in his writings concerning the human condition; he has one set of arguments for life as it might be lived, uncomfortably in the state of nature, and another set describing life lived comfortably in civil society. On the one hand, the description of the state of nature, and of the sort of "natural" person we can expect to find there, is an analytical tool to demonstrate the worst form of human existence. The description of civil society, on the other hand, is meant to highlight an alternative form of existence that everyone can agree is better than life without the rule of law. One could also demonstrate this dualism in relation to the laws of nature. One description fits life lived according to the second clause of the first law, that is, the right of nature. The alternative description shows us how life can be lived when all the rest of the laws of nature dictate human interactions. As Hobbes is much more interested in how people live together in society rather than how they might live together in an "ideal" type state of nature, it seems reasonable to assume that his descriptions of freedom, contract, and so forth, as they pertain to civil society are his actual views on these issues.

Most of the arguments presented throughout this book have been supported by textual evidence. Here I wish to be more speculative. I am not claiming that Hobbes specifically states the dualism identified here (although I do not think that it goes against any textual evidence); I wish to make the lesser claim that this is one way to understand and make sense of the wide range of issues that Hobbes deals with, and it does so in a manner that does not simply write him off as an incoherent thinker. I will now use four examples to illustrate my point.

Determinism

We have seen how Hobbes's more sophisticated theories of freedom and voluntarism allow us to rebut the claim that he supports a theory of psychological egoism and how this in turn opens the door to reading Hobbes as a theorist of morality. But these gains do come at a cost to other aspects of his political philosophy. As noted in chapter 2, Hobbes often describes the world generally and human movement in particular in a mechanistic fashion. All movement and all thought is caused by something *external* to the thing moving and hence everything is determined by a prior cause. Hobbes's "science" of motion depends on demonstrating that determinism and freedom are compatible. He argues originally that they are not in conflict because things internal to the moving object do not enter into the discussion of liberty, and hence we cannot demonstrate that the movement was unfree. Freedom is only concerned with external obstacles to the thing moving and not with the thing itself.

However, once Hobbes is forced by his own arguments into considering internal/mental conditions such as fear and moral obligations, as shown in chapters 4 and 5, he can no longer claim quite so easily that will and determinism are compatible. The reason for this doubt is because Hobbes has surreptitiously added concerns about the genesis of movement into his discussion. Movement is no longer exclusively a question of motion caused by things external to the individual, but now involves the calculations of a thinking being.

When Hobbes discusses freedom in civil society he is forced by his own arguments to concede that freedom is also linked to the *choices* open to the agent. But the more we allow for choice, and the more we allow internal conditions of the agent to influence our judgments of the freedom of actions, the less we can hold to a deterministic view of the world. Under Hobbes's original definition of freedom, choice does not feature at all. This is no longer the case for the extended version of freedom, which is a theory of *action* rather than of movement. Hobbes does not treat humans as billiard balls with set trajectories of movement, but allows for choice and hence some unpredictability in human actions. What he ends up presenting us with is a fairly comprehensive theory of the self that fits with modern notions of autonomy. This causes tension in Hobbes's work between a causal description of the world on the one hand and a vocabulary of moral and voluntaristic concerns on the other.

What we discover in *Leviathan* is an ideal of the self that includes a demand for rationality and reasonableness, the priority of reason over the passions, the capacity to make authoritative statements, the ability to formulate and act upon life-plans, the facility to judge means as well as ends, and the capacity to make moral judgments. These features can be summed up as an aptitude for deliberative self-rule, an aptitude that would be missing from a being solely determined by external forces. At best, the problems raised for the possibility of a compatibilist account of freedom and determinism are much more complicated once we revise our understanding of Hobbes's theory of freedom. The answer to the puzzle may perhaps lie in the fact that most of Hobbes's deterministic-sounding statements take place in the first part of *Leviathan* that culminates in a discussion of the state of nature whereas the more sophisticated concept of the rationally willing self is to be found in the second part of the text dealing with life in a well-ordered commonwealth.

Consent

Once we uncover Hobbes's theory of volition, more than his theory of determinism is challenged. By extending the theory of the will to a rational choosing will, Hobbes can no longer argue persuasively that all contracts are obligatory. If the only valid form of contract is a voluntary, authoritative, contract, but fear limits freedom and hence volition, then Hobbes is no longer in a position to claim that contracts made through fear are still obligatory. Only contracts that are made without coercion can be properly said to be binding and they can only be binding because they have a moral content to them, which in turn requires that they are voluntary. As Hobbes makes clear throughout *Leviathan* the *only* way we can be obliged is through an act of the will. A theory of deterministic motion is therefore useless for the task Hobbes sets for himself, which is to provide good reasons for binding obligations.

This poses a particular difficulty for Hobbes's claim that sovereignty through acquisition is legitimate, and also for his claim that contracts made in the state of nature through fear are binding. The political obligation we owe the sovereign suddenly loses legitimacy if we can demonstrate that it was not made in an authoritative (i.e., free) manner. Hobbes ultimately is left with a better theory of contract and consent because it becomes more voluntaristic, but one that will no longer supply the kind of blanket obligation he demands. Or, rather his argument can explain such obligation, but not in the manner he wishes; he tells us that fear and obligation are not contradictory and hence we can be obliged under any conditions, but his theory of volition does not allow for such a conclusion. It follows that justice can no longer be defined simply in terms of promise keeping irrespective of the conditions under which the promise was made. A promise made in fear, while perhaps retaining some validity, is less obligatory than one made without coercion and cannot be fully binding.

We can say, therefore, that Hobbes's theory of extended freedom produces tension between, on the one hand, fear and coercion and on the other hand, voluntary action. This raises questions about the legitimacy of our obligations created by promises made in fear. It seems to affect any promise made concerning the imposition of sovereignty through acquisition, and to a lesser degree, the promise made in the state of nature to obey the sovereign, for if there is tension between fear and obligation then the political obligation we owe the sovereign is morally tainted. What this suggests is that when Hobbes talks of civil society he has to abandon some of his original arguments that he thought necessary for creating peace, order, and justice. It is no wonder, then, that he does not advertise the changes he makes in his theory of freedom throughout *Leviathan*.

Hobbes has to make subtle changes in his view of freedom because he has to demonstrate that freedom in civil society is more limited than the abstract freedom found in the state of nature. Nevertheless, we are much better off because our natural freedom is replaced by civil freedom that is limited by laws and obligations. He cannot demonstrate this, however, if he continues to maintain that what limits freedom are external obstacles. Hence Hobbes is forced into a duality in which freedom means something different in society than it does in nature. As Hobbes's main concern is with society rather than the state of nature, we should regard his extended theory of liberty as expressing his most important ideas on the subject and not, as has often been thought, his theory of pure negative freedom. Once we do this, however, the systematic character of his thought is significantly compromised. Hobbes subtly abandons his empirical psychology and replaces it with a theory of moral volition. As a consequence, his extended theory of freedom performs the valuable task of rescuing his moral theory from the scrap heap but it does so at some cost as to what can be counted as a political obligation. Because we do not usually count obligations to conquerors as legitimate, this is a small cost to pay.

As has been noted, Hobbes seems to have a very confused view as to what counts as free action and his description wanders all the way from the most rigid definition of freedom solely related to the lack of external obstacles to a description of action that I have argued fits well with the idea of autonomy. One way to understand why Hobbes seems to have such a confusing view on the topic is to think of him as presenting not two different types, but two fundamentally different kinds of freedom depending on the conditions in which humans find themselves. His description of freedom expunged of all considerations of fear, coercion, rationality, and life-plans, is really the form of freedom we associate with nonrational and/or inanimate objects; we do not expect a dog to be able to give cogent reasons for preferring chewing on a bone as opposed to the leg of a chair. This is because it does not possess the rational faculties necessary for such evaluations. Similarly, humans who inhabited a world such as the state of nature would not have the capability to give a coherent description of their actions in the same manner as, for example, Plato's philosopher-king. In other words, life in the state of nature would deaden the faculties that we think make us persons and capable of rational action.

It is only when we have the comfortable existence provided by civil society that freedom becomes something to be valued, pondered over, and limited in such a way as to make each person's freedom compatible with the freedom of everyone else. Also, it is only in such conditions that rationality becomes a defining feature of liberty. This does not fit exactly with what Hobbes has to say about the state of nature because he thinks that we can still grasp the laws of nature and hence that we are still capable of reason. But such reason plays a very minimal role in the state of nature in comparison to civil society; it is only in the latter that we are able to gather our thoughts, desires, and purposes into a coherent plan that guides our day-to-day actions. This is perhaps why Hobbes himself differentiated between natural liberty and the liberty of subjects.

Equality

As with the topic of freedom, Hobbes has different things to say about equality depending on the conditions under which it is exercised. In the state of nature, our natural equality, or at least our perception that we are equal to everyone else, leads to a nasty and brutish life. When combined with absolute freedom from law and authority the results exclude any chance at a long and successful life. Hence the combination of *natural* freedom and equality in the state of nature leads to our downfall. What is needed is an alternative notion of constrained civil equality before the law that makes the exercise of this equality safe for everyone. In the state of nature our equality is largely an equality to cause harm, whereas in civil society it is an equality that prevents us from harming others.

When Hobbes discusses equality he focuses on the equality of "body and mind,"[1] of "strength," "quickness," and so forth, such that "the weakest has strength enough to kill the strongest,"[2] and most importantly has an equality of experience and prudence. There are, however, unfortunate consequences of this equality: "From this equality of ability, ariseth equality of hope in the attaining of our Ends. And therefore if any two men desire the same thing . . . they become enemies and . . . endeavour to destroy, or subdue one another."[3] The result of unconstrained equality is war.

The outcome is very different in civil society where Hobbes discusses equality in terms of natural and civil law. In society our natural equality, identified in the ninth law of nature, is acknowledged but also controlled. It is controlled by the tenth law of nature: "On this law [the ninth], dependeth another [the tenth] *That . . . no man require to reserve to himselfe any right, which he is not content should be reserved to every one of the rest."*[4] When equality is defined by law and each is treated equitably by the sovereign, equality now creates the most conducive conditions for peace. As with Hobbes's discussion of freedom, when equality is defined in legal rather than natural terms, the concept is transformed from one that leads to war to one that promotes commodious living.

Power

There is a tendency to think of Hobbes's notion of power simply in political terms. Michael Foucault, for example, suggests that Hobbes's notion of power is insufficient because it is a top-down concept in which the sovereign imposes his will from his position of political authority. Instead, Foucault suggests that power is a more fluid, pervasive phenomenon that rises from the bottom as well as falls from the top. He wants to highlight

> The manifold forms of domination that can be exercised within society. Not the domination of the King in his central position, therefore, but that of his subjects in their mutual relations: not the uniform edifice of sovereignty, but the multiple forms of subjugation that have a place and function within the social organism. [We] should be concerned with power at its extremities, in its ultimate destinations, with those points where it becomes capillary. . . . In other words, one should try to locate power at the extreme points of its exercise, where it is always less legal in character. . . . What is needed is a study of power in its external visage, at the point where it is in direct and immediate relationship with that which we can provisionally call its object, its target, its field of operation, there—that is to say—where it installs itself and produces its real effects. . . . Let us ask how things work at the level of ongoing subjugation, at the level of those continuous and uninterrupted processes which subject our bodies, govern our gestures, dictate our behaviors. . . . This would be the exact opposite of Hobbes' project in *Leviathan* . . . for whom the problem is the distillation of a single will—or rather, the constitution of a unitary, singular body animated by the spirit of sovereignty—from the particular wills of a multiplicity of individuals. . . . Well, rather than worry about the problem of the central spirit, I believe that we must attempt to study the myriad of

bodies which are constituted as peripheral *subjects* as a result of the effects of power.[5]

In fact, Hobbes has a much more sophisticated concept of power than Foucault suggests, and when he talks of power he rarely discusses it in strictly political terms; instead he notes its pervasive qualities in civil society, and in the state of nature. If power resides in the latter condition then it clearly cannot only refer to the exercise of political authority. If we carefully examine what Hobbes says about power we find that he focuses on the individual and on complex social relations not on the sovereign. The overriding, albeit instrumental drive for Hobbes, is the desire for power, broadly defined as a person's "present means, to obtain some future apparent Good."[6] This definition is broken down into instrumental and natural power, the latter being the "eminence of the Faculties of Body, or Mind,"[7] and the former the instruments that our natural capacities have helped us acquire and that in turn help us to gain even more power, that is, more means of attaining future goods. The primary sources of power, therefore, are the natural faculties and in particular dexterity of mind. Power itself is seen by Hobbes as the primary means to living well, and to living a fulfilling and long life. There is nothing intrinsically political about this definition at all; the use of political power is just one among many means of attaining one's ends.

The problem in the state of nature is that we pursue and utilize our power with little thought of long-term consequences. The result is that the quest for power actually prevents people from living the good life. It is important to remember, however, that Hobbes does not see everyone as a maximizer. Many have suggested that our drive for power is the same as our supposed pursuit of the objects of our desires, that is, uncontrolled by reason. I have already demonstrated that this is not the case with our desires and I think it is also a false interpretation of what Hobbes has to say about power. In the state of nature a person will strive for power "because he cannot assure the power and means to live well, which he hath present, without the acquisition of more."[8] Because we are unsure about the power available to other individuals under the conditions of uncertainty found in the state of nature, it becomes rational to try and accumulate more for oneself. This leads to a systemic problem of power inflation because with each new acquisition of power a person becomes more of a threat to others and hence they have to safeguard themselves by acquiring more in turn. Given the condition of the state of nature is a condition of war, it is particularly dangerous forms of power that are accumulated; the power to defend oneself and harm others is the power most prized.

It is the fear of powerful enemies, therefore, which makes us so acquisitive of power; remove the fear and our passion for power will be tempered and controlled by reason so that the realm of instrumentally effective action is greatly expanded. The drive for power is not that "a man hopes for a more intensive delight, than he has already attained to; or that he cannot be content with a moderate power"[9] but comes from fear and uncertainty. Remove this uncertainty and the drive for power will diminish to reasonable levels. We need, therefore, a passion for power only in its broadest sense as a means to attain goals, and we act virtuously when we pursue it in a rational manner. Power is the first requisite of a rational and autonomous life, but such a life is only possible when the pursuit of power is subordinate to reason and it is, of course, only possible to pursue power in a reasonable fashion once one is living under the protection of the sovereign in civil society. To pursue power in a reasonable fashion is to pursue it for well-being not for greed, or for insatiable appetites. As has been noted earlier, the drive to fulfill one desire over all others is a form of madness, and to use power in such a manner is to abuse its use. The goal of an autonomous person should be to use power reasonably in the pursuit of reasonable ends. The objects pursued as sources of power will also dramatically change in a well-ordered civil society; it is economic goods, intellectual abilities, and social manners that give one power, not forms of coercion. Hence the sources of power change from those of physical force to those of social usefulness. It may be the case, therefore, that Hobbes's concept of power will not find favor with the likes of Foucault, but it is clear that Hobbes viewed power as a fluid, dynamic, social, and pervasive force that is expressed in all areas of human interaction.

Conclusion

This book has examined Hobbes's thoughts on the topics of internal and external freedom. It is the relationship between the two that Hobbes addresses in *Leviathan*. Liberalism teaches us to differentiate in a broad manner between freedom and autonomy based on internal and external requirements for action. At one level, freedom exists by and large to the extent that we are unimpeded by external obstacles. At another level, full freedom or autonomy rests upon the further consideration of the internal conditions of the agent. It has been my intention to demonstrate that Hobbes was one of the first to understand and formulate this relationship, later to be picked up by Rousseau, Kant, and others. The reason why it has not previously been identified in Hobbes is, I think, because he was unclear as to the precise formulation of the dichotomy. To repeat a quote from an earlier chapter, Hobbes thought that "we have no name in our tongue" to adequately describe what he had in mind. We are blinded to the argument if we concentrate solely upon Hobbes's definition of natural liberty; probably the reason why Hobbes is so cavalier in discussing this type of freedom is simply that it was never his major concern to promote it. Natural liberty is inherently dangerous; as one component of the state of nature it contributes to fear, destruction, and even death, and should be abandoned for the benefits of autonomous living in a peaceful society.

Notes

Chapter 1

1. J. R. Pennock, "Hobbes's Confusing 'Clarity'—The Case of 'Liberty,'" in *Hobbes Studies*, ed. Keith Brown (Cambridge: Harvard University Press, 1965); A. Wernham, "Liberty and Obligation in Hobbes," in *Hobbes Studies*, ed. Brown; Ralph Ross, Herbert Schneider, and Theodore Waldman, *Thomas Hobbes in His Time* (Minneapolis: University of Minnesota Press, 1974); Brian Barry, "Warrender and His Critics," in *Hobbes and Rousseau: A Collection of Critical Essays*, eds. Maurice Cranston and Richard S. Peters (New York: Anchor, 1972); J. W. N. Watkins, *Hobbes's System of Ideas* (London: Hutchinson, 1973).

2. Richard Flathman, *The Philosophy and Politics of Freedom* (Chicago: University of Chicago Press, 1987).

3. Ibid., 322.

4. Ibid.

5. Joel Feinberg, "The Idea of a Free Man," in *Rights, Justice and the Bounds of Liberty* (Princeton: Princeton University Press, 1980).

6. Flathman, *Philosophy and Politics of Freedom;* Charles Taylor, "What's Wrong with Negative Liberty?" in *Philosophy and the Human Sciences* (Cambridge: Cambridge University Press, 1985).

7. Thomas Hobbes, *Leviathan,* ed. C. B. Macpherson (London: Penguin Books, 1968), 262.

8. Flathman, *Philosophy and Politics of Freedom,* 322.

Chapter 2

1. Taylor, "What's Wrong with Negative Liberty?"

2. Isaiah Berlin, *Four Essays on Liberty* (Oxford: Oxford University Press, 1969).

3. Taylor, "What's Wrong with Negative Liberty?" 213.

4. Ibid., 215.

5. By "framework" Taylor means a heuristic tool that "provides the context within which the question of meaning has its place . . . and without which one's life would be . . . spiritually senseless." Taylor, *Sources of the Self: The Making of the Modern Identity* (Cambridge: Harvard University Press, 1989), 17.

6. Taylor, "What's Wrong with Negative Liberty?" 219.

7. Taylor, *Sources of the Self,* 224.

8. Taylor, "What's Wrong with Negative Liberty?" 224.

9. Ibid.

10. Ibid.

11. Ibid., 225.

12. Ibid., 224.

13. Ibid., 225.

14. Ibid.

15. Ibid., 215.

16. Ibid., 228–229.

17. Ibid., 216.

18. Ibid., 227.

19. Ibid., 215, my emphasis.

20. Ibid., 210.

21. Ibid., 221.

22. Ibid.

23. Ibid.

24. Ibid., 224.

25. Ibid., 222.

26. Ibid., 238.

27. Flathman, *Philosophy and Politics of Freedom,* 100.

28. Ibid.

29. Ibid., 102.

30. Ibid., 43.

31. Ibid., 206.

32. Ibid., 93. (my emphasis)

33. Ibid., 95.

34. Ibid., 206.

35. Taylor, "What's Wrong with Negative Liberty?" 215.

36. Flathman, *Philosophy and Politics of Freedom,* 178.

37. Joseph Raz, *The Morality of Freedom* (Clarendon: Oxford University Press, 1986), 369.

38. Ibid., 373.

39. Feinberg, "Idea of a Free Man," 6.

40. Gerald C. McCallum Jr., "Negative and Positive Freedom," in *Liberty,* ed. David Miller (Oxford: Oxford University Press, 1991).

41. Feinberg, "Idea of a Free Man," 5.

42. McCallum, "Negative and Positive Freedom," 102.

43. Ibid.

44. Hobbes, *Leviathan* (1968), 261.

45. Feinberg, "Idea of a Free Man," 5.

46. Ibid., 6.

47. Ibid., 9.

48. G. A. Cohen, "Capitalism, Freedom, and the Proletariat," in *Liberty,* ed. David Miller (Oxford: Oxford University Press, 1991), 163–164.

49. Raz, *Morality of Freedom,* 373.

50. Hobbes, *Leviathan* (1968), 261.

Chapter 3

1. Pennock, "Hobbes's Confusing 'Clarity' " Barry, "Warrender and His Critics."

2. Watkins, *Hobbes's System of Ideas,* 128.

3. Alan Ryan, "Hobbes and Individualism," in *Perspectives on Thomas Hobbes,* eds. G. A. J. Rogers and Alan Ryan (Oxford: Clarendon Press, 1988), 199.

4. Quentin Skinner, "The Paradoxes of Political Liberty," in *Liberty,* ed. David Miller (Oxford: Oxford University Press, 1991), 14. He makes a similar point in his book *Liberty before Liberalism* (Cambridge: Cambridge University Press, 1998).

5. Thomas Hobbes, *English Works* Vol. 4, ed. Sir William Molesworth (London: John Bohn, 1966), 240.

6. Ross et al., *Thomas Hobbes in His Time;* Maurice Cranston and Richard S. Peters, eds., *Hobbes and Rousseau* (New York: Anchor, 1972).

7. Hobbes, *Leviathan* (1968), 261.

8. Ibid., 38.

9. Ibid., 262.

10. Hobbes, *English Works* Vol. 5, 79.

11. Ibid., 82.

12. Hobbes, *Leviathan* (1968), 118.

13. Hobbes, *English Works* Vol. 4, 272.

14. Ibid., 246–247.

15. Hobbes, *Leviathan* (1968), 262.

16. Ibid., 261–262.

17. Ibid., 262.

18. Ibid.

19. Ibid., 150.

20. Ibid., 263.

21. Ibid., 128.

22. Ibid., 127.

23. Hobbes, *English Works* Vol. 5, 34.

24. Hobbes, *Leviathan* (1968), 262.

25. Ibid., 263.

26. Ibid., 198.

27. Ibid., 252.

28. Ibid., 263.

29. Hobbes, *De Cive* (London: Appleton-Century-Crofts, 1949), 110.

30. Ibid.

31. Ibid., 109

32. Hobbes, *Leviathan* (1968), 348.

33. Ibid., 317.

34. Ibid., 264.

35. Ibid., 314, my emphasis.

36. Ibid., 192, my emphasis.

37. Ibid., 196.

38. Hobbes, *English Works* Vol. 4, 261–262.

39. Ibid., 263.

40. Hobbes, *Leviathan* (1968), 262, my emphasis.

41. Ibid., 264.

42. Hobbes, *Behemoth or the Long Parliament,* ed. Ferdinand Tonnies, introduction by Stephen Holmes (Chicago: University of Chicago Press, 1990), 157.

43. Hobbes, *Leviathan* (1968), 270.

44. Ibid., 271.

45. Ibid., 269.

46. Ibid., 198, my emphasis.

47. Ibid., 162.

48. Ibid., 189.

49. Ibid., 192.

50. Ibid., 262.

51. Ibid., 198.

52. Ibid.

53. Ibid., 190.

54. Ibid., 189.

55. Ibid., 84.

56. Wernham, "Liberty and Obligation in Hobbes."

57. Pennock, "Hobbes's Confusing 'Clarity.' "

58. Hobbes, *Leviathan* (1968), 190.

59. Ibid.

60. Barry, "Warrender and His Critics."

61. Pennock, "Hobbes's Confusing 'Clarity,' " 105.

62. Hobbes, *Leviathan* (1968), 192.

63. Ibid., 268.

64. Ibid., 271.

65. Ibid., 269.

66. Ibid., 190.

67. Ibid., 191.

68. Ibid., 113.

69. Ibid., 364.

70. Ibid., 278.

71. Ibid., 349.

72. Ibid., 245.

73. Ibid., 118.

74. Ibid., 331, my emphasis.

75. Ibid., 163, my emphasis.

76. Ibid., 271.

77. Ibid., 196.

Chapter 4

1. Flathman, *Philosophy and Politics of Freedom,* 322.

2. Ibid.

3. Jurgen Habermas, *The Theory of Communicative Action: Volume One* (Boston: Beacon, 1984); Habermas, *Justification and Application* (Cambridge: Massachusetts Institute of Technology Press, 1993).

4. Donald P. Green and Ian Shapiro, *Pathologies of Rational Choice Theory: A Critique of Applications in Political Science* (New Haven, CT: Yale University Press, 1994).

5. Morris P. Fiorina, "Rational Choice, Empirical Contributions, and the Scientific Enterprise," *Critical Review* 9, nos. 1–2 (1995): 87.

6. Green and Shapiro, *Pathologies of Rational Choice Theory,* 13.

7. Kenneth J. Arrow, *Social Values and Individual Values* (New York: Wiley, 1951); Mancur Olson Jr., *The Logic of Collective Action* (Cambridge: Harvard University Press, 1965); David Gauthier, *Morals by Agreement* (Oxford: Oxford University Press, 1986); William Riker, *Liberalism Against Populism* (Prospect Heights, Il: Waveland, 1982).

8. Gauthier, *Morals by Agreement,* 27.

9. Jeffrey Friedman, "Economic Approaches to Politics." *Critical Review* 9, nos. 1–2 (1995): 2.

10. Dennis Chong, "Rational Choice Theory's Mysterious Rivals." *Critical Review* 9, nos. 1–2 (1995): 39.

11. Ibid., 40.

12. Green and Shapiro, *Pathologies of Rational Choice Theory,* 14–15.

13. Gauthier, *Morals by Agreement,* 22–23.

14. Jon Elster, *Rational Choice* (New York: New York University Press, 1986), 16.

15. Chong, "Rational Choice Theory's Mysterious Rivals," 39.

16. James Buchanan and Gordon Tullock, *The Calculus of Consent* (Ann Arbor: University of Michigan Press, 1962), 20.

17. Green and Shapiro, *Pathologies of Rational Choice Theory,* 3.

18. Gauthier, *Morals by Agreement,* 159.

19. Stanley I. Benn, *A Theory of Freedom* (Cambridge: Cambridge University Press, 1988), 173.

20. Leo Strauss, *The Political Philosophy of Hobbes* (Chicago: University of Chicago Press, 1952); Michael Oakeshott, *Hobbes on Civil Association* (Oxford: Blackwell, 1975); A. P. Martinich, *The Two Gods of Leviathan: Thomas Hobbes on Religion and Politics* (Cambridge: Cambridge University Press, 1992).

21. Flathman, *Philosophy and Politics of Freedom,* 115.

22. Gregory S. Kavka, *Hobbesian Moral and Political Theory* (Princeton: Princeton University Press, 1986), 12.

23. Ibid.

24. Ibid., 14.

25. Gary Herbert, *Thomas Hobbes: The Unity of Scientific and Moral Wisdom* (Vancouver: University of British Columbia Press, 1989), 26.

26. Hobbes, *Leviathan* (1968), 139.

27. Herbert, *Thomas Hobbes;* 65.

28. Hobbes, *Leviathan* (1968), 81.

29. Ibid., 183.

30. Benn, *Theory of Freedom,* 154.

31. Hobbes, *Leviathan* (1968), 134.

32. Ibid., 135, my emphasis.

33. Ibid., 140.

34. Ibid., 140–141.

35. Ibid., 134–135.

36. Ibid., 135.

37. Ibid.

38. Ibid., 137.

39. Ibid., 136.

40. Ibid., 95.

41. Ibid.

42. Ibid., my emphasis.

43. Ibid., 96.

44. Ibid.

45. Ibid.

46. Hobbes, *English Works* Vol. 5, 186.

47. Ibid., 186–187.

48. Ibid., *Leviathan* (1968), 95.

49. Ibid., 122.

50. Ibid., 97.

51. Ibid., 136.

52. Ibid., 139.

53. Ibid., 139–140.

54. Ibid., 139.

55. Ibid., 140–141, my emphasis.

56. Ibid., 146.

57. Ibid., 140.

58. Ibid.

59. Ibid., 142, my emphasis.

60. Ibid., 82–83.

61. Ibid., 342.

62. Ibid., 138–139.

63. Ibid., 139.

64. Ibid., 142.

65. Ibid., 155

66. Ibid., 97.

67. Ibid., 96, my emphasis.

68. Ibid., 130.

69. Ibid., 103.

70. Hobbes, *English Works* Vol. 5, 357.

71. Ibid., 80.

72. Ibid., 325.

73. Flathman, *Philosophy and Politics of Freedom,* 298.

74. Hobbes, *Leviathan* (1968), 160–161, my emphasis.

75. Ibid., 169, my emphasis.

76. Ibid., 130.

77. Ibid., 137–138, my emphasis.

78. Ibid., 129.

79. Ibid., 124.

80. Ibid., 131.

81. Ibid., 164–165.

82. Ibid., 96.

83. Ibid., 98.

84. Ibid., 129, my emphasis.

85. Ibid., 135.

86. Ibid., 136.

87. Ibid., 122, my emphasis.

88. Ibid., 116.

89. Flathman, *Philosophy and Politics of Freedom*, 218.

90. Benn, *Theory of Freedom*, 163–164.

Chapter 5

1. John Finnis, *Natural Law and Natural Rights* (Oxford: Clarendon Press, 1980), 104.

2. Ibid.

3. Ibid.

4. Flathman, *Philosophy and Politics of Freedom*, 322.

5. Finnis, *Natural Law and Natural Rights*, 176.

6. John Rawls, *A Theory of Justice* (Cambridge: Harvard University Press, 1971), 418.

7. Flathman, *Philosophy and Politics of Freedom*, 206.

8. Benn, *Theory of Freedom*, 159.

9. Habermas, *Justification and Application*, 9–10.

10. Gauthier, *Morals by Agreement*, 6.

11. Ibid., 7.

12. Habermas, *Theory of Communicative Action: Volume One*, 17.

13. Simone Chambers, *Reasonable Democracy* (Ithaca: Cornell University Press, 1996), 90.

14. Ibid., 24.

15. Ibid., 25.

16. Gauthier, *The Logic of Leviathan* (Oxford: Clarendon Press, 1969), 8.

17. Hobbes, *Leviathan* (1968), 214.

18. Ibid., 215–216.

19. Ibid., 115.

20. Ibid., 112.

21. Ibid., 112.

22. Ibid., 717.

23. Ibid., 124.

24. Hobbes, *English Works* Vol. 6, 14.

25. Hobbes, *Leviathan* (1968), 717.

26. Hobbes, *English Works* Vol. 6, 122.

27. Hobbes, *Leviathan* (1968), 340.

28. Ibid., 337–338.

29. Jean Hampton, *Hobbes and the Social Contract Tradition* (Cambridge: Cambridge University Press, 1986), 35.

30. Hobbes, *Leviathan* (1968), 718.

31. Ibid., 377.

32. Ibid., 223.

33. Ibid., 215.

34. Ibid., 210.

35. Alan Ryan, "Hobbes, Toleration, and the Inner Life," in *The Nature of Political Theory*, eds. David Miller and Larry Seidentop (Oxford: Clarendon Press, 1983), 217.

36. Rawls, *Theory of Justice*, 240.

37. Hobbes, *De Cive*, 114.

38. Ibid., 162.

39. Hobbes, *Leviathan* (1968), 186.

40. Ibid., 187.

41. Theodore Waldman, "Hobbes on the Generation of a Public Person," in *Thomas Hobbes in His Time*, eds. Ralph Ross, Herbert W. Schneider, and Theodore Waldman (Minneapolis: University of Minnesota Press, 1974), 74.

42. Taylor, *Philosophy and the Human Sciences*, 1985.

43. Herbert, *Thomas Hobbes;* 85.

44. Flathman, *Philosophy and Politics of Freedom*, 322.

Chapter 6

1. Patrick Riley, *Will and Political Legitimacy: A Critical Exposition of Social Contract Theory in Hobbes, Locke, Rousseau, Kant and Hegel* (Cambridge: Harvard University Press, 1982).

2. A. E. Taylor, "The Ethical Doctrine of Hobbes," in *Hobbes Studies,* ed. Brown; Howard Warrender, *The Political Philosophy of Hobbes: His Theory of Obligation* (Oxford: Clarendon Press, 1957).

3. Gauthier, *Logic of Leviathan;* Thomas Nagel, "Hobbes's Concept of Obligation," *Philosophical Review* 68 (1959): 68–83; Hampton, *Hobbes and the Social Contract Tradition.*

4. Dana Chabot, "Thomas Hobbes: Skeptical Moralist," *American Political Science Review* 69, no. 2 (1995): 401.

5. Nagel, "Hobbes's Concept of Obligation."

6. Kavka, *Hobbesian Moral and Political Theory,* 42.

7. Ibid.

8. Ibid.

9. Richard S. Peters, *Hobbes* (Harmondsworth, Penguin, 1956); Nagel, "Hobbes's Concept of Obligation"; J. W. N. Watkins, "Philosophy and Politics in Hobbes," in *Hobbes Studies,* ed. Brown; M. M. Goldsmith, *Hobbes's Science of Politics* (New York: Columbia University Press, 1966).

10. Hampton, *Hobbes and the Social Contract Tradition,* 56.

11. Gauthier, *Logic of Leviathan,* 7.

12. Kavka, *Hobbesian Moral and Political Theory,* 20.

13. Riley, *Will and Political Legitimacy,* 23.

14. Ibid., 33.

15. Ibid., 49.

16. Ibid.

17. Hobbes, *Leviathan* (1968), 120.

18. Ibid., 192.

19. Ibid., 209.

20. Ibid., 121.

21. Ibid., 120, my emphasis.

22. Ibid., 123.

23. Ibid., 303.

24. Oakeshott, *Hobbes on Civil Association,* 75.

25. Flathman, *Thomas Hobbes: Skepticism, Individuality and Chastened Politics,* (Newbury Park: Sage, 1993), 76.

26. Hobbes, *Leviathan* (1968), 216, first italics my emphasis.

27. Bernhard Gert, "Hobbes, Mechanism and Egoism," *Philosophical Quarterly* 15 (1965): 341–349; F. S. McNeilly, *The Anatomy of Leviathan* (New York: St. Martin's, 1968).

28. Nagel, "Hobbes's Concept of Obligation," 69.

29. Ibid.

30. Hobbes, *Leviathan* (1968), 218.

31. Riley, *Will and Political Legitimacy,* 43.

32. Hobbes, *Behemoth,* 44.

33. Hampton, *Hobbes and the Social Contract Tradition,* 56.

34. Hobbes, *Leviathan* (1968), 203.

35. Ibid., 194–195.

36. Ibid., 196.

37. Ibid., 198.

38. Ibid.

39. Ibid., 191.

40. Ibid., 196.

41. Ibid., 138.

42. Hobbes, *Behemoth,* 44.

43. Hobbes, *Leviathan* (1968), 93–94, first italics my emphasis.

44. Hobbes, *Behemoth,* 38.

45. Ibid., 159.

46. Ibid., 63.

47. Ibid., 39.

48. Barry, "Warrender and His Critics."

49. Hobbes, *De Cive,* 157.

50. Hobbes, *Leviathan* (1968), 340.

51. Richard Tuck, "Hobbes and Locke on Toleration," in *Thomas Hobbes and Political Theory,* ed. Mary Dietz (Lawrence: University of Kansas Press, 1990), 64.

52. Hobbes, *Leviathan* (1968), 215.

53. Watkins, "Philosophy and Politics in Hobbes," 173–174.

54. Hobbes, *English Works* Vol. 4, 255–256.

55. Hobbes, *English Works* Vol. 5, 191.

56. Ibid., my emphasis.

57. David Boonin-Vail, *Thomas Hobbes and the Science of Moral Virtue* (Cambridge: Cambridge University Press, 1994).

58. Hobbes, *Leviathan* (1968), 190.

59. Ibid., 216, my emphasis.

60. Ibid.

61. Ibid., 215.

62. Ibid., 109.

63. Ibid., 165–166.

64. Ibid., 337.

65. Ibid.

66. Ibid., 336.

67. Chabot, "Thomas Hobbes," 404.

68. Hobbes, *Leviathan* (1968), 385.

69. Ibid., 214.

70. Hobbes, *English Works* Vol. 5, 192.

71. Ibid., 193.

72. Ibid., 194.

73. Ibid., 359.

74. Ibid., 193.

75. Bentham, Jeremy, *John Stuart Mill and Jeremy Bentham: Utilitarianism and other Essays,* ed., Alan Ryan, (London: Penguin, 1987), 65.

76. Hobbes, *De Cive,* 58.

77. Ibid., 45, my emphasis.

78. Oakeshott, *Hobbes on Civil Association,* 147–148.

79. Kavka, *Hobbesian Moral and Political Theory,* 14.

80. Oakeshott, *Hobbes on Civil Association,* 148.

Chapter 7

1. Hobbes, *Leviathan* (1968), 160.

2. Ibid., 186.

3. Ibid., 214.

4. John Stuart Mill, *On Liberty* (New York: Penguin, 1974), 63–64.

5. Ibid., 63.

6. Ryan, "Hobbes, Toleration and the Inner Life;" Flathman, *Philosophy and Politics of Freedom.*

7. Hobbes, *Leviathan* (1968), 190.

8. Ibid.

9. Ibid., 191.

10. Ibid., 201.

11. Ibid., 202, my emphasis.

12. Ibid., 209.

13. Ibid.

14. Hobbes, *De Cive,* 135.

15. Hobbes, *Leviathan* (1968), 296.

16. Ibid.

17. Ibid., 374.

18. Macpherson, C. B. *The Political Theory of Possessive Individualism:* Hobbes to Locke. (Oxford: Clarendon Press, 1962).

19. Hobbes, *Leviathan* (1968), 213.

20. Hobbes, *Behemoth,* 4, my emphasis.

21. Hobbes, *Leviathan,* 210.

22. Ibid., 211.

23. Ibid., 132.

24. Ibid., 211.

25. Ibid.

26. Ibid., 385.

27. Hobbes, *English Works* Vol. 6, 4.

28. Ibid., 26.

29. Hobbes, *Behemoth,* 37.

30. Hobbes, *Leviathan* (1968), 211.

31. Ibid., 212.

32. Ibid., 315.

33. Ibid., 212.

34. Ibid., 214.

35. Nancy Rosenblum, ed., *Liberalism and the Moral Life* (Cambridge: Harvard University Press, 1989).

36. Judith Shklar, "The Liberalism of Fear," in *Liberalism and the Moral Life,* ed. Rosenblum, 24.

37. Susan Moller Okin, "Humanist Liberalism," in *Liberalism and the Moral Life,* ed. Rosenblum, 257.

38. Benjamin Barber, "Liberal Democracy and the Costs of Consent," in *Liberalism and the Moral Life,* ed. Rosenblum, 261.

39. Gauthier, "Public Reason," *Social Philosophy and Policy* 12 (1995): 19–42; Michael Ridge, "Hobbesian Public Reason," *Ethics* 108 (1998): 538–568.

40. Ridge, "Hobbesian Public Reason," 538.

41. Hobbes, *Leviathan* (1968), 75.

42. Ibid., 376.

43. Ibid., 209.

44. Ibid., 264.

45. Ibid., 269.

46. Ibid., 138.

47. Ibid., 385.

48. Ibid., 388.

49. Hobbes, *English Works* Vol. 6, 34.

50. Hobbes, *Leviathan* (1968), 81.

51. Ibid., 238.

52. Hobbes, *Behemoth,* 68.

53. Ibid., 180.

54. Hobbes, *Leviathan* (1968), 241.

55. Ibid.

56. Deborah Baumgold, *Hobbes's Political Theory* (Cambridge: Cambridge University Press, 1988), 106.

57. Ibid., 81.

58. Hobbes, *Leviathan* (1968), 232.

59. Hobbes, *Leviathan,* ed. Edwin Curley (Indianapolis: Hackett, 1994), 113.

60. Hobbes, *Leviathan* (1968), 199.

61. Ibid., 223.

62. Ibid., 188.

63. Baumgold, *Hobbes's Political Theory,* 60.

64. Ibid., 101.

65. Hobbes, *Leviathan* (1968), 81.

66. Ibid., 388.

67. Ibid.

68. Ibid., 333.

69. Hobbes, *English Works* Vol. 6, 13.

70. Ibid., 14.

71. Ibid., 16.

72. Ibid., 23.

73. Hobbes, *English Works* Vol. 5, 178.

74. Hobbes, *English Works* Vol. 6, 29.

75. Hobbes, *Leviathan* (1968), 215.

76. Ibid., 314.

77. Ibid.

78. Mary Dietz, ed., *Thomas Hobbes and Political Theory* (Lawrence: University of Kansas Press, 1990), 95.

79. Hobbes, *Leviathan* (1968), 312.

80. Ibid., 389.

81. Hobbes, *Behemoth,* 45.

82. Hobbes, *Leviathan* (1968), 338.

83. Ibid., 358.

84. Hobbes, *English Works* Vol. 5, 177.

85. Hobbes, *Leviathan* (1968), 359.

86. Ibid., 360.

87. Ibid., 390.

88. Ibid.

89. Hobbes, *Behemoth,* 51.

90. Hobbes, *Leviathan* (1968), 376.

91. Ibid., 268.

92. Ibid., 142.

93. Ibid., 388.

94. Ibid.

95. Hobbes, *De Cive,* 170.

96. Stephen Holmes, "Political Psychology in Hobbes's Behemoth," in *Thomas Hobbes and Political Theory,* ed. Dietz, 133.

97. Mark Warren, "Democratic Theory and Self-Transformation," *American Political Science Review* 86 (1992): 9–10.

98. Flathman, *Thomas Hobbes.*

99. Hobbes, *Leviathan* (1968), 140–141.

100. Hobbes, *De Cive,* 120.

101. Hobbes, *Leviathan* (1968), 242.

102. Ibid., 271.

103. Ibid., 292.

104. Flathman, *Thomas Hobbes;* 142.

105. Hobbes, *Leviathan* (1968), 239.

106. Ibid., 241.

107. Hobbes, *Behemoth*, 156.

108. Hobbes, *English Works* Vol. 6, 122.

109. Hobbes, *Leviathan* (1968), 217.

110. Ibid., 220–221.

111. Ibid., 286.

112. J. J. Rousseau, *On the Social Contract* in *The Basic Political Writings,* ed. Peter Gay (Indianapolis: Hackett, 1987), 156.

113. Hobbes, *Leviathan* (1968), 246–247.

114. Ibid., 246.

115. Hobbes, *English Works* Vol. 6, 152.

116. Hobbes, *Leviathan* (1968), 233.

117. William E. Connolly, *Political Theory and Modernity* (Oxford: Basil Blackwell, 1988), 28.

118. Ibid., 34.

119. Ibid., 28.

120. Ibid., 29.

121. Holmes, "Political Psychology in Hobbes's Behemoth," 140.

122. Hobbes, *Behemoth,* 110.

123. Hobbes, *Leviathan* (1968), 138.

124. Ryan, "Hobbes, Toleration and the Inner Life," 217.

125. Hobbes, *Leviathan* (1968), 377.

126. Ibid., 383.

127. Ibid.

128. Ibid., 376.

129. Ibid., 377.

130. Amy Guttman, "Undemocratic Education," in *Liberalism and the Moral Life,* ed. Rosenblum, 82.

131. Ibid., 74.

132. Ibid.

133. William Galston, "Civic Education in the Liberal State," in *Liberalism and the Moral Life,* ed. Rosenblum, 90.

134. Ibid., 91.

135. Rosenblum, ed., *Liberalism and the Moral Life,* 4.

136. Hobbes, *Behemoth,* 58.

137. Flathman, *Thomas Hobbes,* 149.

138. Hobbes, *Leviathan* (1968), 233.

139. Connolly, *Political Theory and Modernity,* 33.

140. Ibid., 34.

141. Hobbes, *Leviathan* (1968), 233.

142. Ibid., 369–370.

143. Hobbes, *Behemoth,* 62.

144. Hobbes, *Leviathan* (1968), 285.

145. Ibid., 287–288

146. Ibid., 288.

147. S. A. Lloyd, *Ideas as Interests in Hobbes's Leviathan: The Power of Mind over Matter* (Cambridge: Cambridge University Press, 1992).

148. Hobbes, *Leviathan* (1968), 233.

149. Ryan, "Hobbes, Toleration and the Inner Life," 207.

150. Hobbes, *Leviathan* (1968), 395.

151. Hobbes, *Behemoth,* 63.

152. Ryan, "Hobbes, Toleration and the Inner Life," 204.

153. Ibid., 206.

154. Timothy Fuller, "The Idea of Christianity in Hobbes's *Leviathan,*" *Jewish Political Studies Review* 4, no. 2 (1992): 139.

155. Ibid., 158.

156. David Johnson, *The Rhetoric of Leviathan* (Princeton: Princeton University Press, 1986), 177.

157. Hobbes, *Leviathan* (1968), 264.

158. Connolly, *Political Theory and Modernity,* 27.

159. Ibid., 31.

160. Ibid.

161. Ibid., 32.

162. Ibid., 27.

163. Ibid., 28.

164. Ibid., 29.

165. Carole Pateman, *The Sexual Contract* (Cambridge: Polity Press, 1988), 219.

166. Ibid., 6.

167. Preston King, *The Ideology of Order* (London: Allen and Unwin, 1974); Gabriella Slomp, "Hobbes and the Equality of Women," *Political Studies* 42 (1994): 441–452.

168. Hobbes, *Leviathan* (1968), 220.

169. Shklar, "Liberalism of Fear," 22.

170. Ibid., 21.

171. Ibid., 29.

Chapter 8

1. Hobbes, *Leviathan* (1968), 183.

2. Ibid.

3. Ibid., 184.

4. Ibid., 211.

5. Michel Foucault, *Power/Knowledge: Selected Interviews and other Writings 1972–1977,* ed. Colin Gordon (Harvester Wheatsheaf, 1980), 96–98.

6. Hobbes, *Leviathan* (1968), 150.

7. Ibid.

8. Ibid., 161.

9. Ibid.

Bibliography

Arrow, Kenneth, J. *Social Values and Individual Values*. New York: Wiley, 1951.

Barber, Benjamin. "Liberal Democracy and the Costs of Consent." In *Liberalism and the Moral Life*, ed. Nancy Rosenblum. Cambridge: Harvard University Press, 1989.

Barry, Brian. "Warrender and His Critics." In *Hobbes and Rousseau: A Collection of Critical Essays*, eds. Maurice Cranston and Richard S. Peters. New York: Anchor, 1972.

Baumgold, Deborah. *Hobbes's Political Theory*. Cambridge: Cambridge University Press, 1988.

Benn, Stanley I. *A Theory of Freedom*. Cambridge: Cambridge University Press, 1988.

Berlin, Isaiah. *Four Essays on Liberty*. Oxford: Oxford University Press, 1969.

Bobbio, Norberto. *Thomas Hobbes and the Natural Law Tradition*. Chicago: University of Chicago Press, 1993.

Boonin-Vail, David. *Thomas Hobbes and the Science of Moral Virtue*. Cambridge: Cambridge University Press, 1994.

Brown, Keith. "Hobbes's Grounds for Belief in a Deity." *Philosophy* 37 (1962): 344–366.

———, ed. *Hobbes Studies*. Oxford: Blackwell, 1965.

Buchanan, James and Gordon Tullock. *The Calculus of Consent*. Ann Arbor: University of Michigan Press, 1962.

241

Chabot, Dana. "Thomas Hobbes: Skeptical Moralist." *American Political Science Review* 69, no. 2 (1995): 401–410.

Chambers, Simone. *Reasonable Democracy*. Ithaca: Cornell University Press, 1996.

Chong, Dennis. "Rational Choice Theory's Mysterious Rivals." *Critical Review* 9, nos. 1–2 (1995): 37–57.

Cohen, G. A. "Capitalism, Freedom, and the Proletariat." In *Liberty*, ed. David Miller. Oxford: Oxford University Press, 1991.

Connolly, William E. *Political Theory and Modernity*. Oxford: Basil Blackwell, 1988.

Cranston, Maurice and Richard S. Peters, eds. *Hobbes and Rousseau*. New York: Anchor, 1972.

Dietz, Mary, ed. *Thomas Hobbes and Political Theory*. Lawrence: University of Kansas Press, 1990.

Elster, Jon. *Rational Choice*. New York: New York University Press, 1986.

Ewin, R. E. *Virtues and Rights: The Moral Philosophy of Thomas Hobbes*. Boulder: Westview Press, 1991.

Feinberg, Joel. "The Idea of a Free Man." In *Rights, Justice and the Bounds of Liberty*. Princeton: Princeton University Press, 1980.

Finnis, John. *Natural Law and Natural Rights*. Oxford: Clarendon Press, 1980.

Fiorina, Morris P. "Rational Choice, Empirical Contributions, and the Scientific Enterprise." *Critical Review* 9, nos.1–2 (1995): 85–94.

Flathman, Richard. *The Philosophy and Politics of Freedom*. Chicago: University of Chicago Press, 1987.

———. *Thomas Hobbes: Skepticism, Individuality and Chastened Politics*. Newbury Park: Sage, 1993.

Foucault, Michel. *Power/Knowledge: Selected Interviews and other Writings 1972–1977*, ed. Colin Gordon. Harvester Wheatsheaf, 1980.

Friedman, Jeffrey. "Economic Approaches to Politics." *Critical Review* 9, nos. 1–2 (1995): 1–24.

Fuller, Timothy. "The Idea of Christianity in Hobbes's *Leviathan.*" *Jewish Political Studies Review* 4, no. 2 (1992): 139–178.

Galston, William. "Civic Education in the Liberal State." In *Liberalism and the Moral Life,* ed. Nancy Rosenblum. Cambridge: Harvard University Press, 1989.

———. *The Logic of Leviathan.* Oxford: Clarendon Press, 1969.

———. *Morals by Agreement.* Oxford: Oxford University Press, 1986.

———. "Public Reason." *Social Philosophy and Policy* 12 (1995): 19–42.

Gert, Bernhard. "Hobbes, Mechanism and Egoism." *Philosophical Quarterly* 15 (1965): 341–349.

Goldsmith, M. M. *Hobbes's Science of Politics.* New York: Columbia University Press, 1966.

Green, P. Donald and Ian Shapiro. *Pathologies of Rational Choice Theory: A Critique of Applications in Political Science.* New Haven, CT: Yale University Press, 1994.

Gutmann, Amy. "Undemocratic Education." In *Liberalism and the Moral Life,* ed. Nancy Rosenblum. Cambridge: Harvard University Press, 1989.

Habermas, Jurgen. *The Theory of Communicative Action: Volume One.* Boston: Beacon, 1984.

———. *The Theory of Communicative Action: Volume Two.* Boston: Beacon, 1987.

———. *Moral Consciousness and Communicative Action.* Cambridge: Polity Press, 1990.

———. *Justification and Application.* Cambridge: Massachusetts Institute of Technology Press, 1993.

Hampton, Jean. *Hobbes and the Social Contract Tradition.* Cambridge: Cambridge University Press, 1986.

Hardin, Russell. 'Hobbesian Political Order.' *Political Theory,* 19, no. 2 (1991): 156–180.

Hayek, F. A. *The Constitution of Liberty*. London: Routledge and Kegan Paul, 1960.

Herbert, Gary. *Thomas Hobbes: The Unity of Scientific and Moral Wisdom*. Vancouver: University of British Columbia Press, 1989.

Hobbes, Thomas. *De Cive*. London: Appleton-Century-Crofts, 1949.

———. *English Works* Vols. 1–10, ed. Sir William Molesworth. London: John Bohn, 1966.

———. *Leviathan*, ed. C. B. Macpherson. London: Penguin Books, 1968.

———. *Leviathan*, ed. Edwin Curley. Hackett: Indianapolis, 1994.

———. *Man and Citizen,* ed. Bernard Gert. New York: Doubleday, 1972.

———. *Behemoth or the Long Parliament*, ed. Ferdinand Tonnies, introduction by Stephen Holmes. Chicago: University of Chicago Press, 1990.

———. *The Elements of Law, Natural and Politic,* ed. J. C. A. Gaskin. New York: Oxford University Press, 1994.

Holmes, Stephen. "Political Psychology in Hobbes's Behemoth." In *Thomas Hobbes and Political Theory,* ed. M. G. Dietz. Lawrence: University of Kansas Press, 1990.

Johnson, David. *The Rhetoric of Leviathan*. Princeton: Princeton University Press, 1986.

Kavka, Gregory S. *Hobbesian Moral and Political Theory*. Princeton: Princeton University Press, 1986.

King, Preston. *The Ideology of Order*. London: Allen and Unwin, 1974.

Kraynak, Robert P. *History and Modernity in the Thought of Thomas Hobbes*. Ithaca: Cornell University Press, 1990.

Lloyd, S. A. *Ideas as Interests in Hobbes's Leviathan: The Power of Mind over Matter.* Cambridge: Cambridge University Press, 1992.

Macpherson, C. B. *The Political Theory of Possessive Individualism: Hobbes to Locke.* Oxford: Clarendon Press, 1962.

Martinich, A. P. *The Two Gods of Leviathan: Thomas Hobbes on Religion and Politics.* Cambridge: Cambridge University Press, 1992.

McCallum Jr., Gerald C. "Negative and Positive Freedom." In *Liberty*, ed. David Miller. Oxford: Oxford University Press, 1991.

McNeilly, F. S. *The Anatomy of Leviathan.* New York: St. Martin's, 1968.

Mill, John Stuart. *On Liberty.* New York: Penguin, 1974.

Mill, John Stuart and Jeremy Bentham. *Utilitarianism & Other Essays,* ed. Alan Ryan. London: Penquin Books, 1987.

Mintz, Samuel. *The Hunting of Leviathan.* Cambridge: Cambridge University Press, 1962.

Mitchell, Joshua. "Hobbes and the Equality of All Under the One." *Political Theory* 21, no. 1 (1993): 78–100.

Nagel, Thomas. "Hobbes's Concept of Obligation." *Philosophical Review* 68 (1959): 68–83.

Oakeshott, Michael. *Hobbes on Civil Association.* Oxford: Blackwell, 1975.

Okin, Susan Moller. "Humanist Liberalism." In *Liberalism and the Moral Life,* ed. Nancy Rosenblum. Cambridge: Harvard University Press, 1989.

Olson, Mancur Jr. *The Logic of Collective Action.* Cambridge: Harvard University Press, 1965.

Pateman, Carole. *The Sexual Contract.* Cambridge: Polity Press, 1988.

Pennock, J. R. "Hobbes's Confusing 'Clarity'—The Case of 'Liberty.'" In *Hobbes Studies,* ed. Keith Brown. Cambridge: Harvard University Press, 1965.

Peters, Richard S. *Hobbes.* Harmondsworth: Penguin, 1956.

Plamenatz, John. "Mr. Warrender's Hobbes." In *Hobbes Studies,* ed. Keith Brown. Oxford: Blackwell, 1985.

Rawls, John. *A Theory of Justice.* Cambridge: Harvard University Press, 1971.

Raz, Joseph. *The Morality of Freedom*. Clarendon: Oxford University Press, 1986.

Ridge, Michael. "Hobbesian Public Reason." *Ethics* 108 (1998): 538–568.

Riker, William. *Liberalism Against Populism*. Prospect Heights, Il: Waveland, 1982.

Riley, Patrick. *Will and Political Legitimacy: A Critical Exposition of Social Contract Theory in Hobbes, Locke, Rousseau, Kant and Hegel*. Cambridge: Harvard University Press, 1982.

Rosenblum, Nancy. *Liberalism and the Moral Life*. Cambridge: Harvard University Press, 1989.

Ross, Ralph, Herbert Schneider, and Theodore Waldman. *Thomas Hobbes in His Time*. Minneapolis: University of Minnesota Press, 1974.

Rousseau, J. J. *On the Social Contract* in *The Basic Political Writings*, ed. Peter Gay. Indiana: Hackett, 1987.

Ryan, Alan. "Hobbes, Toleration, and the Inner Life." In *The Nature of Political Theory*, eds. David Miller and Larry Seidentop. Oxford: Clarendon Press, 1983.

———. "Hobbes and Individualism." In *Perspectives on Thomas Hobbes*, eds. G. A. J. Rogers and Alan Ryan. Oxford: Clarendon Press, 1988.

Shklar, Judith. "The Liberalism of Fear." In *Liberalism and the Moral Life*, ed. Nancy Rosenblum. Cambridge: Harvard University Press, 1989.

Skinner, Quentin. "The Paradoxes of Political Liberty." In *Liberty*, ed. David Miller. Oxford: Oxford University Press, 1991.

———. *Reason and Rhetoric in the Philosophy of Hobbes*. Cambridge: Cambridge University Press, 1996.

———. *Liberty before Liberalism*. Cambridge: Cambridge University Press, 1998.

Slomp, Gabriella. "Hobbes and the Equality of Women." *Political Studies* 42 (1994): 441–452.

Sorell, Tom. *Hobbes*. London: Routledge and Kegan Paul, 1986.

Steiner, Hillel "Individual Liberty." *Proceedings of the Aristotelian Society,* 75 (1974–1975): 33–50.

Strauss, Leo. *The Political Philosophy of Hobbes.* Chicago: University of Chicago Press, 1952.

Taylor, A. E. "The Ethical Doctrine of Hobbes." In *Hobbes Studies,* ed. Keith Brown. Oxford: Blackwell, 1965.

Taylor, Charles. *Human Agency and Language.* Cambridge: Cambridge University Press, 1985.

———. *Philosophy and the Human Sciences.* Cambridge: Cambridge University Press, 1985.

———. *Sources of the Self: The Making of the Modern Identity.* Cambridge: Harvard University Press, 1989.

Tuck, Richard. *Hobbes.* Oxford: Oxford University Press, 1989.

———. "Hobbes and Locke on Toleration." In *Thomas Hobbes and Political Theory,* ed. Mary Dietz. Lawrence: University of Kansas Press, 1990.

Waldman, Theodore. "Hobbes on the Generation of a Public Person." In *Thomas Hobbes in His Time,* eds. Ralph Ross, Herbert W. Schneider and Theodore Waldman. Minneapolis: University of Minnesota Press, 1974.

Warren, Mark. "Democratic Theory and Self-Transformation." *American Political Science Review* 86 (1992): 8–23.

Warrender, Howard. *The Political Philosophy of Hobbes: His Theory of Obligation.* Oxford: Clarendon Press, 1957.

Watkins, J. W. N. "Philosophy and Politics in Hobbes." In *Hobbes Studies,* ed. Keith Brown. Oxford: Blackwell, 1965.

———. *Hobbes's System of Ideas.* London: Hutchinson, 1973.

Wernham, A. G. "Liberty and Obligation in Hobbes." In *Hobbes Studies,* ed. Keith Brown. Cambridge: Harvard University Press, 1965.

Index

249